THE COMING OF AGE
OF THE PROFESSION

Issues and Emerging Ideas
for the Teaching
of Foreign Languages

THE COMING OF AGE
OF THE PROFESSION

Issues and Emerging Ideas
for the Teaching
of Foreign Languages

Jane Harper
Madeleine G. Lively
Mary K. Williams

HH Heinle & Heinle Publishers
An International Thomson Publishing Company
I(T)P The ITP logo is a trademark under license.
Boston, Massachusetts 02116 U.S.A.

New York • London • Bonn • Boston • Detroit • Madrid • Melbourne • Mexico City • Paris •
Singapore • Tokyo • Toronto • Washington • Albany, NY • Belmont, CA • Cincinnati, OH

The publication of *The Coming of Age of the Profession* was directed by the members of the Heinle & Heinle College Foreign Language Publishing Team:

Wendy Nelson, Editorial Director
Tracie Edwards, Market Development Director
Gabrielle B. McDonald, Production Services Coordinator
Amy Baron, Associate Developmental Editor

Also participating in the publication of this program were:

Publisher: Vincent P. Duggan
Project Manager: Lisa W. LaFortune
Assistant Market Development Director: Rossella Romagnoli
Production Assistant: Lisa W. LaFortune
Manufacturing Coordinator: Wendy Kilborn
Cover Designer: Perspectives/Sue Gerould
Assistant Editor: Beatrix Mellauner
Compositor: Esther Marshall

Library of Congress Catalog-in-Publication Data

The Coming of Age of the Profession: issues and emerging ideas for the teaching of foreign languages / editors, Jane Harper, Madeleine G. Lively, Mary K. Williams.
    p.   cm.
    ISBN 0-8384-8224-4
    1. Language and Languages—Study and teaching. I. Harper, Jane, 1924–   . II. Lively, Madeleine G.. III. Williams, Mary K. (Mary Karen), 1948– .
P51.C6215 1997
418' .007—dc21   97–36707
                                                   CIP

Manufactured in the United States of America

ISBN: 0-8384-8224-4

10 9 8 7 6 5 4

TABLE OF CONTENTS

ACKNOWLEDGMENTS

We would like to express our sincere thanks and appreciation to our colleagues in the teaching of foreign languages who have shared ideas, concepts, concerns, and instructional materials with us during the last three decades. We are particularly indebted to the hundreds of teachers of novice- and intermediate-level students who spent parts of their summers with us in teacher-training workshops at Tarrant Country Junior College. We remain convinced that we always learned more than we taught.

We are greatly appreciative of the response of our colleagues and friends in the profession who have generously granted us the benefit of their thoughts on the current issues in foreign language education through their contributions to this volume:

Patricia A. Aplevich, University of Waterloo
Terry L. Ballman, University of Northern Colorado
Jeannette Bragger, Pennsylvania State University
Jorge H. Cubillos, University of Delaware
Vicki Galloway, Georgia Tech University
Michael Geisler, Middlebury College
JoAnn Hammadou, University of Rhode Island
David Herren, Middlebury College
Ana Martínez-Lage, Middlebury College
Linnéa McArt, Middlebury College
June K. Phillips, Weber State University
Lee Ann Rawley, Utah State University
Donald B. Rice, Hamline University
Alfred N. Smith, Utah State University
Robert M. Terry, University of Richmond
Fred Toner, Ohio University
Erwin Tschirner, The University of Iowa
Jo-Anne H. Willment, Society for Teaching and Learning in Higher Education in Canada

We would like to thank Charles H. Heinle for his continuing belief in the value of our work. We owe a special debt of gratitude to the members of our team at Heinle & Heinle: to Vince Duggan for his understanding of the development of the profession which gave the volume its title; to Wendy Nelson for her strategic guidance and consistent encouragement; to Amy Barron for her attention to detail; and to Esther Marshall for carefully copyediting the manuscript. We also offer our sincere appreciation to Joel Deutser who originated the concept of this work.

J. H., M. G. L., M. K. W.

Dedication

We dedicate this book to foreign language teachers entering the profession, who will confront these issues and further develop these ideas in their classrooms.

FOREWORD

The last twenty-five years have been a time of continuous change in the teaching and learning of foreign languages. During this time we have seen (and used), among others, the grammar/translation method, the audio-lingual method, individualized instruction, role-playing, Total Physical Response (TPR), the Natural Approach, tacit learning, authentic materials, oral proficiency interviews, task-based language teaching, content-based instruction, pair work, cooperative learning, and constructivism, with attention to higher order thinking skills and to various learning styles and multiple intelligences of students. We have moved from discussions of language teaching to language learning to language acquisition to the communication of ideas. We have progressed from the Latin grammar-based syllabus to the functional/notional syllabus to the theme-based syllabus. We have modified assessment from exclusive discrete-point correction to encompassing responses to student meaning. We have changed from our role of "Sage on the Stage" to that of "Guide on the Side."

And, rather than rely strictly on classroom observation by our supervisor, we now do much reflection on our teaching/learning experiences with our students and rely primarily on self-evaluation to measure our own professional development. This growth marks **the coming of age of our profession**.

The publication of the *Standards for Foreign Language Learning: Preparing for the 21st Century* provides an opportunity for continued growth and development within the profession. This articulation of the agenda for the next decade—and beyond—offers a vantage point from which to anticipate our next incremental stages of change.

With that in mind, we asked several of our professional colleagues and friends to join us in exploring the **issues and emerging ideas in the teaching of foreign languages**. Together we examine possibilities in the continuing evolution of the profession.

For convenience we have organized the materials into four sections: Teacher-Learner Roles, Presentation, Activities, and Evaluation. At the end of each section we have provided sets of suggested activities for reflection, self-assessment, and application of the ideas presented. We hope that completion of these exercises will provide insight both to teachers in training and to teachers in-service. Through your development of ideas, we invite you to join us in this continuing development of the profession.

Jane Harper
Madeleine G. Lively
Mary K. Williams

Part I

Teacher-Learner Roles

Including articles by:

June K. Phillips
Alfred N. Smith and Lee Ann Rawley
Jorge H. Cubillos
Patricia A. Aplevich and Jo-Anne H. Willment

Changing Teacher/Learner Roles in Standards-Driven Contexts

June K. Phillips, *Weber State University*

June K. Phillips (Ph.D, The Ohio State University) is Dean of Arts and Humanities at Weber State University in Utah. She served as project director for the K–12 Standards for Foreign Language Education Project under the auspices of ACTFL, AATF, AATG, AATSP. She is a former chair of the Northeast Conference on the Teaching of Foreign Languages and recently edited the Northeast Conference Report that featured case studies of standards in classrooms. Professor Phillips serves on the Foreign Language Advisory Committee of the College Board and has served as a faculty coordinator for the Summer Leadership Seminar of the Modern Language Association. She has edited and written numerous articles on instructional and policy issues and has presented hundreds of papers and workshops at conferences.

INTRODUCTION

The publication of *Standards for Foreign Language Learning: Preparing for the 21st Century* occurred after three years of intensive discussion through a number of professional formats: formal questionnaires and surveys, focused invitational meetings, and informal follow-up to conference presentations. The prepublication involvement with the profession at large created at least a level of awareness, even anticipation, so that many teachers and teacher-educators had begun to identify ways in which the standards would have an impact on teaching and learning. The reality has been, with some exemplary exceptions, that teaching has been highly concentrated on beginning levels of instruction with high-school age students. Both classroom research and methodological focus have centered on these traditional areas of instruction; teacher and student roles revolved around a relatively limited set of behaviors that focused largely on language systems and some cultural content. If the profession experiences the desired increase in the numbers of programs with extended sequences of study, the need for teachers prepared to work with younger learners, in middle school programs, and in more advanced language instruction for a wider range of learners will call for additional teachers and new roles. Teachers must now begin to open their curriculum to other learners, other content, other purposes; students will have to expand their vision of what foreign language learning entails.

3

> "Teachers must . . . open their curriculum to other learners, other content, other purposes . . ."

In part, the standards have built upon the movement toward functional language proficiency begun in the mid-1980s. The sometimes contentious debate that surrounded that major paradigm shift has resulted in rather dramatic changes in both purposes and objectives for curriculum and instruction. Along with curricular changes has come a recognition of proficiency levels needed by classroom teachers if targeted student levels were to be achieved. Students, too, have had to change their perceptions of the tasks appropriate to a foreign language class. Now, and before much of that work has been grounded in classrooms as the norm, standards are likely to pose more questions and make greater demands on teacher and student roles, responsibilities, and competencies.

Major changes are attached to the very notion that foreign languages are connected to the other areas of the curriculum as never before; traditionally, our discipline has been at the fringe, a nice elective but rarely central to the mission of the district or the school. That may remain the case for a period of time in many individual districts, but slowly the impact of being one of the subject areas with content standards will be felt if the profession perseveres in being active and visible in the larger arena of educational issues. Continued work with and pressure created by the standards keep us center stage.

WHAT ARE THE STANDARDS FOR FOREIGN LANGUAGE LEARNING?

The fact that the standards were developed with significant input from the field has led to a generally strong acceptance of them at state and local levels. As curricular revision occurs, classroom teachers will be confronted by the standards in their daily work; it is also highly likely that materials and assessments will reflect the broadened vision of foreign language learning. Teacher education programs and professional development will be setting a challenging agenda for projects focused on the *Five Cs* of foreign language education (National Standards in Foreign Language Education Project).

- ♦ *Communication* in languages other than English
- ♦ *Cultures*, understanding the perspectives of other cultures
- ♦ *Connections* with other disciplines
- ♦ *Comparisons* with one's own language and culture
- ♦ *Communities* in which to use languages at home and abroad

The eleven standards that are derived from these goals provide the framework for assessments and draw in broad terms the scope of curricular content. For students to perform credibly in these areas will require that their teachers increase their own understandings of the content and direction of these standards, which have evolved from recent trends of the past, but that go well beyond conventional definitions of the field as language- or skill-based content. Similarly, students will be challenged to *do*, to use language meaningfully in a wide variety of real world contexts.

TEACHER COMPETENCIES

Before discussing teacher roles, it is critical to address the base competencies (for which the base will be higher) that enable the teacher to work comfortably and effectively with students in a standards-driven environment. For years the profession has been struggling to identify the levels of language proficiency recommended for teachers in classrooms where goals are centered on functional language outcomes. It has been rare for a teacher to be able to get students to achieve beyond the teacher's own proficiency level. In order to help students communicate in the interpersonal mode (Standard 1.1), the teacher must have the facility to manage classroom communication through negotiated meaning with students, that means possessing the ability to work spontaneously and creatively in the target language. To assist students to interpret texts as readers or listeners (Standard 1.2) and to present information or creative works (Standard 1.3), teachers have to be highly skilled themselves in order to understand many kinds of texts and to create a variety of discourses. In order to support the learning of interdisciplinary content (Standards 3.1, 3.2), teachers will have to expand their lexicons to content areas beyond traditional groupings in textbooks or literary studies.

> ". . . (T)he *ACTL Provisional Program Guidelines for Teacher Education* recommend that programs verify that their teacher education candidates are performing at the **advanced high** level in speaking, listening, and reading, and at the **advanced** level in writing."

How this could be achieved without a minimal speaking proficiency equivalent to the Advanced Level on the Oral Proficiency Interview is questionable. In fact, the *ACTFL Provisional Program Guidelines for Teacher Education* (in Guntermann, 213–227) recommend that programs verify that their teacher education candidates are performing at the **advanced high** level in speaking, listening, and reading, and at the **advanced** level in writing. Yet few states or higher education programs have been willing to implement that standard for their own graduates. Lafayette (p. 137) makes a strong plea to teacher preparation institutions first to prepare their student-teachers with high levels of proficiency. He states: "If the recommended proficiency levels are to be achieved by prospective teachers, either emphasis in the major language area must focus on language proficiency itself, or all literature and other content-based courses must include a language component."

It is not just the goal areas of the standards that require higher levels of proficiency by teachers, but the growth of programs with extended sequences of study envisioned by the standards also underscore the pivotal nature of this issue. Teaching younger children requires that teachers be prepared to do story-telling and demonstrations in order to immerse learners in a rich flow of language; they cannot limit their classroom talk to exercises or sentence-level discourse. While several program models exist for elementary school language instruction, the "best teachers in both language-arts FLES (Foreign Language in the Elementary School) and content-enriched FLES programs use only the target language in the classroom" (Tedick, Walker, Lange, Paige, and Jorstad, 49). This requires proficiency at least at a level to sustain narration. On the other end of the spectrum, more students in upper level courses will also make greater demands on teacher proficiency. Higher education must accept the challenge to graduate future teachers whose proficiency level is solid and capable of meeting the pedagogical demands of their chosen career.

Teachers currently in the classroom must exercise the responsibility to assess their own proficiency levels. Many have made systematic efforts to increase their language abilities and cultural knowledge, or to maintain high levels, during their working careers. Study abroad, continuing professional development, summer seminars all contribute to the lifelong learning that is part of this profession. If one entered the profession at a time when knowledge about the language system was more of a priority than functional language use, then today awareness of the changing orientation of curriculum coupled with the immediacy of language samples from electronic and print media is powerful motivation for self-development efforts. Indeed, the bottom line is that teachers must be able to conduct multiple tasks in all the modalities at a high level of competency. If not, students will not be able to achieve the challenging standards set forth in the professional document, *Standards for Foreign Language Learning: Preparing for the 21st Century*.

Another major area in which teacher competencies must be substantially more developed than in the past is that of cultural knowledge and contexts. No teacher can know well all aspects of the many cultures that house the languages being taught; however, teachers should have knowledge in depth of at least one of the target cultures and the skills to learn about additional cultures through observation and planned study. The standards themselves set forth a model for students to gain understandings of the perspectives of cultures by studying their products and practices. That might well provide a vehicle for teachers as well. A reality that must be faced is the fact that study/travel abroad, not just once but regularly, is not a luxury for the foreign language teacher, it is a necessity, not only for linguistic immersion but also for immersion in the culture as well. As Glisan (p. 73) points out, "Teachers cannot teach culture effectively from a textbook; they must also be able to bring their own real-life cultural experiences to the classroom. . . . It is imperative that teachers keep abreast of current happenings in the cultures of the languages they teach and benefit from travel and study abroad experiences continually."

CHANGING TEACHER ROLES IN THE CONTEXT OF STANDARDS

□ CONSUMERS OF RESEARCH

One of the first roles that teachers will need to assume to a greater extent than in the past will be that of thoughtful reader and user of research. It is essential that teachers thoroughly understand the theoretical and practical premises upon which the standards have been built. While the profession has accepted the standards from the beginning, and much activity is being generated around them, there remains a certain amount of superficiality in implementation that must be converted to a deeper understanding. Ideally, teacher participation in research projects, especially classroom action research, will provide the most compelling tests of the strengths of the standards and of weaknesses to be readdressed. (See Phillips for a volume built upon action research projects and standards.) The majority of teachers who may not have opportunities to participate in well-conceived research studies might still become avid consumers of articles and studies that promote theory to practice as well as practice to research.

Paradigms for language learning throughout history have promoted research as the necessary base for instructional practice. Teaching toward standards demands a greater grasp of research findings for several reasons: First, the five goal areas have expanded the types of learning identified as important to students' functioning in language in real world 21st-century contexts. The communication standards encompass several theoretical frameworks, including interpersonal communication with negotiation of meaning, a complex set of linguistic, social, and cultural features, at its core. The ways in which learners acquire language in interpersonal modes has distinct features and draws heavily from research in the discipline of communication. The interpretive standard builds on acquisition processes, and the presentational standard builds on how learners organize ideas and express themselves in writing or speech. Of course, the research for one framework feeds into the others; at the same time, an increased complexity rules the field. Teachers/researchers will continue building the knowledge base in these areas since the final answers are not yet established. In addition to communication, teachers will be investigating how to teach cultural content, how to do interdisciplinary work, and how to arrange conditions so that learners make the comparisons suggested for Standards 4.1., 4.2. These standards require that students use comparison insights gained by studying second languages and cultures to reflect back upon their first language. These reflections serve to focus on the nature of language systems and patterns of cultures, outcomes rarely achieved by monolinguals, monoculturalists.

Secondly, over the years, the more we know about language learning, the more complex we recognize it to be. There is a temptation to suspect that each new paradigm is a trend or a fad that will soon pass without our instruction having to change. The very opposite is true. Most paradigm shifts occur as new knowledge comes forth. The effective teacher will always continue to integrate research findings into practice.

☐ INSTRUCTIONAL LEADERS WITH A REPERTOIRE OF APPROACHES

In the past teachers frequently associated their teaching with a method or an approach that was fairly prescriptive for them and for learners. Probably the strongest instance of a dominant method was exemplified in audiolingualism, which held sway in the profession for a substantial time. In a standards-driven world the focus will shift to student performance, and the varying levels of instruction and goal areas lend themselves not to single approaches but to many. Consequently, teachers will need to control a repertoire of approaches that effectively target specific goal areas or standards. The approach used to develop a learner's interpretive abilities may be quite different from those most useful for another area. Or the repertoire may be played in specific sequences in order to lead learners from one area to another such as reading to write, writing to read, or whole language approaches. The main point is that the teacher will have to choose carefully in terms of interrelated factors such as the goal, the individual learner, the level of the course, and age-appropriate content. No single approach or prescription will suffice to do the job.

> "No single approach or prescription will suffice to do the job. . . . (T)he teacher will have to choose carefully in terms of interrelated factors such as *the goal, the individual learner, the level of the course, age-appropriate content.*"

☐ DECISION-MAKERS

Given the variety of performance outcomes and armed with multiple approaches, teachers will make a myriad of both planned and spontaneous decisions daily in the classroom. Those decisions will be based upon a clear definition of goals and an understanding, gained through research and experience, of anticipated results of their actions. An example of planned decisions and spontaneous ones can be drawn from a collaborative project described by Haas and Reardon (pp. 213–241). A middle school Spanish class was doing a unit on Chile. Students began by studying the geography of the country; they worked with maps and did some library or Internet research (Connections standard 3.1). The teacher planned how she would teach the geography using visuals and Total Physical Response (TPR) sequences. Students demonstrated comprehension by generating a *language experience story* in class. They also corresponded by e-mail with students in a Chilean town (Standard 1.1.). The children used collaborative learning to design an *arpillera* (Culture/ Products standard 2.2) to exchange with their new friends from Chile. They prepared to take a field trip to a Chilean bakery in the neighborhood (Communities standard 5.1). The teacher used dialogues and role-plays to prepare the students for the transactional situation (Communication/Interpersonal standard 1.1). The teacher was able to plan situational dialogues (shopping in a bakery) and develop general vocabulary for baked goods and purchasing. In sum, the teacher chose specific approaches for these related activities which included: TPR, language experience story, collaborative learning techniques, and role-plays.

Even with this high degree of planning on the part of the teacher, the very approaches chosen will introduce unforeseen or unexpected events into the classroom. Approaches that allow for, or even encourage, students to use language to convey their own meanings inevitably require teachers to react with insights that probe the thinking processes of learners. In the Haas and Reardon study, the language experience story is co-constructed by teacher and learners; as students try to create the story about Chile, they may make errors that are sometimes opaque, they may introduce ideas that seem to come out of nowhere (in reality from somewhere in the student's head), and they may introduce an idea from their backgrounds that had not been dealt with in the linguistic preparation in the classroom. The success with which the teacher manages this kind of communication and cognitive construction is reflected in the learning that occurs. The e-mail correspondence also brought to light many instances where actual communication evolved in its own direction.

Frequently, the way one makes spontaneous decisions greatly contributes to the richest learning; one can plan lessons, but one must also be ready to handle the convergent thinking that may result. All teachers can, however, become better observers of how their decisions affect learning by periodically videotaping and analyzing their behaviors, by having peers observe them and provide feedback, and by reflecting on the conduct of a class shortly after it has ended.

□ CREATORS OF ASSESSMENTS AND ASSESSORS

The new standards for foreign language learning were developed with assessability as a major criterion. However, the writers were not bound by conventional measures or standardized tests. Assessment, as envisioned by the standards, is open to alternative measures, project-type or problem-solving activities; the performance measure may be holistic, criterion-referenced, or descriptive in nature. Teachers will be urged to experiment with ways of describing how students are performing in the Five Cs goal areas. The standards publication contains sample progress indicators which can be readily converted into assessment activities. The profession has been among the leaders in having broken restrictive psychometric constraints through recent emphases on proficiency testing and holistic scoring of language samples. Inserting objectivity into subjective measures requires training and practice. Teachers will learn to identify and evaluate the key components of these more global assessments so that students become aware of their strengths and of the areas in which they need to improve.

Sample assessments already being piloted in states and districts might include:

- Oral interviews or tape-mediated ones

- Student writing portfolios or portfolios with evidence of a wide range of accomplishments

- Problems posed to a collaborative group with solutions presented to the teacher/class (e.g., planning a summer camp experience)

One can expect that the immediate future will explore many ways of aligning standards-based outcomes and assessments. Just as teachers acquire a repertoire of teaching approaches, so too will they become proficient at a variety of performance measures.

☐ TEACHERS AS KNOWERS, DOERS, AND KNOW-HOW-TO PERSONS

Certainly, the reader of this article quite perceptively could be wondering how it is possible to play out effectively the combination of roles identified as being critical if challenging standards are to be achieved by learners. Exemplary teachers have always performed the multiple tasks outlined above; they have always pushed the boundaries of current practice to experiment and investigate new ways of teaching because they are keen observers of their students' learning. They have taken pride in improving and maintaining their language skills and their knowledge of target cultures. They have attended professional meetings and kept up with professional literature. Beyond this, they have been willing to admit to what they do not know by allowing students to pursue research and projects of personal interest; as teachers they have recognized that they do not have to be the source of all knowledge but only have to know how to point the way.

Given the increasing complexity of research, practice, goals, curriculum, and assessments, teachers will want to have the best knowledge base possible upon entrance into the field and a lifelong commitment to expand it. They will use that "knowing" to develop pedagogical practices that facilitate the many kinds of learning outlined in the standards for all students. Finally, they will become adept at processes of learning (e.g., communication strategies, learning strategies) so that they can help students direct much of their own learning. And that leads us to students.

CHANGING STUDENT ROLES IN THE CONTEXT OF STANDARDS

Even the very best instruction requires that students engage in the search for excellence. Standards are not something that can be done to students or for them. Attaining high levels of performance in the five goal areas depends upon a student buy-in. In many of the schools and districts working with standards aligned with the national ones, one of the first initiatives involves showing students the standards and working through them. In a large urban district (Springfield, MA) that piloted the standards, Riordan and Oleksak (p. 25) report that students were not only informed about the content of the standards but were periodically asked to reflect upon their progress in goal areas during the process. Introducing students to the standards from the beginning may lay valuable groundwork that enables them to make real progress toward the performances outlined. Learners of all ages can understand the standards if their teachers explore the meanings with them. In fact, without that understanding, we cannot expect students to assume the responsibilities for the learning embedded in the standards.

□ STUDENTS AS ACTIVE PARTICIPATORS AND PLANNERS

Students have always been expected to participate in language classes. Going through the paces by giving choral responses, reciting dialogues, conjugating verbs, and memorizing poetry, as well as writing exercises, have all involved students fully in classroom activities. Much of this type of participation will continue to shape language learning to some degree, but the level of cognitive and creative thinking required of this kind of recitation is relatively low. In the last decade, as a proficiency orientation has gained prominence in many classrooms, teachers have noted that some students were content to do the rote tasks and hesitant to partake in the more creative—and more challenging—tasks of meaning making. It is important to recognize that students may not all be eager to engage in negotiated meaning and the sometimes frustrating situations that occur when one has to strive to communicate in spite of language deficiencies. Teachers will have to create the communicative tasks, the cultural investigations, and the community events that will motivate and intrigue students to persevere. Learners will have to accept the invitation to use language creatively and to be active planners in the direction of their own learning.

> "...(S)tudents must be prepared to receive and to send messages, to interact with texts, and to convey individual thoughts and opinions that preclude the word-for-word preparation common to classrooms in the past."

☐ STUDENTS AS STRATEGISTS

In all their courses, students are being called upon to hone the strategies with which they approach learning, and to gain hold of the processes of various disciplines so that they can continue to learn beyond the immediate instructional task. The rapidity with which knowledge builds in today's world is but one reason supportive of knowing "how" and not just "what." In language learning, the knowledge explosion is technologically driven; students now have access to information from the Internet, satellite, and print media of all kinds. This open access to a great variety of materials coupled with the expanded goal areas for foreign language study means that students must be prepared to receive and to send messages, to interact with texts, and to convey individual thoughts and opinions that preclude the word-for-word preparation common to classrooms in the past.

Many students may initially find this challenge overwhelming for reasons cited above; it is easier to learn just facts than to problem solve and to take risks. In addition to the strategy learning important to all disciplines, foreign language study will require some specialized training in strategies relevant to the communicative modes set out in *Standards for Foreign Language Learning* (p. 33): Interpersonal, Interpretive, and Presentational. Students will not only need to control a range of strategies but also to know which to choose for specific tasks. Being able to negotiate one's meaning in an interpersonal transaction requires strategies and attitudes distinct from those most useful for interpretive tasks. In the latter, for example, the ability to tolerate ambiguity while searching for meaning permits students to tackle authentic texts.

☐ STUDENTS BEARING KNOWLEDGE AND EXPERIENCE

Students entering a foreign-language classroom may be prone to leave the rest of their learning behind. They do not, however, come as *tabula rasa*, they come as bearers of tablets filled with knowledge from schooling and life. Interdisciplinarity of curriculum is being underscored throughout the schools so it will come as less of a surprise as students experience this in foreign language courses as well. However, the initial response to content in geography or art or history in the language classroom will be: "Will I be tested on that? I thought this was a language class." Our students may have judged us to be without content or with content limited to forms of the target language. The attempt to shift them to a recognition that the content of a language class is meaningful, i.e., full of meaning, will not be achieved without effort (and of course, as teachers, we, too, must be convinced that the message is the ends and language the means). All educators hope that students ultimately see the connections with all the subjects they study; students who are willing to bring their questions, their interests, their experiences to the foreign-language classroom will infuse all those areas with a cross-cultural dimension.

□ STUDENTS AS WORLD CITIZENS

For a very long time, the rationale for the study of the world's languages in schools has been to prepare our students for an increasingly international society. Students are well aware that almost everything that touches their lives is global: entertainment, sports, ecology, market. As tomorrow's leaders, they enter this arena in one of two ways: as monolinguals or as ones with a high enough degree of competency in a second (or third) language to interact with another group in that group's language and culture. In the simple but loaded words of the standards publication, students who chose to gain skills in "knowing how, when, and why, to say what to whom" (p. 11) will be enriched and rewarded by the experience. However to achieve results that ease entrée into another culture, students must take much of the responsibility for directing their learning toward Communities standards (5.1, 5.2). In the view of many members of the public, being able to use the target language at home and abroad subsumes all other standards. Teachers cannot do that for students; students must do that for themselves.

COOPERATIVE ROLES, COLLABORATIVE ROLES

The message in this article is purposefully repetitive. Recurring themes of individual responsibility on the part of teacher and student, of diversity and choice in content to be learned, and of personal development of strategies and processes do not equate with learning in isolation. In fact, the opposite holds true, for achieving the standards will require greater cooperation among teachers and students than ever before. As classroom tasks focus more on real-world issues, texts, or events, students will be increasingly involved with solving problems together by scanning reports, documentaries, and web pages to find information that can be synthesized and discussed again. Teachers will guide more and be less all-knowing in that the finiteness of language systems as content gives way to a vast array of potential topics. Students will collaborate not just with peers in the classroom but electronically with youth from around the world. The very smallness of our technologically linked globe should both motivate and reward students who know other languages, other cultures. Teachers and students have already made progress toward the learning outcomes envisioned in the standards; as roles continue to change for both the journey will proceed more quickly.

REFERENCES

Glisan, Eileen W. "A Collaborative Approach to Professional Development," *National Standards: A Catalyst for Reform.* ACTFL Foreign Language Education Series. Robert W. Lafayette, ed. Lincolnwood, IL: National Textbook Co., 1996.

Guntermann, Gail, ed. *Developing Language Teachers for a Changing World.* ACTFL Foreign Language Education Series. Lincolnwood, IL: National Textbook Co., 1993.

Haas, Mari, and Margaret Reardon. "Communities of Learners: From New York to Chile." *Collaborations: Meeting New Goals, New Realities.* Northeast Conference Reports. June K. Phillips, ed. Lincolnwood, IL: National Textbook Co., 1997.

Lafayette, Robert. "Subject-Matter Content: What Every Foreign Language Teacher Needs to Know." *Developing Language Teachers for a Changing World.* ACTFL Foreign Language Education Series. Gail Guntermann, ed. Lincolnwood, IL: National Textbook Co., 1993.

National K–12 Standards for Foreign Language Education Project. *Standards for Foreign Language Learning: Preparing for the 21st Century.* Yonkers, NY: Author, 1996.

Phillips, June K., ed. *Collaborations: Meeting New Goals, New Realities.* Northeast Conference Reports. Lincolnwood, IL: National Textbook Co., 1997.

Riordan, Kathleen M., and Rita A. Oleksak. "The Teacher's Voice: A View from a National Standards Pilot Site. *Collaborations: Meeting New Goals, New Realities.* Northeast Conference Reports. June K. Phillips, ed. Lincolnwood, IL: National Textbook Co., 1997.

Tedick, Diane J., Constance L. Walker, Dale L. Lange, R. Michael Paige, and Helen L. Jorstad. "Second Language Education in Tomorrow's Schools." *Developing Language Teachers for a Changing World.* ACTFL Foreign Language Education Series. Gail Guntermann, ed. Lincolnwood, IL: National Textbook Co., 1993.

Teachers Taking the Lead: Self-Inquiry as Professional Development

Alfred N. Smith and Lee Ann Rawley,
Utah State University

Alfred N. Smith is Professor of French and Language Education at Utah State University, where he teaches French, linguistics, cross-cultural studies, and does teacher training and supervision. He has presented numerous papers and workshops on language teaching and teacher education and has published articles on reading, writing, culture, and developing critical thinking skills. He has served as president of the Pacific Northwest Council on Foreign Languages and of the Utah Foreign Language Association and is currently editor of the journal HANDS ON *Language. He has directed study programs and tours for American students in France.*

=== ||| ===

Lee Ann Rawley is Assistant Director of the Intensive English Language Institute at Utah State University, where she teaches ESL courses specializing in cross-cultural perspectives of American culture and building critical thinking skills through the use of authentic video. She is a doctoral student in Educational Leadership and Innovation, University of Colorado at Denver. She has made numerous presentations at local, regional, and national conventions and has served as Chair of the TESOL Awards Committee. Her research interests include teacher decision-making and language policy. She is the 1992 recipient of the TESOL Newbury House Excellence in Teaching Award.

INTRODUCTION

The image of the second and foreign language teacher normally projected by the profession and by teachers themselves is that of a classroom manager responsible for implementing language instruction and facilitating language learning (Richards, 1996). The view of the classroom teacher as a qualified theorist and researcher, however, is less common. Even though there have been recent movements to encourage classroom investigation of teaching and learning by teachers themselves (Burnaford, 1996; Cochran-Smith, 1993; Goswami, 1987; Hubbard, 1993; Kincheloe, 1991; Knoblauch, 1993; Richards, 1994), the language teacher's role is mainly perceived by the public and the profession alike as that of classroom practitioner.

Administrators, policy makers, researchers, theorists, and teacher educators regularly issue standards, regulations, methodological procedures, and research findings to teachers whom they expect will use these principles, theories, and teaching techniques in their classrooms, often in accordance with specific modes of implementation. Those who make the pronouncements do not always recognize that the daily work of teachers with learners in classrooms builds a knowledge base which renders teachers experts and creators of theory in their own right. Moreover, because teaching is an enormously complex endeavor (Calderhead, 1993), it is far from being an activity that can be explained, learned, or taught as a set of techniques, methods, or behavioral prescriptions. Who the teacher is as a person, who the students are, what particular constraints they face, and the context within which they live and learn together impact how learning takes place and is understood. Cochran-Smith and Lytle (1993) argue that "the increasing diversity of America's schools and schoolchildren and the increasing complexity of the tasks that educators face render global solutions to problems and monolithic strategies for effective teaching impossible" (p. 63). What is needed, they say, are teacher/researchers who can "construct their own questions and then begin to develop courses of action that are valid in their local contexts and communities" (p. 63). Teachers seeing themselves as researchers creates the potential for blurring the traditional, stereotypical boundaries between researchers and teachers and between theory and practice. By advocating that more credence be given to the teacher's voice, we are not at the same time suggesting that what researchers have to say about teaching and classrooms is unimportant. We are not speaking in favor of substituting a bottom-up approach for the traditional top-down view. Rather we speak in favor of a leveling of the hierarchy, a collaborative view that validates the contributions of experience and empirical research equally. Making research on teachers a cooperative venture, however, requires not only that administrators, researchers, and policy makers look at teachers differently, but that teachers begin to trust and value themselves as contributors to the profession's knowledge base.

The purpose of this article is to encourage the reconceptualization of "the language teacher" and "teacher development" by focusing on teachers as experts on language learning and teaching. We further suggest that when teachers reflect on their actions and conduct inquiry on their practice, they develop the confidence needed to add their voices to on-going professional conversations about language teaching, learning, and classrooms. In this article we let teachers take the lead by presenting the voices of language teachers engaged in reflective practice and inquiry, telling their stories and portraying their views of what is important in their work.

WHAT TEACHERS KNOW

Successful language teachers have learned about linguistic and pedagogical theory, but they also possess a wealth of knowledge gained from experience (Knezevic and Scholl, 1996). This knowledge-from-experience is most often tacit. It is revealed through the thousands of decisions and negotiations played out in the classroom each day. A good language teacher knows what activities keep his or her students in the target language, how to handle unexpected questions, when to move from an activity that seems to be dragging to a new one, and how to connect the two so they make sense to students. Yet the knowing is often in the doing; that is, a good teacher knows what to do, but may not be able to articulate his or her knowledge. It is common for expert practitioners to be capable of performing with skill, but at the same time be unable to explain what they do or how they know how to do it (Schön, 1987). Gregory Bateson (1972) relates a quote from Isadora Duncan that conveys this message succinctly: "If I could tell you what it meant, there would be no point in dancing it" (p. 137).

Bringing this experiential, tacit knowledge to awareness and putting it into words so it can be examined and shared "lies at the heart" of becoming a skilled teacher (Shulman, 1988, 33). According to Shulman, teachers become better educators when they know how they know what they do and the reasons behind their actions; furthermore, making tacit knowledge explicit "also requires a combining of reflection on practical experience and reflection on theoretical understanding" (p. 33). Freeman (1991) adds that making the tacit explicit is not a linear process of revealing what teachers already know; rather, his work with in-service language teachers has led him to the conclusion that tacit knowledge interacts with newly explicit understandings gained from teacher training, graduate courses, and study and discussion of theory in a dialectical process that reshapes a teacher's knowledge base.

THE ROLE OF INQUIRY

Teachers have typically been seen as the recipients of research conducted by outsiders (Clarke, 1994; Cochran-Smith and Lytle, 1993). Even the movement toward recognizing the importance of the teacher's knowledge base and ways of thinking has tended to objectify teaching and ignore the teacher as a theorist and an interpreter and critic of practice (Cochran-Smith and Lytle, 1993). Teachers who engage in inquiry in their own schools and classrooms, however, begin to recognize themselves as creators of theory and new knowledge. Knoblauch and Brannon (1993) characterize research conducted by teachers as a program of critical literacy which aims not only to construct new knowledge from an insider perspective, but also to enfranchise teachers as "authentic makers of that knowledge" (p. 186). Cochran-Smith and Lytle (1993) concur that teacher research, by giving teachers centrality in constructing the knowledge base of teaching, disrupts traditional assumptions of who possesses expert knowledge about teaching.

In our own classrooms and in our work with other language teachers, we have come to value teacher inquiry as a means for understanding our teaching, ourselves as professionals, and our colleagues in the language teaching profession. By inquiry we mean paying attention to our work and lives, asking questions about what we do and why, and processing the things we notice. We process what we notice about our practice in a variety of ways. We engage in conversations with colleagues, family members, and students about what happens in our classrooms and what we think about it. Sometimes these conversations are in the form of e-mail with colleagues at other schools. We observe peers' classes and have them observe ours to stimulate discussions. We have students audiotape class sessions for us. We videotape one another's classes. We engage in writing journals, often in response to transcribing or viewing the videotapes of our classes. How a teacher chooses to process what he or she notices depends on personal preferences and constraints. However, it is our view that good language teachers conduct inquiries all the time. Sometimes inquiry is directed at discovering who the teacher is as a person, what his or her values are, and how they are translated into classroom actions. Inquiry also focuses on learning and students since teaching has no meaning apart from learners and what is being learned (Clarke *et al*, 1996). Good teachers ask questions to learn why one lesson worked and another did not, why students responded to an activity in a certain way, how a particular student's behavior changes from oral practice activities to writing workshop, and what role the teacher plays in the classroom dynamics.

DISCOVERING SOURCES OF TEACHERS' KNOWLEDGE THROUGH STORIES

The educational lives of teachers are rich sources of narrative, and telling and sharing personal accounts of classroom events can contribute to the professional development of a teacher. Mattingly (1991, 236) sees stories as a basis for reflection:

> Storytelling and story analysis can facilitate a kind of reflecting that is often difficult to do, a consideration of those ordinarily tacit constructs that guide practice. Stories point toward deep beliefs and assumptions that people often cannot tell in propositional or denotative form, the 'practical theories' and deeply held images that guide their actions.

Bruner (1986) describes narrative as a primary mode of thought through which humans order experience and construct reality; Clandinin (1991) claims the deliberate storying of one's life is a basic method for social and personal growth. The deliberate telling of an educational happening can be both informative and therapeutic. When information is put in story form, the context of the tale connects facts to psychological and emotional realities and therefore renders the meaning more profound and significant. Inquiring into teaching experiences through storying also requires active recall and promotes the making of connections. In authoring a story, teachers recapture an educational moment by reconstructing events, recalling the actions of the main characters, and describing the setting or context. Once the story is authored (told, recorded, shared) it can be studied and analyzed to determine motivations underlying specific teaching behaviors (Clandinin, 1991, 264).

A story can also be a voyage of transformation, helping teachers break out of old patterns of perception that can block development and imagine new ways of thinking. For example, a teacher who would like to have a classroom where language learning is a more social and collaborative process could begin by creating a story about such a place or by listening to or reading a story by a colleague who has already created such a place. Hearing others' stories, says Clandinin (1993), is a way to gain "new possibilities for writing our lives differently" (p. 2).

Sometimes teachers live stories in which they are faced with difficult realities that complicate their work. They may be expected to use prescribed materials or certain instructional procedures that are in their eyes less than adequate. They may not have access to the latest technology and, therefore, not be able to involve their students in Internet, e-mail, video, or computer assisted learning suggested in journals and in-service workshops. In telling and sharing "problem stories" teachers can gain insights on how to cope with difficulties and how to be resourceful in the face of uncontrollable constraints (Johnson, 1996).

In this article we share teacher stories collected from portfolios of in-service teachers we have worked with and from data gathered from case studies, teacher training experiences, and collaborative inquiry projects.[1] All of the teacher voices presented here come from real language teachers in real settings. They include public elementary, middle, and high school teachers, a teacher from a private language school, and university language teachers. Four story plots that reveal how teacher knowledge and inquiry are connected to classroom practice emerge in the telling of their stories:

1) The connection between teacher and person: Extracts from teacher histories and personal metaphors about teaching show how teachers' past experiences, backgrounds, talents, and interests determined their career choices and continue to influence how and what they teach.

2) The connection between the "apprenticeship of observation" and teachers' beliefs about teaching: Teachers' stories reveal the strong connection between how they learned and were taught and how they now teach.

3) The connection between theory and practice: Teachers react to theories about learning and language acquisition. In their stories they relate what they have done to incorporate theory into practice and how they have modified and constructed their own versions of parts of theories that were not always validated in their particular contexts through practice.

4) The connection between classroom practice and inquiry (research): In their inquiry stories, teachers write about the type of research they do or are interested in doing and the approaches to classroom investigation that best suit them and their situations.

THE CONNECTION BETWEEN TEACHER AND PERSON

> We do best as teachers by being real, whole people relating to students as real, whole people . . . living our daily realities.
> (Melanie, a high school Spanish teacher)

The primary focus in most discussions about learning and teaching ESL and foreign languages is on the learner. Teachers are encouraged to consider how students' interests, backgrounds, learning style preferences, personality characteristics, aptitudes, attitudes, and psyches influence their behaviors as learners. The learner is presented as a complex individual whose idiosyncrasies need to be perceived and appreciated by teachers in order for meaningful and relevant instruction to take place. When teachers become the center of discussion about teaching or learning issues, the descriptors are much more impersonal. Teachers are usually described in terms of their functions and roles. They are planners, assessors, disciplinarians, motivators, facilitators, target language users and modelers, and creators of positive learning environments. When teachers' personal traits are mentioned, they are usually idealized and stated in terms of student needs. Brosh (1996) summarizes descriptions of the effective teacher as "someone who comes to know his or her students, who is sensitive to the ways in which students receive and process information, and who establishes a classroom environment that stimulates and supports students' innate motivation" (p. 127). When individual teaching style preferences are acknowledged, it is usually in the context of understanding the negative results of mismatches with incompatible learning styles (Nunan, 1991). Teachers, then, are seldom described as complex individuals with varied backgrounds, specific likes and dislikes, diverse personality traits, representing a wide range of attitudes and competencies.

> "Teachers can be more effective participants in this process (interaction with students) only when they begin to see **how what is distinctive about them and about each of their students combines to create the unique milieu** that characterizes their particular classroom learning/teaching situation."

It is not realistic to think that teachers can respond to students' needs without considering who they are and how they operate as people.

Teachers and students interact together in a social context in which all participants play a vital role in determining what shape the learning process will take. Teachers can be more effective participants in this process only when they begin to see how what is distinctive about them and about each of their students combines to create the unique milieu that characterizes their particular classroom learning/teaching situation.

As we work with teachers in our training, supervising, and collaborative capacities, we explore with them through journals, portfolios, and interviews how who they are as people influences who they are as teachers. As they discover how aspects of their personal lives connect to their teaching worlds, they become more aware of the inseparability of the two worlds and the ways they intersect. Beyond this it makes no sense to attempt to generalize about what teachers' stories reveal because it is in their particularity that they have value. We offer the following as examples of the explorations language teachers have made into the connection between personal and teaching worlds.

Lila[2] is an ESL (English as a Second Language) teacher who works with university-bound international students in an urban intensive English program in Colorado.

> "It is the total woman who walks through the classroom door every morning, and it is as much **her philosophy of life** as any pedagogical principle that **shapes her teaching**."

The story of Lila as a teacher is the story of Lila as a person. It is the total woman who walks through the classroom door every morning, and it is as much her philosophy of life as any pedagogical principle that shapes her teaching. In a portfolio/journal entry she describes the way she sees her beliefs influencing her teaching:

> . . . what I believe about human nature and the meaning of life is a necessary part of my existence. Two pieces of this philosophy particularly influence how I deal with students. The first is that I believe in the inherent good of people and their desire to reach toward perfection. Each student deserves to be given every opportunity to succeed. I also believe that each individual is responsible for making his/her own choices. This translates into action in the classroom by my providing choices every day and in many ways and by my helping students realize that they are responsible for their own learning.

Just as her beliefs shape her teaching, her teaching and her students have an impact on her life outside the classroom. In an interview Lila explained, "I read the newspaper every day with an eye to what I can use in the classroom. And often my dinner conversation with my kids is about the corny things people said and did in my class that day." Her classroom life is woven into the fabric of her home life, and in turn her life experiences find their way into the classroom. She tells her students stories about her travels, for example, relating what happened on a trip to Europe when she put her almost-out-of-gas rental car on the wrong ferry boat crossing from Denmark into Germany and found herself without the proper currency and without gas in a strange city. Her students reacted to this story with questions and comments, relating it to other stories she had told them about herself. They know who she is; she is a real person to them.

Tina, a high school French teacher in Alaska, characterizes herself as someone who is easily bored. As a result she sees herself using a wide variety of visuals, music, stories, and games in her classes. In a group discussion she described herself as loving "a good laugh." Later in a journal entry she explores how her enjoyment of humor goes into the classroom with her:

> I use [humor] in everything I do—including disciplining students. (Yes, in high school this is still a big factor.) Saying things like, "Oh, no! Put that science book away before the teacher sees it!," usually gets a laugh and good results. Students know I tease them, but only gently. And I'm quite happy to direct the joke at myself as well. I think all of us function better together when we can relax and share a few smiles. We're more receptive. And my cats (whom I adore) figure often in the funny stories I tell in French.

Hannah teaches high school Spanish, German, and ESL in Alaska. She identifies herself as a person who loves the outdoors, open spaces, and freedom. She sees who she is as a person reflected in her work in subtle ways; she speaks of the "geographical layout" and visual impact of how the room is arranged so that she and her students can move through it without running into obstacles, and so that she can get close to any student at any time. She says she is also "very waste-aware at home and at school." In a journal entry she shares how valuing the environment shows up in her teaching:

> I try to be accountable for the paper I use. I try to teach the students this sense of accountability by stamping homework assignments with a "Recycle" stamp and giving an extra credit point if they have two stamps on one paper.

□ METAPHORS

In their preservice and in-service education, teachers are using metaphors more and more in telling their stories about how their personal beliefs and behaviors are linked to their teaching (Bullough, 1991).

> "We have encouraged teachers to use **metaphors** to explore the motivations behind their teaching decisions, to conceptualize their commitments to students and to look critically at perceived teaching problems."

The common view is that a metaphor is a figure of speech used mainly by literary folks to enrich and poeticize their texts. However, Lakoff and Johnson (1980) see the metaphor as an essential device used by all of us to interpret our experiences and interactions with others: "Just as we seek out metaphors to highlight and make coherent what we have in common with someone else, so we seek out personal metaphors to highlight and make coherent our own pasts, our present activities, and our dreams, hopes, and goals as well" (pp. 232–3). We have encouraged teachers to use **metaphors** to explore the motivations behind their teaching decisions, to conceptualize their commitments to students, and to look critically at perceived teaching problems. Here are some of their efforts.

Andy, a veteran university French teacher in Utah, sees teaching and learning as a sculpting process. He explains his metaphor in this way:

> I see myself being shaped daily by my interactions with my students, molded by the group dynamics and class-room culture, and see my lesson chiseled out by content choices, perceptions of student needs, my proficiency in the language, and the class' shared psychological state.

Another of Andy's journal entries shows his reflections about a class that he has just taught. He is disappointed that he monopolized the talk and avoided student involvement because he feared that students would go off in "wrong" directions if he did not stay in control. He goes back to his original metaphor to analyze his understanding of the event:

> I horded the hammer and chisel; instead of being an interactive "sculptor," being sculpted as well as sculpting, I had played the teacher who was a total "chiseler," swindling my students out of their role in the creative process.

Angie has taught high school Spanish, biology, and general science for seven years. She was part of a group that used metaphors to explore how their conceptions of teaching had changed over the course of their careers. When she started teaching, she said, her metaphor for a teacher was a venetian blind open to let the light in. In her journal she explains the metaphor this way:

> I began teaching fresh out of college; I never student taught in Spanish—just jumped right in with experienced teachers as mentors. At that time I believed that if I presented the material in an interesting and logical

manner the students would learn and grow intellectually. All I was responsible for was to open the blind, by presenting the material, and let the knowledge soak in. I now believe that that metaphor is narrow and that a teacher's role and responsibility go well beyond presenting material. I now consider myself to be a gardener where presenting the material is merely planting the seed. My role as a teacher goes well beyond sowing to the cultivation and ultimately to the enjoyment of the mature plant. Cultivation represents the continuing concern and interest in my students' development, not only as language learners but as productive members of society. I want them to grow into mature and responsible adults who take the knowledge gained in my classroom, both in language and in general life skills, out into the world with them.

Nicole, a 14-year veteran of the language teaching profession, was part of the same group using metaphors to tap into how their conceptions of teaching had changed. As a beginning Spanish teacher she saw herself as "the fountain of knowledge, brimming with excitement, eager to fill every student's cup with the same passion, energy, and possibility" that she felt. Now her metaphor is that of a "river guide." Instead of flooding students with information every class period, she sees herself encouraging her students to grab a paddle and join her in the boat as they float down the river. She feels she can help them avoid rough spots and teach them to paddle better as they negotiate the river together. In her words, "Teaching is a journey. I don't really think I know how far each student will get, but we'll have fun getting there and will work together."

Jeannie, a Spanish teacher for twenty years, viewed herself as a "sales rep" in the early years of her career. Her product was the Spanish language and culture and she "was out to sell it with every trick imaginable." Being a great actor played into this image, and she measured success by how much the students loved her classes, whether or not they bought the product and her act. Now she sees herself more as an "orchestra conductor" and her students as the diverse individual musicians who come together under her orchestration to perform as one. The music, she says, comes from the musicians, not the conductor. Her job is to facilitate their learning, set the scene, and encourage excellence so they can improve both individually and as a group.

THE CONNECTION BETWEEN THE "APPRENTICE-SHIP OF OBSERVATION" AND TEACHERS' BELIEFS ABOUT TEACHING

"But I don't want to learn Spanish!" That's what I told the 9th grade counselor, but I took it anyway and guess what? The teacher changed my life. She was my first language teacher and under her influence, I fell in love with the Spanish language and culture.

(Carla, a Spanish and ESL teacher)

Novice teachers do not enter the classroom as blank slates. The teachers they have had throughout their years as students provide models that shape their expectations and notions of what teachers are and do. Lortie referred to this lengthy classroom tenure as the "13,000-hour apprenticeship of observation" (1975). Examining this apprenticeship permits teachers to see where some of their practices and philosophies have come from. Bailey, *et al.* (1996) also suggest that such an examination of the past can help teachers break out of the cycle of teaching as they were taught rather than as they have been trained. Mahabir (1993, 19), in describing her student teaching experience, makes this case for reflection into past educational experiences:

> Reflection helps me to weave the connections between my past experiences of education and my present understanding of negotiating curriculum. As I write about and share these stories I become aware of where I come from, where I am, and where I would like to be in the future.

> "Whether **former teachers** were **models of perfection** or **the antithesis they have helped shape the way teachers think** about what students need, how classrooms should be structured, and what education should mean."

Teachers' stories of inquiry and reflection on their student years are seldom neutral. Whether former teachers were models of perfection or the antithesis they have helped shape the way teachers think about what students need, how classrooms should be structured, and what education should mean.

The stories language teachers have told us reveal that liberation as well as appreciation can be the result of investigating the influence of one's own educational experiences. There are four categories into which most of the stories we have collected about student years fall:

1) Stories of apprenticeships where examples of teaching were basically negative.

2) Stories of apprenticeships where examples were initially negative, but in the long term were also salutary in some ways.

3) Stories of apprenticeships where reflection on the learning process was more central than any reaction to teaching.

4) Stories of apprenticeships where examples were positive and inspirational.

The accounts below represent each of these story types.

Angie is a high school Spanish teacher, but she did not set out to be. After what she considered negative experiences in language classes, she changed her college major to biology. In Angie's words:

> My first experiences with learning a second language were in high school where I studied French. I had always wanted to learn a second language and was very eager to get started in 9th grade. It was, as it turned out, boring, difficult, straight from the book, totally teacher directed- and very grammar-based. I struggled through three years. In college, scared off from French, I switched to Spanish. Again it wasn't very interesting; I came away with a good knowledge of grammar, but would not/could not speak a word.

As a language teacher now, Angie tries to avoid what her early teachers did; she also found "wonderful mentors" in three language teachers at the high school where she was hired. She spent many hours observing their classes and talking to them about teaching and still considers them a major source of her knowledge of what works in a language classroom. She has been able to create another apprenticeship, using these more recent models as a bridge between the negative models in her past and the teacher she has become.

Vanessa is another teacher who has developed her own teaching priorities partially in reaction to a negative experience as a student:

> . . . whenever a student made an error, [the teacher] modeled with her puckered lips, "Non!" and then went on to another victim . . . I was horrified at her cold demeanor and knew that I could *never* do that.

Now in the French classes she teaches, Vanessa says she corrects errors by repeating students' inaccurate words or phrases correctly, but she does not interrupt their attempts at communication; she reacts first to the content of the students' utterances and then tends to the errors.

Geraldine is an experienced language teacher of 24 years. During one of those years she was a Fulbright exchange teacher in Germany. The story she tells about one of her teachers relates the negative reaction she had to the teacher's instructional style and values but also demonstrates how she later came to view the experience of being in this woman's classroom. A demanding person who "used a textbook at least 30 years old," Geraldine's first German teacher never gave her a grade higher than a "B" no matter how hard Geraldine worked. However, Geraldine does recognize several positive influences that the tutelage of this teacher had on her:

Thanks to her I can read Fraktur, the old style of printing and writing, which thoroughly amazed my college professors. I can also recite any number of lengthy German poems, which impresses my students!

Over the years, Geraldine has distanced herself considerably from the model of this teacher. She characterizes her teaching now as communicative ("providing lots of opportunities for hearing, speaking, and using the language") and student-centered ("personalizing activities and focusing on content of interest to students").

Novice teachers and student teachers who are still very close to their apprenticeships often have more vivid memories of how they learned than how they were taught. During her student teaching experience, Julia affirmed that the main sources of her teaching knowledge came from remembering how she learned and taught herself as a student:

> I might have been taught methods in the secondary education classes, but I find that I have to keep reminding myself of those. They don't come to mind as quickly or as naturally as the techniques I contrived to get myself to learn. And this is what helps me to come up with ways to help my students now.

Some fortunate teachers have followed in the footsteps of exemplary mentors who were their first language teachers. Bonnie, who moved around a lot during her school years because her father was in the military, gives this account of how lucky she was to be at one school where she had an excellent Spanish teacher after whom she tries to model herself now:

> This teacher introduced and reintroduced vocabulary and grammar and gave us opportunities to use the language and create with the language. We sang, we did art projects, we wrote skits based on stories read. She was always prepared and organized for class. We moved from one related activity to another almost seamlessly. Our activities included seeing, touching, listening, reading, writing, recombining material in new and ever increasingly creative ways. Much of the way I teach today is based on how I was taught then.

THE CONNECTION BETWEEN THEORY AND PRACTICE

> I don't want to mess around with things that I don't think will work. I like to read, go to workshops, talk to other teachers, then follow my instincts as to what I think might work. Then I try it out.
>
> (Lisel, a high school Spanish teacher)

One way teachers learn theory about language and learning is through academic course work, readings in the professional literature, and conferences and workshops, often called "received knowledge" (Wallace, 1991, 52). However, the theoretical positions that teachers take are often greatly influenced by their own language learning and teaching experiences, often called "experiential knowledge" (Wallace, *ibid.*). Teachers also construct theory as they reflect upon practice to confirm or reject hypotheses they have about effective teaching, i.e., teachers reflect on "received knowledge" in the light of "experiential knowledge" and thereby reform and reconstitute theory. As the carriers of teaching knowledge acquired in practice and refined through reflection upon that practice, teachers rarely view the theories they have as never-changing ultimatums. They use them in search of ways to help students learn. They try them out, integrate them into their current knowledge systems, reject them, or find them adequate and in harmony with what they see as working well with a certain group of students in the context of the culture of that group of people at a particular moment in the learning/teaching continuum. Like Clarke (1994) we believe that teachers' experience should be central to the development and application of theory. In this section teachers from our studies talk about their reactions to theories, their own understandings of theories, and the ways in which they modify and implement theory in their classrooms.

Donna has been teaching French and English at the high school level for 12 years. She describes her way of deciding what instructional activities to use with students as putting something to the "acid test." Donna is open to trying new techniques based on "the theory of the day." If a technique works and students are successful, then Donna will continue to use it and make it a part of her repertoire of activities. On the other hand, "if it doesn't [work], I try tweaking and changing, and if it still doesn't work, I toss it out and try something else," says Donna. As a novice teacher, Donna was introduced to TPR (Total Physical Response) and describes the encounter this way:

> When I first started teaching, TPR was the "big" new theory, and the idea that students should just listen and not write, speak (at first) or have books for the first few weeks of language learning. I tried it. It drove me crazy! Some students wanted desperately to know how to spell words, others wanted to talk instead of just listen, others were very threatened because they didn't have a book to use. Over the years I've found that balance is the key for me. All students do not learn in the same way, and my methods need to reflect that. Now we spend time listening, but I also write words down so those spellers can begin learning. And when students want to speak I encourage them to do so. Now, I give out textbooks sooner than I used to.

Jamie, who has taught high school German, English, and art for twenty-four years, also tried TPR out in her classroom. She developed a unit for beginning students based on objects in the classroom and expressions they would use throughout the year. She reports that in the beginning she tried to follow Asher's guidelines "to the letter," but through "trial and error" discovered that her students were "wilting." She says, "The novelty wears off, and teenagers are social beings who *need* to talk." Her knowledge of her students and her observations of how they responded to the activities led her to integrate TPR with other activities.

Jenna is an experienced high school and adult education teacher of Spanish and ESL. Her story of how she came to view "method" is an example of one person's reaction to experiential knowledge coming together with received knowledge. Armed with theories learned in methods courses, theories she identified strongly with, Jenna took over a high school Spanish class from another teacher at mid-year. She went to class ready to apply the notions that "language learning is a social, collaborative process" and that "the target linguistic system is learned best through the process of struggling to communicate." The former teacher, on the other hand, had used a grammar-based approach; students applied grammatical rules by writing correct sentences. Jenna was shocked that the students couldn't communicate in Spanish and struggled to get them to do so. She had assumed that her methods were "correct" and "best." However, the students' reluctance to collaborate and communicate led her to question the assumption that one method is superior to another. The students were learning Spanish, they just could not use it in the ways she valued.

> Due to the students' negative reaction to me, however, I began to question who was using the "correct" method. I have found that some students excel in oral language yet struggle with the written form and vice versa. Therefore, I now strongly believe that a constant and consistent variety of instructional methodologies should be implemented to be as effective as possible for all students.

Jenna still thinks language learning is a social, collaborative process and that much is gained from attempts to communicate in the target language. She arranges students into "families" that collaborate on projects and she asks them to use Spanish in class from "day one." But she is also sensitive to the needs of students who prefer to work individually and need rules and written forms to anchor them.

THE CONNECTION BETWEEN CLASSROOM PRACTICE AND INQUIRY

> Having someone observe me and my interaction with students has opened up a new picture and enabled me to reflect about teaching in a way I have never been able to do before.
> (Jeannie, a Spanish teacher and district supervisor)

It is our assertion that good teachers conduct inquiries in their classrooms all the time, though they and the profession in general may not acknowledge that teachers are "researchers." The day-to-day experiences of teachers in classrooms with real students and real constraints lead naturally to questions about effective teaching practices, the way classes are scheduled, the type of homework assignments teachers require, what they want students to be able to do at the end of the year. Finding answers to these questions forms the framework of teachers' inquiries, inquiries that help them make sense of their work, their students, and themselves. As the following teachers take the lead in telling what questions they are seeking answers to, and how they conduct their inquiries, they also tell of the constraints they face.

Jenna is concerned about students who are doing poorly in her Spanish classes and is considering ways to approach the issue:

> I know that it helps for me to be able to converse and meet with my peers concerning individual students; I would like to have more time in order to do this on a regular basis. I also need to talk to counselors about individual backgrounds and personal lifestyles and families . . . and make it a point to conference with students to let them know I am concerned and care about them now and about their futures. I need to constantly remind myself that students' behaviors are usually not the result of my teaching ability but rather due to occurrences in their own lives.

When Jenna talks about conducting an inquiry into her concerns about students, she does not separate "a study" or "inquiry" from her day-to-day concerns and work with students. She includes information about her time constraints, her emotional links to her students, and her understanding that her question (why are students doing poorly?) is likely to have a myriad of answers for each individual student. She is not looking for a single cause, and she cannot separate her question from the realities of the people involved.

Monica is concerned that students in her Russian classes do not perceive that they have made progress. She wants to find ways to make them aware of their growth and has decided to do some simple end of week/day/unit evaluations to help them begin thinking about what they have learned. Tina is interested in finding effective ways to move her French students from speaking to writing. Lila wants to investigate patterns of relationship in her multicultural ESL class; Sara is evaluating the relative frequency of student talk to teacher talk and plans to involve students in helping her collect data. The issues teachers address in their classroom inquiries are as diverse as the teachers and students involved. To have value, the inquiry must address the questions of the particular players, not aim for generalizable universals. Bassey (1986) calls this the "study of singularities" (p. 21).

Jessie has developed a number of very successful content-based courses in her German program. She has noticed that her students stay in the target language when activities are teacher fronted and they are talking about the content (Botany in German). However, she is aware that during group work and other non-teacher-fronted activities there is considerable English being spoken. She wants to determine when and why students are using English and then explore ways to encourage more target-language use.

> First, I'll try to determine *when* the English is being used (beginning of period as I do clerical duties, during transitions, during group work?). Perhaps I can find a colleague to come and observe and take notes on a grid, or videotape. Then I'll analyze to see whether they speak English because:
>
> 1) they can't express their thoughts in German;
>
> 2) they don't consider that class has begun;
>
> 3) they don't know how to ask for help;
>
> 4) the stress of speaking German all the time is too great;
>
> 5) my expectations for them are too high;
>
> 6) their motivation is too low.
>
> I think I'll put the problem before the class for their input as well and ask for possible solutions. I'll also brainstorm with colleagues in my department. Consulting with the immersion teachers may also be a good idea to see how they keep kids "in the language."

Jessie has identified an area that concerns her. Her first plan is to gather data which will give her a better understanding of the behavior (speaking English). She will seek the collaboration of her students and colleagues in pursuit of a plan that may increase target-language use. As she contemplates implementing her inquiry procedures, she continues to question her feelings about the issue: "Can I change this? Is it too much to ask of kids after one or two years of a language? Maybe both sides must make more of an effort???"

For Jessie, and for most of the teachers we work with, inquiry is not a sterile, objective process that leads to absolute truths and irrefutable conclusions. Inquiry is messy. The researcher does not distance himself or herself from his or her subject, but realizes that he or she is part of the process and cannot be divorced from it since understanding his or her role in an inquiry issue is as important as understanding the role of the students, the subject matter content, and the context in which all of these factors come together.

Any discussion of teachers conducting inquiry must consider the constraints they face. The constraint most frequently cited by the teachers we have worked with is *time*. As Tina points out, it is not just time to plan her inquiry on helping students move from speech to writing that she needs, it is time to find the dictations she wants to use, time to assess writing samples, analyze results, and discuss it all with students. Other teachers mention the value of consulting with colleagues, but always with the *caveat* that time is a factor. Lisel mentions "lack of time to think, lack of practical information for teachers, lack of understanding by people outside the field of language teaching, and isolation" as major constraints facing public school language teachers conducting inquiries. In addition, teachers have told us that budget, degree of support from administrators, scheduling, equipment, and logistics are constraints they must confront in conducting classroom inquiry. Hannah's suggestions for facing constraints are enlightening:

> *Time*: A scheduled block of time should be incorporated within the work day [to allow teachers to pursue research interests] (not the conventional conference period in which counselors' and administrative demands and parent contacts are made).

> *Logistics*: A language department needs to be geographically located together in the building to facilitate sharing equipment and consulting.

> *Equipment*: We need access to equipment; television, VCR, audiocassette recorders, screens, and overhead projectors *should* be standard equipment in each language class. The standard sign-up for equipment in the library is time-consuming and ineffective. I'd gladly pay for all photocopying I do in exchange for this equipment.

> *Schedule*: Language teachers' conference periods in such a way that peer coaching would be possible.

Hannah's comments point to Clarke's (1994) stand that much in the system must change in order to bring teachers to the center. Teachers may well conduct inquiry all the time, but they cannot get peer feedback on their work, disseminate it, or facilitate inquiry projects without the acknowledgment and support of others in their buildings and districts. Gina, who teaches French, English, and ESL at the high school level, talks about the difference administrative support made for peer coaching teams at her school:

> It took a lot of time, and it was hard to give up a prep period. But because the principal considered this program very important, substitutes were also hired to free teachers during class periods so that they didn't always have to use their prep hours. Money dried up, the prin-

cipal moved on, and the program disappeared. I'd love to have this program reinstituted. I learned a tremendous amount about the craft of teaching.

Melanie, who teaches at the same high school, adds that without funding and leadership from the administration, they are struggling to keep the process alive. She sees her colleagues reeling from the time and energy demands of trying to sustain the peer coaching program on their own and becoming isolated once again into their individual classrooms. She wants "continued funding and recognition" of the good they have accomplished through the program.

CONCLUSION

> "To get ahead you need a good theory . . . The
> most important one is a theory about yourself."
> (Bruner and Weisser, 1991)

The teachers who have told their stories here have developed personally and professionally through the use of self-inquiry; their inquiry has helped them understand themselves as people, as teachers and learners, and as creators of theory. It is our hope that they have demonstrated that teachers are not passive recipients of theory and method, that teaching requires thought, that the particularity of context is important, and that good teachers have much to contribute to discussions of theory and practice in the language teaching profession.

We think hearing what practitioners have to say is instructive for those who train teachers, conduct research, make policy, and administer educational programs. Teachers want and need to have their efforts acknowledged and valued. Teachers who are involved in self-inquiry say they feel better informed, more energized, less isolated, and committed to their work in new ways—all of which bring benefits to individual schools, school districts, communities, and students. However, these teachers do not operate inside vacuums any more than administrators or students do. Supporting teachers and facilitating opportunities for them to conduct inquiry requires that all levels of the educational system acknowledge the value of teacher inquiry and at the same time address the constraints that teachers say interfere with their inquiry processes.

Getting the educational system at large to recognize the value of teacher inquiry and of teachers as researchers is no simple matter. Despite the growing number of teachers who engage in inquiry, the idea has not gained wide acceptance. Wells (1994) sees two main reasons for this. First, tradition says that decisions about curriculum, method, and organization are made at the top by university-based researchers and education and government policy makers and passed on, through building-level administrators, to teachers. Status and power are far removed from classroom teachers; proposals to "democratize decision-making" by recognizing the expertise of teachers threatens this *status quo*

(p. 1). Second, according to Wells, the nature of teacher research itself impedes its being accepted. The wide variety of issues teachers choose to investigate results in their inquiries being varied in form and method. Furthermore, the methods they use are often not typically part of traditional educational research, making teacher studies difficult to describe to those with a traditional frame of reference and difficult to reduce to a set procedure or method.

To this we would add that if teachers are to take the lead in helping the profession reconceptualize who they are, what they know, and how their work adds to the production of theory, they must begin to see themselves as researchers and recognize themselves as a dynamic in the system. This will allow them to see that they, individually and collectively, can take a part in bringing about a redefinition of teacher and researcher roles.

ACKNOWLEDGMENTS

We would like to thank the following colleagues for their insights on inquiry-based teaching: Mark Clarke, University of Colorado at Denver, Janice Gullickson, Anchorage School District, Alaska, Janice Oldroyd, Spring International Language Center, Aurora Campus, and the many language teachers in Alaska, Colorado, and Utah who have shared their stories with us.

NOTES

1. The sources of these stories include: language teachers in Alaska who participated in a workshop the authors conducted on inquiry-based teaching in October 1996; student teachers of Spanish, French, and German who taught under the supervision of Al Smith during the 1995–1997 academic years; Janice Oldroyd who is part of an ethnographic study of teaching being conducted by Lee Rawley, as well as a partner in a collaborative inquiry project with Lee; and the authors' own collaborative inquiry in their language classrooms.

2. All of the names used here are pseudonyms.

REFERENCES

Bailey, K. M., *et al.* (1996). "The Language Learner's Autobiography: Examining the 'Apprenticeship of Observation.'" In D. Freeman and J. C. Richards (Eds.), *Teacher Learning in Language Teaching*, (11–129). New York: Cambridge University Press.

Bassey, M. (1986). "Does Action Research Require Sophisticated Research Methods?" In D. Hustler, T. Cassidy, and T. Cuff (Eds.), *Action Research in Classrooms and Schools*. London: Allen and Unwin.

Bateson, G. (1972). *Steps to an Ecology of Mind*. New York: Ballantine Books.

Brosh, H. (1996). "Perceived Characteristics of the Effective Language Teacher." *Foreign Language Annals*, 29(2), 125–138.

Bruner, J. (1986). *Actual Minds, Possible Worlds*. Cambridge, MA.: Harvard University Press.

Bruner, J., and S. Weisser. (1991). "The Invention of Self: Autobiography and its Forms." In D. Olson & N. Torrance (Ed.), *Literacy and Orality*. New York: Cambridge University Press.

Bullough, R. V., Jr. (1991). "Exploring Personal Teaching Metaphors in Preservice Teacher Education." *Journal of Teacher Education* 42(1), 43–51.

Burnaford, G., J. Fischer, and D. Hobson. (Eds.). (1996). *Teachers Doing Research*. Mahwah, NJ: Lawrence Erlbaum Associates, Inc.

Calderhead, J. (1993). "The Contribution of Research on Teachers' Thinking to the Professional Development of Teachers." In C. Day, J. Calderhead, and P. Denico (Eds.), *Research on Teacher Thinking: Understanding Professional Development*, 11–18. London: The Falmer Press.

Clandinin, D. J. (1993). "Teacher Education as Narrative Inquiry." In D. J. Clandinin, A. Davies, P. Hogan, and B. Kennard (Eds.), *Learning to Teach, Teaching to Learn: Stories of Collaboration in Teacher Education*, 1–15. New York: Teachers College Press.

Clandinin, D. J., and F. M. Connelly. (1991). "Narrative and Story in Practice and Research." In D. A. Schön (Ed.), *The Reflective Turn: Case Studies in and on Educational Practice*, 258–281. New York: Teachers College Press.

Clarke, M. A. (1994). "The Dysfunctions of the Theory/Practice Discourse." *TESOL Quarterly* 28(1), 9–26.

Clarke, M. A., A. Davis, L. K. Rhodes, & E. D. Baker. (1996). *Creating Coherence: High Achieving Classrooms for Minority Students* (Research report). Denver: University of Colorado at Denver.

Cochran-Smith, M., and S. L. Lytle. (Eds.). (1993). *Inside/Outside: Teacher Research and Knowledge*. New York: Teachers College Press.

Freeman, D. (1991). "'To Make the Tacit Explicit': Teacher Education, Emerging Discourse, and Conceptions of Teaching." *Teaching and Teacher Education* 7 (5/6), 439–454.

Goswami, D., and P. R. Stillman. (Eds.). (1987). *Reclaiming the Classroom*. Upper Montclair, NJ: Boynton/Cook Publishers, Inc.

Hubbard, R. S., and B. M. Power. (1993). *The Art of Classroom Inquiry: A Handbook for Teacher-Researchers*. Portsmouth, New Hampshire: Heinemann.

Johnson, K. E. (1996). "The Vision Versus the Reality: The Tensions of the TESOL Practicum." In D. Freeman and J. C. Richards (Eds.), *Teacher Learning in Language Teaching* 30–49. New York: Cambridge University Press.

Kincheloe, J. L. (1991). *Teachers as Researchers: Qualitative Inquiry as a Path to Empowerment*. New York: The Falmer Press.

Knezevic, A., and M. Scholl. (1996). "Learning to Teach Together: Teaching to Learn Together." In D. Freeman and J. C. Richards (Eds.), *Teacher Learning in Language Teaching*, 79–96. New York: Cambridge University Press.

Knoblauch, C. H., and L. Brannon. (1993). *Critical Teaching and the Idea of Literacy*. Portsmouth, NH: Boynton/Cook Publishers.

Lakoff, G., and M. Johnson. (1980). *Metaphors We Live by*. Chicago: The University of Chicago Press.

Lortie, D. (1975). *Schoolteacher: A Sociological Study*. Chicago: University of Chicago Press.

Mahabir, H. (1993). "Autobiography as a Way of Knowing." In D. J. Clandinin, A. Davies, P. Hogan, and B. Kennard (Eds.), *Learning to Teach, Teaching to Learn: Stories of Collaboration in Teacher Education*, 19–27. New York: Teachers College Press.

Mattingly, C. (1991). "Narrative Reflections on Practical Actions: Two Learning Experiments in Reflective Storytelling." In D. A. Schön (Ed.), *The Reflective Turn: Case Studies in and on Educational Practice*, 235–257. New York: Teachers College Press.

Nunan, D. (1991). *Language Teaching Methodology: A Textbook for Teachers*. Hemel Hempstead: Prentice Hall International.

Richards, J. C. (1996). "Teachers' Maxims in Language Teaching." *TESOL Quarterly* 30 (2), 281–296.

Richards, J. C., and C. Lockhart. (1994). *Reflective Teaching in Second Language Classrooms*. New York: Cambridge University Press.

Schön, D. A. (1987). *Educating the Reflective Practitioner*. San Francisco: Jossey-Bass Publishers.

Shulman, L. (1988). "The Dangers of Dichotomous Thinking in Education." In P. Grimmet and G. Erickson (Eds.), *Reflection in Teacher Education*, 31–39. New York: Teachers College Press.

Wallace, M. J. (1991). *Training Foreign Language Teachers: A Reflective Approach*. Cambridge: Cambridge University Press.

Wells, G. (Ed.). (1994). *Changing Schools from Within: Creating Communities of Inquiry*. Portsmouth, NH.: Heinemann.

Technology: A Step Forward in the Teaching of Foreign Languages

Jorge H. Cubillos, *University of Delaware*

> Nothing is ever done until everyone is convinced that it ought to be done, and has been convinced for so long that it is now time to do something else.　(F.M. Cornford)

Jorge H. Cubillos is a native of Colombia and a Ph.D graduate in Spanish Applied Linguistics from Pennsylvania State University. At the present time he is an Assistant Professor at the University of Delaware, where he supervises Elementary and Intermediate Spanish instruction, as well as the training of Teaching Assistants. He is the author of several materials for the teaching and learning of Spanish, among them Siempre adelante *(textbook and CD-ROM reading assistant for Intermediate Spanish) and* Mundos Hispanos 2 *(CD-ROM program). His research interests are in the areas of culture, technology, and student assessment.*

INTRODUCTION

It was not so long ago that teachers had to lobby to get an overhead projector in their classrooms or to persuade a school administrator to provide them with a VCR or a tape recorder. Lately, however, many teachers are struggling with the question of what to do with the new technologies (multimedia computers, Internet connections, etc.) that are almost literally being thrown their way by administrators eager to benefit from the promises of the new media systems. The focus must not be on what to do with the new technology that is being provided but rather on how valid its introduction is into the communicative foreign language classroom of today. Teachers must be the ones making the decisions about their materials and equipment, and they should be doing so on the basis of available research evidence with regard to the pedagogical benefits of the new tools.

　The interest of administrators in computer technologies is perhaps grounded in their desire to respond to the changing ways in which today's students access and process information. The sale of personal computers has skyrocketed in recent years (according to the U.S. Bureau of the Census, the number of households with computers went from 6.9 million in 1984 to 22.8 million in 1993), and the proliferation of Internet access providers is evidence of the changing ways in which the new generation

37

learns and interacts with the world (Nickerson, 1988). School administrators are also very interested in the financial promise of a transformed classroom landscape. The new technologies are perceived as a source of instructional efficiency since these projected technology-enhanced courses seem to require less classroom seat-time and potentially less faculty.

The publishing industry has not been immune to the growing interest in technology and appears to be in a rush to develop electronic tutorials, CD-ROM's, and experiments of all kinds to take advantage of Internet communications. Just five years ago none of the leading college Spanish or French textbooks included multimedia ancillaries. Today it is hard to find any important foreign language publication without accompanying instructional software. In fact, book representatives indicate that their sales often depend on providing software to their customers as part of the textbook adoption process.

In spite of this anecdotal evidence, teachers' positive reception of the new technologies is far from being the norm. While some faculties have embraced these new tools and teaching materials, many are still unaware of the options and appear reluctant to invest themselves in the new media. Perhaps, there is a fear of jumping on yet another "bandwagon." Perhaps, it is perceived as a passing fad.

The last "technology fad" took place during the 1950s and 1960s, with the proliferation of language laboratories as a result of the theoretical framework provided by the Audio-Lingual Method (ALM). The goal of ALM lab designers was to create ideal conditions for "over-learning" (abundant exposure to native FL [Foreign Language] models, followed by extensive drills). In spite of their good intentions, the miracle in FL learning did not happen. Studies conducted by Smith (1969) found no significant effect on the performance of ALM students in the *MLA* (Modern Language Association) *Cooperative Classroom Listening and Speaking Test* and actually a negative effect compared to the performance of traditional students in the *MLA Reading and Writing Test*. Although the instrumentation in Smith's research has been widely criticized (Valette, 1969), it is clear that the language lab did not live up to its potential. Perhaps it had to do with the fact that the hardware was still under development, or in many cases that the software used was pedagogically unsound. However, Schwartz (1995) points out that perhaps the main problem was the lack of awareness or familiarity of many faculty members with regard to the learning methods and materials used by the students in those language labs.

Technology-assisted teaching tools, as illustrated by the previous example, cannot exist in isolation or at the expense of teachers. It is clear that new media must be at the service of good teaching:

> It is not enough for teachers to purchase expensive equipment in the hope that students will use it and reach higher levels of proficiency. Teachers need to be trained in the appropriate use of the technology so they may

better guide their students to achieve maximum results. (Schwartz, 1995, 534)

In the case of Computer Assisted Instruction (CAI) a healthy dose of skepticism on the part of faculty is warranted and even desirable. We certainly cannot afford to make the financial investment in this kind of technology without a basic sense of its pedagogical effectiveness. However, the fact that these media are invading our teaching space must lead to immediate action. My proposal and challenge to the profession is to gain ownership over these technologies so that they can be incorporated into our curricula in ways that are consistent with our current understanding of Second Language Acquisition (SLA) processes.

But, how exactly are we to accomplish this lofty goal? To answer this question, let us first examine the current Foreign Language Instruction (FLI) paradigm.

THE CURRENT FLI PARADIGM

Any discussion of foreign language materials must be placed in the context of current views of FL pedagogy. The pedagogical paradigm that has evolved on the basis of the past 20 years of SLA research could be summarized as follows:

□ INPUT-DRIVEN

Since its introduction the idea that comprehensible input is necessary for the acquisition of a second language (Krashen, 1982) has had a tremendous impact on the profession. Although not without controversy (McLaughlin, 1987), "No explanation of L2 acquisition will be complete unless it includes an account of the role of input" (Ellis, 1994, 288). Recent evidence suggests that input-rich activities such as reading are at the core of successful FL teaching and learning practices (Krashen, 1995).

> "Learners today expect **practical abilities** that will help them **interact** with speakers of other languages . . . "

□ GEARED TOWARD THE DEVELOPMENT OF COMMUNICATIVE SKILLS

The profession continues to move away from teaching practices aimed at providing *information* about the TL (Target Language) to teaching practices that emphasize the *use* of the TL for the interpretation and expression of real-life messages. Learners today expect practical abilities that will help them interact with speakers of other languages abroad and at home (Rivers, 1992). The Standards Movement (which seeks to promote the establishment of guidelines for the teaching of foreign languages for all K–12) is a good indicator of this concern with outcomes and account-ability. Delaware, in its *Content Standards* document released in September of 1996, already proclaims that the number one goal for foreign language education in the state is to "communicate in languages other than English through listening, speaking, reading, and writing in various cultural contexts" (1996, 2).

> "Teachers are beginning to conceptualize their roles in different terms: **support rather than lead, orient rather than dictate.**"

□ STUDENT-CENTERED

The profession clearly recognizes the need to put students at the center of the FL learning process (Nunan, 1988). Teachers are beginning to conceptualize their roles in different terms: support rather than lead, orient rather than dictate (Lee and Van Patten, 1995). Teaching is no longer limited to classroom delivery of information, but it now encompasses significant responsibilities in the design and support of individual/personalized learning tasks (Scarcella and Oxford, 1992).

□ CONCERNED ABOUT THE AFFECTIVE ENVIRONMENT IN WHICH LEARNING TAKES PLACE

The affective domain plays a crucial role in SLA (Krashen, 1982). Research evidence suggests that the learning of foreign languages encompasses more than cognitive processes and that the impact of these learner variables is at the core of effective language instruction. Motivation, attitudes, anxiety, self-esteem, tolerance of ambiguity, risk-taking, cooperation, and competition are key variables that explain individual differences in SLA (Ellis, 1994).

□ INTERESTED ABOUT CULTURAL AWARENESS

The teaching and learning of languages is no longer a task devoid of con-text. Decoding the foreign language requires understanding the cultural context in which the message was generated. Seelye (1984) suggests seven goals for cultural instruction in the FL classroom:

1. The exploration of the sense or functionality of culturally condi-tioned behavior;

2. The study of the interaction between language and social variables;

3. Conventional behavior in common situations;

4. The cultural connotation of words or phrases;

5. The evaluation of statements about a society;

6. The development of skills needed to locate and organize information about the target culture; and

7. The development of intellectual curiosity and empathy towards the TL community (adapted from Seelye, 1984, 43).

Learning more about life in the TL community is a very important expectation among students with regard to their required FL courses. "A number of recent surveys of college and university students have shown generally positive attitudes toward required language study, especially if the cultural component is sufficiently emphasized" (Omaggio, 1993, 356). More than facts or tourist information about the TL community, FL teachers need to direct their efforts to the development of the learners' cultural self-awareness and their ability to appreciate culturally-derived differences (Lafayette & Schulz, 1975).

WHAT DOES TECHNOLOGY HAVE TO OFFER?

Although research into the effectiveness of technology for the teaching of foreign languages is still limited, the following tendencies can already be identified in the literature:

> " . . . L2 vocabulary learned in a **multimedia environment** leads to **higher retention rates**."

□ TECHNOLOGY CAN FACILITATE THE ACQUISITION OF VOCABULARY

The importance of images and associations in learning L2 vocabulary has been well documented (Kellogg & Howe, 1971), as well as the need to promote deep processing of the new lexical items by embedding them in context (Bahrick & Phelps, 1987). Because of the ability of multimedia technologies to deliver a variety of visual and oral input, they are ideally suited for the contextualization of lexical items and therefore have the potential to result in significant vocabulary gains for the learner. Danan (1992) examined the relationship between visual input (video) and bimodal verbal input (audio plus L2 subtitles). Her research findings suggest that L2 vocabulary learned in a multimedia environment leads to higher retention rates. Lyman-Hager, *et al.* (1993) studied the impact of exposure to interactive reading software (text plus on-line glosses and pictures) and found greater mastery of vocabulary among students exposed to the computerized treatment. Chun and Plass (1996) also found that the learning of vocabulary was significantly higher for students working on reading passages with the help of *CyberBuch* (computer software designed to support reading tasks by means of glosses, images, and videos). The previous results indicate that multimedia technologies have a great potential in the area of vocabulary acquisition.

☐ TECHNOLOGY CAN INCREASE STUDENTS' LANGUAGE AWARENESS

The ability of technology to present, elicit, and evaluate learner responses (both written and oral due to voice recognition technologies) can be a great help in directing students' attention to the structural aspects of the language. In the literature we can find examples of the use of videodiscs to help students better understand the French sound system (Jamieson, 1994), video to enhance students' learning of vocabulary and idiomatic structures (Secules, Herron, and Tomasello, 1992), and multimedia instructional tools such as *Teacher Partner* developed at the University of Michigan to facilitate the exploration of lexical and structural aspects of video texts in the FL classroom (Johnston & Milne, 1995). However, intelligent computer feedback is perhaps the most promising option available in the area of learner consciousness-raising. In the initial stages of CAI, programs were only able to respond with general error messages when the learner's response did not match the stored "correct" answer. The positive or negative feedback (frequently presented in terms of bells and whistles) revealed the behaviorist orientation of their designers but failed to provide meaningful information about the nature or the location of the problem (Garret, 1987).

With the advent of the *Pattern Mark-Up* technique the computer was able to provide the learner with more concrete information regarding the nature of the error by pinpointing the location of the mismatch between the correct stored and provided response (Nagata, 1993). *Pattern Mark-Up* became even more helpful in view of the development of the *Error Anticipation* technique, which allowed for the provision of error messages that explained the nature of the problem and its solution based on the list of possible errors stored in the system.

Today, *Natural Language Processing* (NLP) represents a more sophisticated alternative to program feedback, allowing the program to analyze students' output and to generate very specific responses as to the location, nature, and solution(s) to their errors. Nagata (1993) studied the impact of NLP on the production of learners of Japanese and found that the scores on achievement tests of students who used the intelligent feedback version of the Nihongo-CALI system (a computer program for the practice of Japanese passive structures) were significantly higher than those of students exposed to the conventional feedback version of the same system. Similar results were obtained by Nagata & Swisher (1995) who studied the performance of students in achievement and retention tests of Japanese particles and passivization. Their study revealed that students exposed to intelligent computer feedback benefited significantly from the metalinguistic instruction offered by the computer. Today's CAI materials should take advantage of NLP to provide specific and informative feedback on students' output.

□ TECHNOLOGY CAN EFFECTIVELY SUPPORT INPUT-RICH ACTIVITIES SUCH AS READING AND WRITING

The ability of technology to facilitate the exposure of students to authentic language is widely documented (Altman, 1989). In recent years, the potential of these new media to foster the development of comprehension skills has come under scrutiny with very positive and encouraging results. In the case of listening, a great deal of attention has been given to video in its many forms (videotape, laser disc, CD-ROM, etc.) due to its ability to combine aural and visual cues and to illustrate the dynamics of communication among speakers of the target language (Altman, 1989). In the words of Di Carlo (1994): "Students seem to learn best when all their senses and emotions are engaged" (p. 468). Secules, Herron, & Tomasello (1992) found that the use of the video series "French in Action" with second-semester university students of French resulted in greater listening comprehension skills. In a subsequent study, learners exposed to video showed significant difference in listening comprehension tests, a difference that did not come at the expense of other skills (Herron, *et al.*, 1995). Multimedia technologies have given even more control over this video input to FL learners in view of their ability to provide not only audio-visual stimuli but also a number of additional resources such as transcriptions, glosses, translations, and grammar presentations.

> ". . . (T)he **images and sounds contained in videos** serve as powerful preparatory activities that explain the **superior performance in reading comprehension** tests of learners exposed to them."

In the case of reading, multimedia technologies and the Internet offer great promise as well. Two important concerns when it comes to reading comprehension are: a) how to provide choices in order to approach the "Free Voluntary Reading" ideal advocated by Krashen (1993); and b) how to support the learners as they try to derive meaning from authentic texts. The Internet has been suggested as a source of unlimited and engaging reading opportunities (Armstrong & Yetter-Vassot, 1994). To support the reading process, video can be used as an advance organizer (Hanley, *et al.*, 1995). Hanley's research results indicate that the images and sounds contained in videos serve as powerful preparatory activities that explain the superior performance in reading comprehension tests of learners exposed to them. Sharma (1993) suggests that beyond the basic activation of schemata, multimedia technologies are in a unique position to provide FL readers with the necessary tools for the effective comprehension of culturally displaced texts. The database that can be accessed through hypertexts (texts that interface large bodies of information) are, in his view, an absolute requirement for getting to the "essence" of literary texts.

☐ TECHNOLOGY CAN SUPPORT AND FACILITATE OUTPUT ACTIVITIES

While technology is ideally suited for the delivery of L2 samples in diverse and flexible formats, it is also quite capable of supporting and promoting output activities inside and outside the foreign language classroom. Take for instance the case of local area networks (LAN). Beauvois (1992) describes the experience of incorporating real-time, synchronous discussions on a LAN as part of an intermediate Portuguese course. The willingness of students to use the target language for real communication in the computer-mediated discussion sessions (much like the popular "chat rooms" offered by Internet access providers), as well as their positive perceptions of the course, are two promising signs of the benefits of this type of application. Beauvois' findings are consistent with those reported by Kern (1995), who found that the use of real-time discussion through *Daedalus InterChange* with a second-semester French class created a non-threatening atmosphere that encouraged the participation of all students and fostered their creative expression—a very strong case indeed for the use of this kind of material in the communicative classroom:

> Compared to oral discussions, *InterChange* was found to offer more frequent opportunities for student expression and to lead to more language production. Furthermore, students' language output in *InterChange* was of an overall greater level of sophistication than in oral discussion, in terms of its morphosyntactic features and in terms of the variety of discourse functions expressed. Direct student-to-student interaction stimulated students' interest in one another, contributed to peer learning, and decreased students' reliance on the instructor. Moreover, a large majority of students enjoyed using *InterChange* and found it motivating. Finally, there was some indication that the *InterChange* environment reduced communication anxiety (Kern, 1995, 470).

When it comes to oral skills, there is also evidence in the literature regarding the benefits of available multimedia technologies. Borrás & Lafayette (1994) found that fifth-semester students of French exposed to a multimedia package that allowed for student-control of fully duplicating intralingual subtitles (literal transcriptions of the video text in the target language) resulted "in both better comprehension and subsequent better productive use of the foreign language" (p. 70). The impressive results of this first study on the impact of hypertexts on receptive and productive L2 skills speaks for the quality of the learning experience afforded by these new learning tools.

□ TECHNOLOGY CAN GIVE TEACHERS AN INSIGHT INTO THEIR STUDENTS' SLA PROCESSES

The ability of computer programs to keep track of students' progress provides teachers and researchers with invaluable data about SLA. Programs such as *Système-D* (writing assistant for French) and the Spanish (*Atajo*) and German counterparts (*Quelle*) allow for the creation of detailed logs of students' activity while using the program (time on task, type of searches, etc.). Based on data obtained from student logs, Bland, *et al.* (1990) have been able to identify three stages in the development of L2 writing proficiency: **Token Matching** (when the learner assumes a one-to-one correspondence between L1 and L2 lexical items), **Type Matching** (when the learner makes use of more abstract representations of the lexical item needed while searching for a TL match); and **Relexicalization** (when learners sense lexical gaps and begin to explore the L2 for alternative ways of expressing a given concept). Student logs and student records of all kinds can provide teachers with unprecedented insights into their students' SLA processes. The ideal of a teacher-researcher is much more feasible today in view of the learner-tracking capabilities of the new technologies.

□ TECHNOLOGY CAN FACILITATE THE EXPLORATION OF THE TARGET LANGUAGE CULTURE

Hypertexts in a multimedia environment combine images and sounds of the TL community with very large databases that explain, expand, or highlight cultural phenomena. A case in point is the *Ça continue...* software developed at The Penn State University by Mary Ann Lyman-Hager. This software combines authentic materials (text, audio, video) with activities that activate students' schemata and explore the text in more detail to allow for deeper comprehension (Lyman-Hager, 1995).

The Internet has also been explored in recent years because of its potential to expose students to real texts from the TL community. Abrate (1996) reports on the use of *Minitel* for a third-year French culture course. Students were asked to access different materials on this network, carry out short assignments, and complete a research project based on these materials. The positive results of this experiment seem to confirm the capabilities of this medium to allow students to interact with the target language community and to enhance their understanding of their current issues and concerns:

> Whether used in a complete course or as a supplement, *Minitel* contains a wealth of resources accessible in no other way. Furthermore, *Minitel* documents lack the analysis and synthesis of most textbooks, and this forces students to perform these tasks themselves, thus developing their cognitive skills as well as increasing their knowledge. (Abrate, 1996, 708)

An exploration of the TL culture that goes beyond simple facts and information to include the investigation and analysis of the functionality of culturally learned behaviors is consistent with the overall need to develop materials that promote the higher order thinking skills of analysis, synthesis, and evaluation advocated by Williams, Lively, & Harper (1994). Technology-assisted cultural materials seem to offer ideal conditions for accomplishing these pedagogical goals.

☐ TECHNOLOGY MAY ENHANCE STUDENTS' MOTIVATION

As mentioned in previous studies, one of the most common outcomes of the introduction of new technologies into the FL classroom is the increased motivation and positive response of the students (Masters-Wicks, Postlewate, & Lewental, 1996). The non-threatening environment created by the computer seems to allow anxious or non-confident learners to try harder, get more involved, and even participate more in technology-mediated activities (Kern, 1995). Interactive interfaces are welcomed by learners, who view them as engaging and stimulating.

☐ TECHNOLOGY CAN MAXIMIZE THE USE OF TEACHING RESOURCES

One aspect of technology that should not be forgotten is its ability to make the teacher's job easier and/or more effective. Tasks such as grade calculations, design of presentation materials, and even communication with students and other colleagues have been facilitated and enhanced with the proliferation and increased user-friendliness of computerized gradebooks, presentation software (such as *PowerPoint* and *Podium*), and of course, e-mail. But beyond the maximization of individual teachers' resources, technology can make it possible to share resources in a fully interactive manner that would have otherwise remained centralized or untapped. I am referring specifically to distance learning. With the advent of fiber optics and fully interactive two-way video it is now possible to reach wider audiences, specifically in cases where teaching resources are scarce or highly centralized. Instead of replacing teachers, these technologies can promote the sharing of resources, create links among faculties, diffuse the teaching of non-European languages, and expand the interaction of otherwise disconnected student bodies (Lambert, 1991).

IS TECHNOLOGY LIVING UP TO ITS POTENTIAL?

Clearly, modern technologies can play a very positive role in our FL programs. However, not every CD-ROM or Internet supplement on the market today takes full advantage of the pedagogical potential of the new media. Teachers and materials designers need to beware of the following pitfalls:

☐ THE "DRILL AND KILL" SYNDROME

Perhaps because of the relative ease of producing basic computer-driven drills, and the willingness of many teachers to accept this limited use of available technologies, there is a proliferation of CAI packages that do not go beyond the mechanical practice of discrete grammar or lexical items. The main limitation of this kind of material is its de-contextualized, meaningless approach to language learning. The student is taken through a series of "challenges" that require only the mechanical manipulation of isolated pieces of language. As discussed before, there is simply no need for the profession to settle for these kinds of CAI materials. We can do much better than that.

☐ FUN AND GAMES

Another dangerous alternative in the area of materials designed for CAI is the "diversion trap." Although originally conceived as engaging learning tools, many software packages present the learner with a stream of games aimed at the recycling of vocabulary, information, or structures. The ability of many of these games to support communicative language instruction goals is, of course, highly questionable. Assigning computers the role of "entertainers" or "baby-sitters" constitutes a gross underutilization of their potential.

☐ GENERIC ADD-ONS

In order to keep up with the demand (and given the lack of selectivity of most consumers at the present time) many publishers are offering what could be called generic software packages (materials that can be shared by several titles). Teachers must be very careful in the selection of these ancillaries and demand the careful articulation of these packages with their selected textbooks. There is no point in asking students to interact with a particular program if its design, content, or pedagogical approach are incongruent with the overall content or direction of a given program.

☐ RIGID AND NON-INTERACTIVE INTERFACES

In the early stages of CAI, all the technology could do was present the student with a linear stream of activities with varying degrees of program feedback (with bells or "bong" sounds to indicate the occurrence of a correct or an incorrect response, respectively). However, at the present time, many authoring programs allow for a truly interactive, non-linear interface. The student can now decide where to go, how long to stay with a given activity, and even receive helpful hints from the program on the type of learning options available. In view of these technical developments, lockstep and behaviorist feedback need no longer be the standard format of instructional software for foreign languages.

CONCLUSION: TOWARDS A PEDAGOGICAL FRAMEWORK FOR THE INCORPORATION AND DESIGN OF TECHNOLOGY-BASED FOREIGN LANGUAGE MATERIALS

As previously outlined, successful incorporation of technology into our FL classrooms depends largely on the ability of teachers to articulate the new media with sound pedagogical goals and principles. The following guidelines constitute the basic framework for eliciting the substance behind the glitz of technology-assisted FL materials.

Technology-assisted materials for the teaching of foreign languages should:

■ **be rich sources of input.** If input is at the core of language acquisition, technology must serve as a rich and flexible source of input. Listening activities can be greatly enriched by the use of interactive video technologies and by the design of strategy-oriented comprehension activities. Reading can also be supported by technology by turning it into a multimedia learning experience (going beyond the simple text to explore images and sounds and other texts that explain, elaborate, or expand on key lexical, structural, or cultural aspects of the original text). Above all, technology should allow teachers to present students with a wealth of choices to suit their diverse interests and needs. That is perhaps the most exciting aspect of the new technologies: For the first time Krashen's idea of Free Voluntary Reading (Krashen, 1993) can be a feasible reality for the average language learner.

■ **be fully interactive.** The interface design of choice must not be the linear but the interactive. Technology should allow learners to take control of their own foreign language learning experience. Students should be able to make decisions as to when and where to go in the system depending on their own interests and needs. The program should also be able to respond intelligently to the learners' progress with practical guidance and adaptive sequences, not simply with behaviorist response reinforcers.

■ **support and encourage independent learning.** FL teachers know quite well that language learning is much more than what takes place in any given classroom. They know that it requires commitment on the part of the learner to spend time with the skill-getting activities that underlie language acquisition and to practice the acquired skills beyond the completion of a given course. FL teachers also know that learners cannot simply be told to study on their own. That is why technology is called upon to facilitate the independent learning experience by means of user-friendly interfaces, clear and informative feedback, and helpful reference tools (including but not limited to vocabulary, phrases, grammar, pronunciation, and spelling tools).

■ **serve as a springboard for interactive and communicative activities.** Unless there is a clear connection between the classroom learning and the self-directed technology-aided experience, there will not be much incentive to work with the new materials. More importantly, the electronic materials must become an integral part of the curriculum either to provide the foundation for open-ended communicative tasks or to assist in their completion.

■ **facilitate the exploration of the target language culture.** The new technologies are in a privileged position not only to present the images, sounds, and texts of the TL culture, but also to help the learners fully understand and appreciate their meaning. Electronic communications also make it quite easy today to interact directly with people from the TL community. Learning and interacting with the TL culture can and must be at the core of technology-driven tasks.

■ **maximize the use of resources.** Technology can make a myriad of materials accessible to a great number of people. The promise of economic use of resources is perhaps one of the long term benefits of investing in these media. The returns, however, must not be examined in the short-term. (The cost of software and hardware will require significant financial disbursements for most institutions.) The economy will reside in the maximization of the communicative and interactive value of the teacher-led language learning sessions.

■ **enhance the role, not substitute the FL teacher.** Teachers must realize that technology is called upon to supplement and enhance, not replace them, in the learning process. Human interaction is at the core of language learning. The contribution of the skilled FL professional cannot be underestimated. Teachers must gain ownership over these new technologies in order to take full advantage of their potential (which means that schools must not only invest in software and hardware, but also in on-going training for the faculty). The role of teachers and the definition of what they do will be expanded as a result of these curricular changes.

■ **facilitate course administration.** The new technologies should make it easier for teachers to keep track of the progress of their students and to maintain an active two-way communication with them and other colleagues. These new technologies should also expand their ability to produce learning materials and to make them easily accessible to all students.

Bringing technology into our curricula can indeed enhance the effectiveness of our FL teaching efforts. It is time for faculty to be proactive by choosing and designing FL teaching tools that are consistent with our current views on SLA.

REFERENCES

Abrate, J. (1996). "A French Culture Course with Minitel: Comme si on était là." *The French Review* 69, 701–09.

Altman, R. (1989). *The Video Connection: Integrating Video into Language Teaching.* Boston: Houghton Mifflin.

Armstrong, K., and C. Yetter-Vassot. (1994). "Transforming Teaching Through Technology." *Foreign Language Annals* 27, 475–86.

Bahrick, H., and E. Phelps. (1987). "Retention of Spanish Vocabulary over Eight Years." *Journal of Experimental Psychology: Learning, Memory and Cognition* 13, 344–9.

Beauvois, M. (1992). "Computer-assisted Classroom Discussion in the Foreign Language Classroom: Conversation in Slow Motion." *Foreign Language Annals* 25, 455–64.

Bland, S., J. Noblitt, S. Armington, and G. Gay. (1990). "The Naïve Lexical Hypothesis: Evidence from Computer-assisted Language Learning." *Modern Language Journal* 74, 440–50.

Borrás, I., and R. Lafayette. (1994). "Effects of Multimedia Courseware Subtitling on the Speaking Performance of College Students of French." *The Modern Language Journal* 78, 61–75.

Chun, D., and J. Plass. (1996). "Effects of Multimedia Annotations on Vocabulary Acquisition." *The Modern Language Journal*, 80, 183–98.

Danan, M. (1992). "Reversed Subtitling and Dual Coding Theory: New Directions for Foreign Language Instruction." *Language Learning* 42, 497–527.

Di Carlo, A. (1994). "Comprehensible Input Through the Practical Application of Video-Texts in Second Language Acquisition." *Italica* 71, 465–83.

Ellis, R. (1994). *The Study of Second Language Acquisition.* Oxford: Oxford University Press.

Garret, N. (1987). "A Psycholinguistic Perspective on Grammar and CALL." In W. Smith ed., *Modern Media in Foreign Language Education: Theory and Implementation*. Lincolnwood, IL: National Textbook Company.

Hanley, J., C. Herron, and S. Cole. (1995). "Using Video as an Advance Organizer to a Written Passage in the FLES Classroom." *The Modern Language Journal* 79, 57–66.

Hennessey, J. (1995). "Using Foreign Films to Develop Proficiency and to Motivate the Foreign Language Student." *Foreign Language Annals* 28, 116–20.

Herron, C., M. Morris, T. Secules, and L. Curtis. (1995). "A Comparison Study of the Effects of Video-based Versus Text-based Instruction in the Foreign Language Classroom." *The French Review* 68, 5.

Jamieson, D. (1994). "Pronunciation Matters—an Experiment in Repurposing Videodiscs." *Computers and Education*, 23, 117–124.

Johnston, J., and L. Milne. (1995). "Scaffolding Second Language Communicative Discourse with Teacher-controlled Multimedia." *Foreign Language Annals* 28, 315–29.

Kellogg, G., and M. Howe. (1971). "Using Words and Pictures in Foreign Language Learning." *Alberta Journal of Educational Research* 17, 87–94.

Kern, R. (1995). "Restructuring Classroom Interaction with Networked Computers: Effects of Quantity and Characteristics of Language Production." *The Modern Language Journal* 79, 457–76.

Krashen, S. (1982). *Principles and Practice in Second Language Acquisition*. New York: Pergamon Press.

Krashen, S. (1993). "The Case for Free Voluntary Reading." *Canadian Modern Language Review* 50, 72–82.

Krashen, S. (1995). "What Is Intermediate Natural Approach." In P. Hashemipour, R. Maldonado, and M. van Naerssen, eds., *Studies in Language Learning and Spanish Linguistics*. New York: McGraw-Hill, Inc. 92–105.

Lafayette, R., and R. Schulz. (1975). "Evaluating Cultural Learning." In R. Lafayette, ed., *The Cultural Revolution in Foreign Languages: A Guide for Building the Modern Curriculum*. Lincolnwood, IL: National Textbook Company.

Lambert, R. (1991). *Distance Education and Foreign Languages*. NFLC Occasional Papers.

Lee, J., and B. van Patten. (1995). *Making Communicative Language Teaching Happen*. New York: McGraw-Hill, Inc.

Lyman-Hager, M. A. (1995). "Multitasking, Multilevel, Multimedia Software for Intermediate-Level French Language Instruction: Ça continue…" *Foreign Language Annals* 28, 179–92.

Lyman-Hager, M., J. Davis, J. Burnett, and R. Chenault. (1993). "Une vie de boy: Interactive Reading in French." In F. Borchardt & E. Johnson, eds., *Proceedings of the CALICO 1993 Annual Symposium on "Assessment."* Durham, NC: Duke University.

Masters-Wicks, K., L. Postlewate, and M. Lewental. (1996). "Developing Interactive Instructional Software for Language Acquisition." *Foreign Language Annals* 29, 217–22.

McLaughlin, B. (1987). *Theories of Second Language Learning*. London: Edward Arnold.

Nagata, N. (1993). "Intelligent Computer Feedback for Second Language Instruction." *The Modern Language Journal* 77, 330–39.

Nagata, N., and M. Swisher. (1995). A Study of Consciousness-Raising by Computer: The Effect of Metalinguistic Feedback on Second Language Learning." *Foreign Language Annals* 28, 337–47.

Nickerson, R. (1988). "Technology in Education in 2020: Thinking About the Not-Distant Future." In R. Nickerson & P. Zodhiates eds., *Technology in Education: Looking Toward 2020*. Washington: Lawrence Erlbaum Associates, Inc.

Nunan, D. (1988). *The Learner-Centred Curriculum*. Cambridge: Cambridge University Press.

Omaggio, A. (1993). *Teaching Language in Context*. 2nd Ed. Boston: Heinle & Heinle Publishers.

Rivers, W. (1992). *Teaching Languages in College: Curriculum and Content*. Lincolnwood, IL: National Textbook Company.

Scarcella, R., and R. Oxford. (1992). *The Tapestry of Language Learning: The Individual in the Communicative Classroom*. Boston: Heinle & Heinle Publishers.

Schwartz, M. (1995). "Computers and the Language Laboratory: Learning from History." *Foreign Language Annals* 28, 527–35.

Secules, T., C. Herron, & M. Tomasello. (1992). "The Effect of Video Context on Foreign Language Learning." *The Modern Language Journal* 76, 480–90.

Seelye, H. (1984). *Teaching Culture: Strategies for Intercultural Communication*. 2nd Ed. Lincolnwood, IL: National Textbook Company.

Sharma, C. (1993). "Teaching Foreign Literature Through Multimedia." *Electronic Library* 11, 5–11.

Smith, P. (1969). *A Comparison Study of the Effectiveness of the Traditional and Audiolingual Approaches to Foreign Language Instruction Utilizing Laboratory Equipment*. Office of Education (DHEW), Bureau of Research, Washington, DC.

Valette, R. (1969). "Some Conclusions to Be Drawn from the Pennsylvania Study." *NALLD Journal* 3, 17.

Van Patten, B. (1995). "Cognitive Aspects of Input Processing in Second-Language Acquisition." In P. Hashemipour, R. Maldonado, & M. van Naerssen eds., *Studies in Language Learning and Spanish Linguistics*. New York: McGraw-Hill, Inc. 170–83.

Williams, M., M. Lively, and J. Harper. (1994). "Higher Order Thinking Skills: Tools for Bridging the Gap." *Foreign Language Annals* 27, 405–26.

Teaching and Learning Language Through Distance Education: The Challenges, Expectations, and Outcomes

Patricia A. Aplevich, *University of Waterloo*; **Jo-Anne H. Willment,** * *Society for Teaching and Learning in Higher Education in Canada*

> "The Department Chair enters your office and announces that enrollment is down, costs are increasing, and the Department has decided to offer language courses at a distance. The Department appoints you to develop the first distance education language course. How would you react? Where would you begin?"

Patricia A. Aplevich is a language teaching specialist in the Department of French Studies at the University of Waterloo. In 1984, she developed the first distance education course in Basic French Language for the University of Waterloo. Since that time, she has revised and developed distance education courses in French language at the Basic and Intermediate levels.

=== ||| ===

Jo-Anne H. Willment is an active participant in the Society for Teaching and Learning in Higher Education in Canada. Her work in instructional design and faculty consultations has provided innovative directions for faculty over the last 15 years. As a curriculum designer in the Ontario college system, and as a past advisor on teaching and learning at the University of Waterloo, Jo-Anne has lead projects involving study groups for campus and off-campus learners, instructional design issues for distance education, and selection of new communication technologies for teaching. She has taught extensively at both the community college and university levels, and is currently completing a doctorate from the Ontario Institute for Studies in Education—University of Toronto.

---

* This paper was coauthored with surnames listed in alphabetical order.

INTRODUCTION

As the scenario above indicates, language departments continue to experience rapidly changing student populations and the imposition of funding schemes that make the expression of "doing more with less" common. The public wants education to be affordable, accessible, and accountable. For the institution and instructor, teaching through distance education provides an opportunity to meet these criteria, to incorporate innovative delivery through new technology, to serve a growing adult student population, and to motivate the new generation of technologically adept learners.

> "For students, distance education is a **flexible, convenient,** and **economical** vehicle that will carry them through the degree process while allowing them to fulfill work and family commitments."

For students, distance education is a flexible, convenient, and economical vehicle that will carry them through the degree process while allowing them to fulfill work and family commitments.

In a recent article of the *American Association of Departments of Foreign Languages Bulletin*, Lively (1997) points out that in the U.S.A., "almost half of all college students today are over the age of 24, up from 30% in the 1970s." This new student population is probably not living on-campus or attending daytime courses full-time as do many of their 18-year-old colleagues. The responsibilities that come with maturity can require a higher income and include supporting more than one person. To quote Lively (1997), "30% are going to school full-time while working and managing families." These adult learners cannot devote four years of their lives to the full-time pursuit of higher education. They seek alternatives such as distance education that allow them to study on their own terms, in their own time, at a considerably reduced cost.

□ DEFINING DISTANCE EDUCATION

Distance education encompasses situations in which teachers and learners are separated in time and place. One can visualize various scenarios in which this is possible:

- ◆ the traditional "correspondence" course where students receive a self-contained package (e.g., print materials, audio and video-cassettes, software) and communicate with the instructor only through written and/or taped assignments;

- ◆ the course that is primarily self-contained but includes regular telephone, or interactive video tutorials, or even "immersion" workshops when students meet face-to-face with the instructor as a group; or

♦ the Internet course in which students interact synchronously or asynchronously with other students and the instructor via e-mail, chat lines, cafés, or discussion groups using conferencing software. The instructor and students may be in far-flung communities, on the same campus, or a combination of both.

> "With the instructor at a distance from the learner, the traditional teaching role changes from that of the authority figure, broadcaster, dispenser of wisdom, to one of a **guide, mentor, coach** and/or **resource facilitator**."

Distance education encourages learners to identify their own needs and ways to address these needs within the context of the course. For example, those with strong oral skills may emphasize structure and vocabulary development, whereas others may identify culture, listening comprehension, oral production, or writing as priorities. Instructors lay a table but do not always know if all dishes have been tasted, the plates cleaned, and the forks used in the "right" order—if at all! Learners, for their part, are given the opportunity to manage their own learning, set their own pace, select course components relevant to their goals, and choose from the course menu.

With the instructor at a distance from the learner, the traditional teaching role changes from that of the authority figure, broadcaster, dispenser of wisdom, to one of a guide, mentor, coach, and/or resource facilitator. To serve in these new capacities, the instructor must learn to relinquish control. The learner, on the other hand, is in a position to accept greater responsibility with the result that both work as a team in a new collaborative, balanced relationship.

This article offers practical suggestions to those about to design a distance education course for the first time. It also examines issues concerning the delivery of language courses outside of the traditional, on-campus classroom.

CHALLENGES IN TEACHING LANGUAGES VIA DISTANCE EDUCATION

□ CREDIBILITY

To prepare a language course for distance education is to believe that such a course will meet the same standards and expectations as other university courses. Many language-teaching faculty worry that students will not be equipped to make the transition from a distance education course to the campus edition of the follow-up course. Aligning the standards and the methods of evaluation can reassure sceptics and assure a seamless transition for students seeking success in both formats.

Today's communication technology offers interactive possibilities unthought of twenty years ago in the days of the traditional print-based correspondence course. The primary challenge today for many language course instructors and their students is to master the technology and employ it effectively in their language courses. Building a training period into the course syllabus to assure that all students start with some sense of control on a level playing field is one response to these challenges.

☐ MEETING A COMPLEX ASSORTMENT OF NEEDS

Knowing the students and recognizing the diversity of language proficiency, level of preparation, and access to resources poses a significant challenge to the planning of a distance education course. These factors must be balanced with the aims of the instructor, the challenges of technology, the language components of the course, and the administrative considerations.

Due to the complexity of these teaching and learning needs, an instructional designer working closely with the content expert/faculty member and support staff (e.g., graphic designer, production and administrative staff) becomes a crucial component to the process. The instructional designer assures that these various needs are met within each facet of the course and across the course as a whole.

☐ ACHIEVING INTERACTION

In the last decade, developments in conferencing software, interactive CD-ROM, e-mail, audio and video conferencing, and the Internet have all opened new paths to communicative and interactive language learning in distance education. The challenge remains, however, to establish how these new technologies can best aid the course development team in producing an effective, high quality, interactive language-learning experience while assuring that costs remain reasonable and that the course be accessible to as broad a range of students as possible.

The recent expansion in the language-learning CD-ROM market, for example, has been a boon to instructors seeking a low-cost, easily accessible, ready-made, and predictable teaching tool. Students can both see and hear native speakers in their own environment, interact with them through structured speaking and listening exercises, as well as practice reading and writing. In the area of basic French, D.C. Heath's *Mais oui!* (1996) and McGraw-Hill's *Vis-à-vis* (1996), for example, both offer an integrated CD-ROM with the text package. Other commercial companies propose similar extensive programs for this market. Students are able to work independently and yet receive corrective feedback. The CD-ROM is self-contained, requires only a media package addition to some computers (many have the media package built-in), and is readily available at reasonable cost and is independent of network delays. The CD-ROM is ideal for inclusion in the distance education course package.

TEACHING AND LEARNING EXPECTATIONS

Developing a distance education course calls for a change in teaching process, not a change in teaching philosophy. Preparing a distance education course for the first time offers the opportunity to examine or reexamine one's personal teaching aims. The challenge then is to select the delivery mode best suited to the course, the instructor, the students, and the resources of the institution, keeping in mind time, distance, and budgetary constraints.

> "Developing a distance education course calls for a change in teaching process, not a change in teaching philosophy."

When experienced distance education instructors reflect upon the process of course development, they confess that their distance education course was more organized, planned, and coherent than their campus course because the process required new ways of planning and implementing course delivery. Instructors cannot rush to the lecture hall with notes tucked under their arm at the last minute. In fact, distance education requires that as much thought be put into planning and delivery as into content. The result is, of course, that one becomes a better campus instructor as a result of the distance education experience. Many use distance education courses as a new basis for their campus courses.

> "... (D)istance education requires that as much thought be put into . . . **delivery** as into content."

DEVELOPING A GOAL-SETTING STATEMENT

To begin the process, answer the following important questions about the course you are about to develop.

- ♦ Who are the distance education students?
- ♦ What are their goals?
- ♦ What are the goals of the course?
- ♦ What teaching strengths does the instructor bring to the course?
- ♦ What skills must the instructor acquire to enhance his or her ability to plan and teach a distance education course?

The answers to these questions provide a guideline for a distance education teaching project, help articulate the goals, select the delivery method, and prepare the instructor for this new challenge. As distance education experience and skills increase, the guidelines may need modification.

PLANNING STRUCTURES NEEDED IN PREPARING A DISTANCE EDUCATION COURSE

In preparing or instructing a distance education course the importance of planning the time frame, content and delivery method, and personnel and administrative components cannot be overstated. It is best to negotiate these at the outset of the project rather than having complications arise later. The following are matters to consider:

□ TIME

Preparing a distance education course is a full-time, intensive activity. Choosing, selecting, and preparing content, assessing available instructional resources, and providing ancillary support services, all relate to course development. Moreover, weighing these factors in relation to student markets, course objectives, and instructor style must also be addressed within the time frame of the course preparation activity. Given the time pressures of the preparatory activities, negotiating sufficient time with administrative personnel (e.g., department chair, distance education office) is critically important to the quality, success, and outcome of the program.

TIPS FOR BUILDING A TIME FRAMEWORK

♦ Create a timetable for distance education course preparation and update it as required. A total of 320 hours, or about 27 hours per week x 12 weeks per term (Kelly & Haag, 1985), was suggested by one course preparation team.

♦ Begin preparation and research as promptly as possible. Since preparation of a course takes time, build a time line that includes checkpoints for periodic reviews of the project.

♦ Arrange blocks of time away from other responsibilities, duties, and distractions.

♦ Brainstorm with colleagues to identify what, when, and who will be responsible for the many aspects of the course development project. Update as the project progresses.

☐ CONTENT AND DELIVERY

A constant challenge in distance education is to select and develop innovative ways to communicate course content to students in an interactive and credible distance education format. The course must also address (and be seen by others to address) the standards, expectations, and work requirements of a similar course delivered in person through traditional face-to-face formats.

In selecting appropriate course content, ask exploratory questions about the learners' backgrounds. For example, what are the academic prerequisites for the course? What level of language proficiency corresponds? What are students' expectations of the course? The answers will help focus on the types of content delivery methods useful in planning a course.

The students' physical location, their technical skills, the type of course, and resources available will influence the manner in which it is presented for distance education delivery. For example, if students do not have access to on-line electronic communication, they cannot use distance education courses delivered on the Internet or Web. Due to limited resources, some institutions offer courses through audiotape, textbooks, and written or taped assignments, while other more technologically advanced universities are rushing to develop a greater "high-tech" focus.

TIPS FOR CONTENT AND DELIVERY

♦ List the academic prerequisites for the course.

♦ Identify goals, level, and depth appropriate for the course.

♦ Arrange to review course preparation literature that includes suggestions on selection guidelines. (See References for suggestions.)

♦ Contact publishers regarding instructional resources on the market.

♦ Establish from the beginning how students will be evaluated (e.g., written exams, oral interviews, tests, reports, presentations, etc.) and by whom (e.g., content expert/faculty member, tutor, grader, individual, team, etc.).

☐ TEAM BUILDING

The availability and selection of support and resource personnel is essential to the course development process. These might include technical resources (e.g., audio-visual personnel, computer resource personnel, broadcast and/or satellite personnel, secretarial support), distance education resources (e.g., copyright staff, reprographics and/or graphics personnel), and instructional resources (e.g., instructional designer, teaching and learning consultant, content experts, administrative coordinator).

TIPS ON TEAM BUILDING

♦ Discuss the course preparation activities with other members of the team. Establish the time frame and discuss additions/revisions/changes.

♦ Meet with the instructional development consultant on a regular basis. Course preparation work is a challenge, and it often helps to have another person's suggestions.

♦ Establish who will grade the course, prepare material, perform tutorial duties.

♦ Input from others experienced in these areas is very useful.

☐ ADMINISTRATIVE CONCERNS

It is essential that the distance education project have the support of academic administrative personnel (e.g., academic vice president's, deans, academic department chairs) who can often help solve problems that develop in the course preparation process. Provide a regular informal written "progress report" to the administrative personnel responsible for the project to help them understand the process and to impress upon them the magnitude of the undertaking.

TIPS ON ADMINISTRATIVE CONCERNS

♦ Negotiate professional credit for curriculum development, teaching, promotion, and tenure.

♦ Assure adequate financial and/or time compensation.

♦ Establish whether the distance education course development is part of the normal teaching load or is considered overload.

♦ Determine time commitment, amount of time, and dates.

□ ACADEMIC NEEDS

In the 1990s distance education course development has seen a rapid expansion of programs, resources, and methods of delivery. For instructors whose institutions are not yet offering distance education programs, we have provided the websites of some institutions providing French courses through distance education. Conversely, if the home institution offers distance education in other departments, it would be useful to contact experienced colleagues to learn what resources are available.

When assuming the challenge of preparing a distance education course, make a list of teaching and learning resources needed to manage and deliver the course. The inventory on the next page will help in the selection of course components.

□ COMMUNICATION

Instructors must be true to their own teaching style. To establish an instructor-learner bond, the instructor must be comfortable with and secure in the method of delivery. Communication between instructor and learner is crucial. In a distance education course, the course package is the first line of communication. It must impress the student upon first encounter that the course has been well-organized and planned so that the student has every confidence in the instructor and in the potential of the course as an effective learning tool suited to his or her needs.

□ THE COURSE OUTLINE

The course outline serves as a map to orient and guide the instructor and students through the course. While this guide will typically evolve through several drafts before completion, this document is the central focus of the course. The outline serves to list objectives, content, and learning resources; it discusses assignments and explains all other components. Some instructors include specific study guides (e.g., study guide for video materials) detailing particular aspects of the course.

□ EVALUATION OF THE COURSE

To guarantee accountability, provide formative and summative evaluation procedures addressing each component in the course. It is important to evaluate and give prompt feedback to learners, but the instructor and the course must also be evaluated. This student feedback is the foundation on which improvements and future course planning are built. See the Bibliography for a reference on evaluation methods.

Course Content Inventory

Component	Content	Description
Course Administration	Course Outline	Course description, evaluation methods, assignment timetable, resource list, academic and administrative contacts, and information
	Study Guide	Approach to the material. The "how to's"
	Instructor's Profile	Introduction and comments
	Course Evaluations	Formative and summative
Course Content	Audio and Video	Many course texts in basic language, for example, are accompanied by videos
	Lectures	Print, Web, audio and/or video format
	Text/Courseware Package	e.g., *Mais oui!* (1996)
	Assignments/Projects	
	Tests/Exams	
	Sample Exams	
	Answer Keys	To text or supplementary exercises
	Readings	Supplementary to text
	CD-ROM	See Bibliography
	Websites	See Websites for examples
	Software	
Personnel	G.T.A./Marker/Tutor	Marking of assignments and exams, student consultation
Computer Support	Technical Instruction Package	Introduce course technology to students

□ TECHNOLOGY NEEDS

Print, audiotape, and video have served the distance education clientele well over the years, but the new generation of the Web, CD-ROM, and laserdisk bring the language to learners in ways never before possible. They open doors to resources that students of the 1960s could only dream about. Through CD-ROM it is possible, for example, to explore the target culture by interacting with native speakers with regional accents from a range of socio-economic groups. The Web can provide the opportunity to find a pen pal, read magazines, visit the Louvre, research historical sites in Paris, or find out what is playing at the Comédie Française—all in French. Students no longer rely on one usually non-native speaking instructor as the only live contact with the language. The variety and extent of comprehensible input is limitless and conveniently available at one's fingertips.

The Internet and the Web can provide resources and collegial contact to the instructor developing a distance education language course. Teaching material in the public domain, research articles, access to colleagues via listservs, newsgroups, and chat lines are just some of the possibilities. Communication technologies facilitate instructor-student, student-student, and student-native speaker interaction. Are telephone tutoring, e-mail, audio, video, or computer conferencing to be considered? These choices are usually made based on the resources of the learner, the instructor, and the institution.

As seen in the Table on the next page, the type of technology selected for course delivery or communication must be carefully explored to provide maximum benefits.

Software, CD-ROM, video, and audio resources are becoming standard in basic language programs published in North America. The instructor considering developing a distance education course would do well to choose a text with integrated ancillaries. These can save time, money, and effort in course preparation. Furthermore, publishers often grant duplication and networking rights without additional cost with the use of these texts.

Selection of Teaching and Communication Technology

Medium	Reading	Listening	Writing	Speaking	Culture	Student/ student interaction	Student/ instructor interaction	Ease of access by student	Cost to institution
Courseware									
Print	✓				✓			1*	1**
Audio cassette		✓			✓			1	1
Video cassette		✓			✓			2	2
Software	✓		✓	✓	✓			2	2
CD-ROM	✓	✓	✓		✓			2	2 or 3***
WWW	✓	✓	✓	✓	✓	✓		3	2 or 3
Communication									
Telephone tutoring		✓		✓	✓		✓	1	2
Audio conferencing		✓		✓	✓	✓	✓	2	2
Video conferencing		✓		✓	✓	✓	✓	3	3
E-mail / Internet	✓		✓	✓	✓	✓	✓	2	2
Computer conferencing	✓		✓	✓	✓	✓	✓	3	3

* 1 = openly accessible re. cost, time, place   2 = reduced flexibility   3 = limited flexibility
** 1 = relatively low cost to set up and run   2 = moderate cost   3 = high cost
*** Cost depends on whether product is purchased or custom produced

For instructors who wish to assemble a courseware package from pre-prepared ancillaries, Prégent (1994) provides recommendations in the Table below.

TIPS FOR USE OF EDUCATIONAL SOFTWARE

♦ Evaluate the program before putting it into the hands of students. First judge its instructional qualities, then its technical qualities.

♦ Verify how much the content of the program and the objectives it allows students to attain conform to those of the course.

♦ Read the documentation that accompanies the program, for both the instructor and the students.

♦ Verify whether the program is flexible enough to allow individualization of instruction in the course material and fosters underlying cognitive developments.

♦ Check that the program is easy and enjoyable to use.

♦ Plan to integrate the program into the instructional activities of the course.

♦ Plan how to evaluate what the students learn using the program.

♦ Evaluate the compatibility of the program with the available hardware.

♦ Plan how your students will use the program: place, dates, length of time, and logistics.

♦ Determine whether extra staff will be necessary.

♦ Evaluate the cost of purchasing copies of a program or licenses necessary to make copies.

♦ Test the program on a small scale before using it with the entire class.

♦ Never design a course solely around individual use of educational software; students need much more than a machine to learn and persevere.

(Prégent, 1994, 110.)

While the new technologies provide exciting opportunities, there are practical considerations including how to make them accessible and affordable to students, integrate them into the course plan, and assure their compatibility with the resources available from the institution and with the comfort level of the instructor. Answers to the key questions below will help the instructor decide whether technology is to be used, and, if so, the type of technology that best fits the needs of the instructor, the learner, and the course.

TIPS ON WHEN AND WHAT TECHNOLOGY TO USE

♦ Why use technology in the distance education course?

♦ Do students have access to the technology and the skills to use it?

♦ Is it integrated with the goals of the course and course materials?

♦ Is there technical support for using these resources?

♦ Are there other ways to provide the same learning opportunities aside from use of technology?

□ PROFESSIONAL DEVELOPMENT NEEDS

It is essential to underscore the critical importance of training instructors in both presentation and technology. Translating a course from the regular campus to the distance education format demands different skills of instructors in audio, video, computer, and Internet presentation and manipulation.

Training includes attendance at workshops offering a range of topics corresponding to the formats available for distance education. Instructors need access to current distance education publications, books, and journals, and they should be encouraged to consult with colleagues experienced in the distance education field.

COMPARATIVE CASE STUDY

Earlier the critical importance of knowing the students, their needs, environment, and expectations was indicated. Interestingly, surveys performed in Australia of 868 "students enrolled in all-language or predominantly language subjects by distance education" in 1985 (S. Williams and P. Sharma, 1988) and of 4,600 distance education students in all subjects in Canada at the University of Waterloo (T. Giguere, 1994) have produced similar results. Included in the grids below are results of an informal tabulation of 150 student evaluations in a basic French language course offered over nine trimesters in 1992, 1993, and 1994 in the University of Waterloo's Distance Education program.

Age and Gender of Distance Education Students

Institution	Australia; 1985; Language courses only	University of Waterloo, Canada, 1994; Courses in Arts, Science, Math, Environmental and Resource Studies, Applied Health Studies	Basic French language course, University of Waterloo, Canada 1992–1994; inclusive (nine trimesters)
Age	(Where Available)	under 25 — 11.6%	20–29 — 19.3%
	25–29 years — 15.0%	25–34 — 30.9%	30–39 — 36.5%
	30–39 years — 32.0%	35–44 — 36.1%	40–49 — 32.2%
	40–44 years — 12.0%	45–54 — 16.1%	50–59 — 5.0%
	45–65 — 27.0%	55–64 — 3.0%	60+ — 6.0%
	65+ — 5.0%	65 + — 2.3%	
Men	29.0%	30.5%	13.3%
Women	71.0%	69.5%	86.7%

Women evidently dominate the student body in distance education, especially in languages. The most significant age range is 30 to 49 years, accounting for about 60% of the students.

Occupation of Distance Education Students

Occupation	Program		
	Australia (% of 356 responses)	University of Waterloo, Canada (% of 4,600 responses)	Basic French language course, University of Waterloo, Canada (% of 150 responses)
Student	6.1%	8.5%	6.6%
Teacher	20.2%	9.0%	14.5%
Home duties	16.0%	7.2%	10.5%
Professional/technical	23.5%	32.4%	25.0%
Executive/manager	3.0%	10.1%	5.9%
Retired	7.3%	2.6%	6.6%
Industry/trade	1.9%	n/a	n/a
Unemployed	3.3%	2.2%	n/a
Clerical/administrative	14.0%	6.6%	n/a
Other	3.3%	13.2%	33.4 %

With the high percentage of women in the distance education program, it is not surprising to see that the occupational distribution leans toward employment areas still dominated by women: teaching, home duties, clerical. In Canada, a bilingual country (French/English), the military, the federal government, social services including nursing, and tourism are areas for which bilingualism is a job requirement in many regions.

Reasons for Enrolling as Distance Education or External Students

Reasons (multiple answers possible)	Australia	Program Basic French language course, University of Waterloo, Canada (% of 150 responses)
1. convenience 2. flexibility (time and place) 3. financial reasons	74.0% indicated courses not offered at convenient times	35.0%
Need language credit for degree	n/a	22.5%
Course not available locally	50.0% live at least 500 km. from a university	11.6%
Prefer not to drive	n/a	5.8% (Winters are harsh and driving difficult in some regions of Canada)
Prefer "independent" learning	38.0%	5.8%
Reduce campus course load. (Students choose distance education in off-campus or summer term)	n/a	2.5%
Age or disability	n/a	4.1%

It seems clear when considering demographic and lifestyle changes in the 1990s that in Canada, at least, adult-learners are increasingly less interested in leaving home after a day's work. Shift work, the movement to irregular part-time jobs, contract employment, and cottage industry work, as well as heavy traffic in urban areas are making traveling to a campus for study less attractive. These students will search out distance education opportunities. As Internet courses require that students sit in front of a computer over long periods of time, it would seem reasonable to speculate that they are more likely to want to do this from home than from the workplace or in the classroom.

REASONS FOR STUDYING LANGUAGE THROUGH DISTANCE EDUCATION

When asked why they chose to study French language using the distance education format, University of Waterloo students enrolled in the Basic French language courses responded as follows (multiple answers were possible):

Pursuing degree studies and must fulfil language requirement	79.7%
General interest/self-development	56.3%
Family reasons (e.g., French ancestry, spouse is French-speaking, children are enrolled in French immersion program)	13.8%
Career change/advancement	12.7%
Needed for present employment	8.5%
Other (e.g., to understand French language television)	2.0%

THE UNIVERSITY OF WATERLOO'S BASIC FRENCH LANGUAGE COURSE AND ITS ASSESSMENT BY THE STUDENTS

The University of Waterloo's basic French language courses have been offered since 1984 to approximately 300 students per year over three trimesters. While 87% of the students live in the province of Ontario, where the University of Waterloo is located in Canada, 13% reside elsewhere in Canada and the world.

The self-contained course package includes the text (*Bonne route! À la découverte du français dans le monde,* 1995), workbook (lab manual and written exercises), and accompanying audio- and videocassettes as well as the following components produced by the instructor: course outline, lecture notes, evaluation forms, supplementary written exercises, audio lecture tapes, assignments, answer keys, and a sample final exam. In a four-month term, students submit five written assignments, three of which include a question to be answered on audiocassette, and write a final exam with no oral or comprehension component. Feedback to the student includes written comments and corrections on the assignments and a thirty-minute tutorial cassette on which the instructor discusses the assignment, common problems, and offers tips for improvement.

The course emphasizes reading, writing, comprehension, culture, and some speaking. Contact with the instructor is primarily through the assignments. A listserv run by the instructor since January 1995 sees participation by only 10–15% of the students in any one term. Students are encouraged to phone the instructor but most only do so to request an extension on the assignment due date.

When asked if the course met their expectations, 86% of students replied that it did while 14% thought it was more difficult than expected, more challenging, gave no answer, or said they had no expectations.

The strengths of the course:	The weaknesses of the course:
27.0% Quality of course components	50.5% Said that they could not name any
23.5% The instructor (encouraging, informal, enthusiastic, created a classroom feeling)	19.1% Would have liked more interaction and personal contact
23.0% Organization and presentation	15.0% Found the workload too heavy
12.5% Self-paced, comprehensive, lots of practice	6.0% Thought the course offered too many components
7.0% Interesting, fun, challenging	5.0% Had pronunciation and/or comprehension difficulties
6.0% Relevant, practical	2.0% Had administrative concerns often indicating that the assignments were due too closely together
	1.0% Did not appreciate the spiraling in the text
	1.0% Thought the text was too French and not Canadian enough.

CONCLUSION

This article presents a brief overview of the decision-making process inherent in the development of a distance education course. Due to the complexity of the issues and the scope of the task, input from all the participants, including learners, is essential to create a network of co-operating individuals and groups. For the instructor charged with developing the language department's first distance education course, the initial steps are to consult, to network, and to build a working team.

For the demographic, lifestyle, and economic reasons outlined earlier, distance education is expanding as an alternative approach in the provision of and access to education. At the same time, the new technology facilitates delivery in accessible, affordable, and convenient ways. Previously unserved populations can now benefit from higher education and lifelong learning. For traditional students and those studying outside the confines of the four-year full-time degree, distance education provides the possibility of managing their own learning in their own time and place, at a reasonable cost, and often at their own pace. For instructors, distance education encourages professional growth and the exploration of new horizons in the realm of content delivery and communication with their students.

REFERENCES

Amon, Evelyne, Judith A. Muyskens, and Alice C. Omaggio Hadley. *Vis-à-vis Beginning French*. New York: McGraw-Hill, 1996.

De Méo, Patricia P., James W. Brown, and B. Edward Gesner. *Bonne route! À la découverte du français dans le monde*. Toronto: Holt, Rinehart and Winston of Canada, 1995.

Finnemann, Michael D. "The World Wide Web and Foreign Language Teaching." *ERIC/CLL News Bulletin*. 20, No.1. (1996), 1–6.

Giguere, Timothy. *University of Waterloo Distance Education Program Student Survey 1994*. Waterloo: University of Waterloo Teaching Resources and Continuing Education, 1995.

Lively, Madeleine. "The Changing Demographics of the Traditional Student: Making Our Classrooms Relevant for the New Generation of Students." *ADFL Bulletin*, Winter Vol. 28, No. 3, Spring 1997, 32–36.

Thompson, Chantal P., and Elaine Phillips. *Mais oui!*. Lexington, MA: D.C. Heath, 1996.

Williams, Sylvia, and Pramod Sharma. "Language Acquisition by Distance Education: An Australian Survey." *Distance Education* 9, No.1 (1988), 127–146.

Worthen, Blaine, and James Sanders. *Educational Evaluation*. New York: Longman, 1987.

RESOURCES

Foster, Geoff. "Lessons from Team Work: Towards a Systematic Scheme for Course Development." *Higher Education*, 24 (1992), 193–211.

Holmberg, Borje. "The Discipline of Distance Education—Character and Scope in the 1990s." *Epistolo Didaktika*, 1 (1996), 5–36.

Howard, Ron, and Ian McGrath, ed. *Distance Education for Language Teachers: A U.K. Perspective*. Clevedon: Multilingual Matters Ltd., 1995.

Kelly, Mavis and Sally Haag. *Teaching at a Distance*. Waterloo: University of Waterloo Teaching Resources and Continuing Education, 1985.

Lewis, Roger, and Nigel Paine. *How to Find and Adapt Materials and Select Media*. London: Council for Educational Technology, 1986.

Morgan, Alistair. *Improving Your Students' Learning*. London: Kogan Page, 1993.

Prégent, Richard. *Charting Your Course: How to Prepare to Teach More Effectively*. Madison, WI: Magna Publications Inc., 1994.

Rowntree, Derek. *Teaching through Self-instruction*. London: Kogan Page, 1986.

WEBSITES: FRENCH RESOURCES

The following websites offer French resources from around the world.

Branchez-vous!: http://www.branchez-vous.com/

Tennessee Bob's Famous French Links: http://www.utm.edu/departments/french/french.html

The French World on the Web: http://www.mmlc.nwu.edu/new/french_links.html

Le Web En France: http://web.urec.fr/France/web.html

French Resources Worldwide: http://www.utexas.edu/depts/french/.web/world/french.html

Bienvenue au Québec: http://www.tourisme.gouv.qc.ca

Francescape (vacationing in France): http://www.france.com/francescape/top.html

WEBSITES: FRENCH COURSE INFORMATION

Athabasca University, Alberta, Canada: http://www.athabascau.ca

French National Centre for Distance Education: http://www.cned.fr

Institute of Modern Languages: Distance Education Courses, University of Queensland, Australia: http://www.cltr.uq.oz.au:8000/iml/imldist.htm

Open Learning Agency, British Columbia, Canada: http://www.ola.bc.ca/ou/cis/

University of Alaska, Alaska, USA: http://dist_ed.alaska.edu/telehtml/index.html

University System of Georgia, Georgia, U.S.A.: http://www.dartnet.peachnet.edu/flcoll.htm

University of Waterloo, Ontario, Canada: http://www.uwaterloo.ca

University of Wisconsin, Wisconsin, U.S.A.: http://www.uwex.edu/disted/welcome.html

APPLICATION OF IDEAS ON TEACHER-LEARNER ROLES

1. Phillips analyzes anticipated change in teachers' roles as the *Standards for Foreign Language Learning* are implemented. She identifies the following roles as significant ones in this new arena:

   ♦ Thoughtful reader and consumer of research

   ♦ Instructional leader with a repertoire of approaches

   ♦ Decision-maker in both planned and spontaneous classroom contexts

   ♦ Creator of assessments and assessor

   ♦ Knower, doer, and know-how-to person

   Taking into consideration your education, your classroom teaching experience, your travels, your level of language proficiency, your cultural knowledge, your teaching style, and your personality traits, describe your potential for comfort and success in this new environment.

   (1) Tell which one(s) of these roles you feel confident of assuming (or extending). Explain what aspects of your background have prepared you for these functions.

   (2) Tell which one(s) of these roles cause you concern. List possible ways that you can get prepared to assume them.

2. Phillips also analyzes anticipated change in students' roles with the new *Standards,* identifying the following as significant components:

   ♦ Active participators and planners

   ♦ Strategists

   ♦ Bearers of knowledge and experience

   ♦ World citizens

   Based on your classroom experiences with students, describe how students can be assisted to learn and assume these roles.

   (1) Identify areas of experience and expertise already in place with your students. Give examples of these behaviors.

   (2) Tell in which areas you feel confident to help students develop the necessary skills. Give examples of possible activities that you might use.

(3) Tell in which areas you are not confident of having the skills/information to assist students in their development. List possible ways you can acquire additional information and skills.

3. According to the *National Standards in Foreign Language Learning,* the following Five Cs represent the goals of foreign language education:

♦ *Communication* in languages other than English

♦ *Cultures,* understanding the perspectives of other cultures

♦ *Connections* with other disciplines

♦ *Comparisons* with one's own language and culture

♦ *Communities* in which to use languages at home and abroad

On a topic that you expect to teach during the next semester (or quarter or month or week), make a chart of possible activities or sources of materials that you could use in developing a unit of instruction which incorporates all Five Cs.

4. Smith and Rawley explore with teachers how who we are as people influences who we are as teachers. They offer several examples of "teachers' stories" in which individual teachers use metaphors "to explore the motivations behind their teaching decisions, to conceptualize their commitments to students, and to look critically at perceived teaching problems."

Consider how your current teaching style is linked to your personal beliefs and behaviors. Develop a personal metaphor to interpret your own classroom experiences and interactions with your students.

5. Smith and Rawley comment that "the teachers we have had throughout our years as students provide models that shape our expectations and notions of what teachers do."

Identify the most powerful influences on your teaching from your former teachers, both in positive and negative terms.

(1) Name three teachers that you have had whom you consider influential on your teaching.

(2) Tell how each has influenced your teaching, as models for emulation and/or as the antithesis of all you wish to be and do with students.

(3) Give specific examples of their classroom practices that you attempt to replicate and/or that you attempt to avoid with your students.

6. Smith and Rawley distinguish between "received knowledge" and "experiential knowledge."

   Describe the most influential example(s) of "received knowledge" which inform your teaching.

   (1) Name one or more workshops that you have attended and/or professional books or articles that you have read and/or courses of study that you have taken that made a significant impact on your teaching.

   (2) Summarize the elements of the theory or practice that you found to be the most interesting/provocative/stimulating/promising for success in the classroom.

   (3) Describe your initial attempts to implement the theory or practice and the results of your efforts.

   (4) Tell how you modified the techniques/activities/materials to improve their effectiveness with your students.

   (5) Analyze why you think that these changes made them work better for you.

7. Smith and Rawley state ". . . that if teachers are to take the lead in helping the profession reconceptualize who they are, what they know, and how their work adds to the production of theory, they must begin to see themselves as researchers and recognize themselves as a dynamic in the system."

   Develop a plan for a research project concerning the teaching/learning process in your classroom.

   (1) Identify an area of concern or special interest that you would like to investigate.

   (2) Write one to three specific questions that you would like to have answered about the situation.

   (3) Decide what kind(s) of information would help you to answer these questions about this concern or interest.

   (4) Determine how to acquire the data that you need (e.g., questionnaire, observation, comments by students, peer evaluation, analysis of grades)

   (5) Make a list of possible changes that might be appropriate based on what your collection of data finds.

   (6) Make a list of constraints that you face in doing "inquiry" projects in your current teaching situation.

8. Make an analysis of the typical interaction in your classroom. Describe the customary roles of teacher and learners in relationship

to each of the factors identified by Cubillos as the current Foreign Language Instruction paradigm:

(1) Input-driven

(2) Geared toward the development of communication skills

(3) Student-centered

(4) Concerned about the affective environment in which learning takes place

(5) Interested in cultural awareness

9. Cubillos states that we as teachers need "to gain ownership over . . . technologies so that they can be incorporated into our curricula in ways that are consistent with our current understanding of Second Language Acquisition (SLA) processes."

How do you foresee that increased use of technologies may change the teacher/learner roles in each area of the paradigm (as listed above) in your own instruction?

10. Aplevich and Willment note that a growth of distance education courses in foreign languages has occurred simultaneously with the demographic and lifestyle changes in the 1990s. If these changes continue to develop, more foreign language faculty will be needed to create and/or teach these distance education courses.

Reflect on your own personal and instructional strengths (and weaknesses) to determine your own potential response to a request or demand that you develop and offer a course through distance learning.

(1) Study your personal metaphor that interprets your own classroom experiences and interactions with your students.

(2) Make a list of your personal and professional qualities, skills, experiences, and philosophies that support the concept of distance education.

(3) Make a second list of your personal professional attributes and beliefs that might hinder you in the development of distance learning programs.

(4) Based on your two lists, determine what role you would be best suited to play in setting up and operating a distance education program (e.g., developer of goals/objectives/scope and sequence, creator of instructional activities for interactive format, designer of evaluation techniques and devices, interactive instructor with students by instructional television or computer modem or other system).

(5) Write a potential personal metaphor that might describe your role with students in this new environment.

Part II

Presentation

Including articles by:

Madeleine G. Lively/Mary K. Williams/Jane Harper
Terry L. Ballman
Erwin Tschirner
Vicki Galloway
Ana Martínez-Lage and David Herren

Mediating Language with Teacher Talk: Bringing Speech to Ideas

Madeleine G. Lively, Jane Harper, Mary K. Williams,
Tarrant County Junior College, Fort Worth, Texas

Jane Harper, Madeleine Lively, and Mary Williams are at Tarrant County Junior College (TCJC), Northeast Campus in Fort Worth, Texas, where Jane chairs the Humanities Division, Madeleine chairs the Department of Foreign Languages, and Mary teaches French. Among them, they have taught students of languages at every level: elementary, secondary, undergraduate, and graduate. At TCJC, in addition to the regular university-parallel program, they have provided annual series of workshops for teachers of foreign languages and a year-round program of languages for children of ages 4 through 12.

The Texas trio makes frequent presentations at international, national, regional, and state conferences on such topics as curriculum development, design of instructional activities, cooperative learning, methods for teaching conversation, testing and grading, teaching critical thinking through languages, bridging the gap between language and literature, changing demographics in language programs, and administration of language departments. They have published articles on these topics in a variety of professional journals, including the ADFL Bulletin, *the* Foreign Language Annals, *and the ACE monograph on mentoring departments of foreign languages. They also author novice- and intermediate-level textbooks.*

Individually, these authors consistently provide service to the profession while keeping current on contemporary issues and emerging ideas by their leadership and participation in professional organizations, such as the Association of Departments of Foreign Languages Executive Board of the Modern Language Association, the MLA Committee on Professional Employment, the Southwest Conference on Language Teaching Executive Board, and the Texas Foreign Language Association Executive Board, as well as by their work on professional projects such as Project ExCELL (Texas) and the development of the Texas Oral Proficiency Test.

INTRODUCTION

It is in the presentation phase of a lesson that the theme is established, giving a *raison d'être* for the ideas, structures, and lexicon to be studied in the L2. In this phase, the instructor seeks to provide thematic input, to make authentic texts accessible, to guide students to construct their own knowledge, and to provide a range of conceptual and linguistic experiences that will support the development of critical thinking and multiple intelligences. These are the topics to be addressed in this article.

> Authentic texts, as total communicative events, invite observation of a culture talking to *itself*, not to outsiders; in its own context; through its own language; where forms are referenced to its own people, who *mean* through their own framework of associations; and whose voices show dynamic interplay of individuals and groupings of individuals within the loose general consensus that is the culture's reality. (Galloway, 133)

The importance of authentic texts as "input" for language learning has been well established. Students learn what and how a language means in its native culture through authentic texts. The very essence of the input text being imbued with the native culture is what makes accessing the language in authentic documents so difficult for students. Moreover, as Rebecca Valette recently noted with regard to the use of authentic documents, "it takes us so long to get the students to understand the vocabulary and grammar in the authentic texts that there is usually no time left to deal with the ideas in the text" (1997). Nevertheless, the language in authentic input texts can, however, become accessible to the students and useful in the development of their own ideas via instructor mediation. Supportive teacher talk in the L2 can play a pivotal role in mediating the three phases of dealing with authentic texts—pre-mapping, processing, and synthesizing texts—and in helping solve the dilemma created by using authentic text.

> "In order to make the language in the authentic input texts accessible enough to students to be ultimately transformed into quality output, a teacher must be ready to provide **meaningful, interactive, L2 teacher talk**. Through this mediation, students can gain access to vocabulary, grammar, and cultural information."

DEFINITION OF MEDIATION

Mediation provides the bridge between the elements to be developed in a lesson and the students' existing knowledge in order to heighten their readiness to access and ultimately use the language as "output." In this way teacher talk renders the language in the authentic texts accessible, enables students to move from meaningful reception of quality input to active manipulation of the new elements of the language, and then guides them to the production of quality, personalized output. Tschirner affirms that, "while input is primary, output does not simply emerge but needs to be learned and practiced separately." (See Tschirner, this volume, p. 120). In order to make the language in the authentic input texts accessible enough to students to be ultimately transformed into quality output, a teacher must be ready to provide meaningful, interactive, L2 teacher talk. Through this mediation, students can gain access to vocabulary, grammar, and cultural information. Carefully designed language mediation can be effectively brought about through teacher talk. It is an essential component of the lesson, serving to achieve understanding of input texts, establishing an environment whereby students can relate to the texts on a personal level, and acting as a catalyst for the development of ideas.

THREE PHASES IN THE TREATMENT AND MEDIATION OF INPUT MATERIAL

As students participate in a lesson, their opportunities for meaningful processing of the input texts can be effectively realized only with the help of the teacher's intervention. Teacher talk provides the *interface* between the students and the lesson itself. During the three different phases in the treatment of the input material—pre-mapping, processing, and synthesizing the texts—the instructor provides the support which guides the students to a sequentially higher level of interaction with the document on each occasion.

> " . . . (M)ediation is what we do with the language to prepare the students to be able to cope with the authentic input, to help them access what the input source has to offer. We help students integrate what they see, hear, and read into the greater body of knowledge in their language repertoire."

LANGUAGE DEVELOPMENT IN THE PRE-MAPPING PHASE

Here supportive teacher talk (*mediation*) is used to prepare the students to be able to cope with the authentic input, to help them access what the input source has to offer. We help students integrate what they see, hear, and read into the greater body of knowledge in their language repertoire. It is the teacher's role to help the students relate the information in the presentation materials to their own experiences to establish a point of insight, a foothold, into a text for interpreting its relevance and usefulness. Using the target language in pre-mapping activities provides the teacher with opportunities for idea-based language development. With cognate-rich language combined with the language recycled from earlier lessons, the instructor can engage students on the theme (central ideas) of the lesson. This is to guide them to determine which main ideas will be treated, who the main characters are or what is going to be happening, and to sensitize them to culturally significant aspects. Heavily contextualized and personalized interaction in the teacher talk can provide frequent, yet natural, repetition of meaningful samples of language that will be heard in the upcoming authentic text. (See the example of interactive L2 pre-mapping below.)

> "The benefit of the teacher talk input can be dramatically enhanced if we take an idea-based approach to the language development rather than a grammar/vocabulary-based approach."

The benefit of the teacher talk input can be dramatically enhanced if we take an idea-based approach to the language development rather than a grammar/vocabulary-based approach. This idea-based approach is particularly engaging when it takes on an interactive nature through personalized questions of the students. For example, consider setting up a unit on transportation and selecting an appropriate text as input for the unit. Here it is necessary to be selective in coordinating the choice of authentic documents with appropriate authentic tasks to follow. For example, if an advertisement is selected about the values of a certain kind of automobile, then the activities should focus on the evaluation of that car and its attributes, as opposed to selecting an excerpt from an owner's manual, in which case the focus would be on the parts of the car and their operation. For the purposes of the case here, imagine that an automobile advertisement has been selected in the L2 culture, either as an audio text (a radio ad), a video text (a television commercial), or a print text (a newspaper ad).

The following class discussion, directed in L2 teacher talk, pre-maps treatment of the authentic document. The students might be polled on where the cars they themselves have come from. The instructor can use the chalkboard "interactively" to tally the results as the discussion unfolds and to organize the responses in categories on a grid. Attributes unique to certain entries can be listed on the board along with the polled results, allowing students to *see* the key words as they are used in discussion. Note that active vocabulary development is going on while students are still in the receptive mode and are actually focusing on ideas.

> " . . . (U)se the chalkboard *interactively* to elicit personalized responses and engage students in class discussions while developing vocabulary and pre-mapping ideas to be treated in the text."

The teacher talk, in L2, might sound like this:

Who has a Japanese car? (*Count hands and record number on board next to Japanese.*)

What brand do you have, Heather, a Honda, a Toyota, an Acura? (*Heather names car.*)

You have a Toyota? How many [students] have a Toyota? (*Count hands and record on board next to Toyota.*)

What is another brand of Japanese car? (*Student says Honda.*) A Honda? How many [people] have a Honda? (*Count, record number, and continue in this mode.*)

Who has an American car? (*Make a new column on the board for American cars with the number of owners.*)

Michael, what kind of American car do you have? (*If student does not answer here because (s)he didn't understand "kind" or "brand," name again a few "brands," like Ford, Buick, Pontiac, to get him or her started. List each model under American and poll for number of owners; record number next to it and continue in this mode.*)

Typically, Japanese cars are smaller than American cars. What is an example of a large American car? (*Elicit name of car from a student and record on board, writing large in L2 next to the name of the car mentioned.*)

A small American car? (*Elicit name of car from a student and write the word for small in L2 next to the cars students mention.*)

Debra, do you have a large car or a small car? (*Student answers with small or large.*)

Typically, are small or large cars more economical to drive? (*Students respond with word small.*)

Name a small, economical car. (*Write the word for economical in L2 next to the cars students mention and continue in this mode.*)

Does anyone have an Italian car? No one? What are some brands of Italian cars? (*Make a new column on the board for Italian cars, and record specific types as they are mentioned by students, adding any you can think of after responses subside.*)

A Ferrari? It is a very fast car, isn't it? (*Write the word for fast in L2 next to it.*)

Name other cars you know of that are fast. (*Add their names to the appropriate columns already established while eliciting students' help, and add attributes discussed next to them.*)

Are fast cars typically small or large? (*Wait for students to answer.*)

Why? Aerodynamics?

Are foreign (European, Japanese) cars typically small or large? (*Wait for students to answer.*)

Why? Because they are economical on gas consumption? Gas is very expensive in Europe and Japan. (*Using several attributes that are transparent cognates in many languages, write them on the board as they come up.*)

Are all small cars fast? What are some small fast cars?

What is a small American car that is fast? Is it economical?

What is an American car that is economical? (*Students answers.*) Is it powerful? (*Add "powerful" to the board.*)

Are American cars typically economical or costly to operate?

Are foreign cars typically economical or costly?

Are large cars sporty or safe?

Are fast cars economical or costly?

(*Continue in this mode, working in such attributes as are doable in the L2 for the availability of cognates, for the level and previous knowledge of the students, etc. Consider: expensive, comfortable, safe, luxurious, beautiful, trendy, quality of general performance, color, interior decor, powerful engine, polluting, level of gas consumption, sportiness, etc.*)

Chalkboard results of the class discussion might look something like the following:

Japanese - 10	American - 13	German - 3	British - 0	Italian - 0
Honda ||||	Ford ||| *economical*	Mercedes || *expensive & powerful*	Rolls-Royce *large & very expensive*	Ferrari *fast, expensive, & small*
Toyota ||| *small*	Buick | *large*		MG *small*	
Acura *expensive*	Dodge ||	Volkswagen *small & economical*		Fiat *small*
Mitsubishi ||	Chevrolet ||||			
Isuzu | *economical*	Chrysler |	BMW || *expensive*		
	Cadillac *expensive*			
	Jeep || *small, not economical*			
Totals: 10	**13**	**3**	**0**	**0**

This type of teacher talk sets the context for the upcoming input text, provides frequent repetition of highly contextualized key vocabulary, and guides students in critical analysis while engaging them on the topic by helping them relate it to their own experiences and knowledge. Next to the poll of types of cars students actually have, the teacher might then create a second grid on the board to record responses to another question.

Now, what kind of car would you *prefer* to have? (*Count and record responses.*)

Japanese - 4	American - 4	German - 7	British - 5	Italian - 4
Honda	Ford	Mercedes ||||	Rolls-Royce |	Ferrari ||||
Toyota	Buick	Volkswagen		
Acura |||	Dodge		Jaguar |||	Fiat
Mitsubishi	Chevrolet	BMW |||	MG |	
Isuzu	Chrysler |			
Lexus |	Cadillac			
	Jeep |||			
Totals: 4	**4**	**7**	**5**	**6**

A follow-up activity to this second poll can be to have students infer in L2 the desired attributes of the class based on which cars they indicated that they would most like to have. The previous high-repetition vocabulary will be the words they will most likely come up with, such as, *large, small, fast, economical, expensive, comfortable, safe, luxurious, beautiful, trendy, of a certain brand, quality of general performance, color, interior decor, powerful engine, polluting, level of gas consumption, sportiness.* List the attributes on the board as they come up in the class brainstorming session. Now, ask the question:

What features are most important to you personally?
(*Here, have students look at the list of attributes on the board and prioritize their top three choices. They can vote with three fingers for their top priority, two for the next, and one finger for their third choice. Record the results of the vote beside each feature.*)

Attribute	# of votes	Order of priority
large	8	last
small	60	*3rd*
fast	64	*2nd*
safe	22	5th
luxurious	70	*1st*
trendy	32	4th
Italian	17	6th

By seeing represented in grids the results of their own class' choices of cars and of their preferences of attributes in purchasing an automobile, the students become personally engaged and begin, at least tacitly, to make comparisons and contrasts and to observe trends as they emerge. The instructor can now help the class analyze how well their vote reflects the inferences they drew about the class in general based on the question about which kind of car they would prefer. In this way they become sensitized to another culture's treatment and response to automobiles since they have just completed an analysis of an American viewpoint in their own classroom.

In sum, students are far better prepared to encounter this language and these ideas in the authentic text, in this case an advertisement in the target culture for a new automobile. If this lesson were about personalities or about the things we treasure most, the students could hear about what others value and make comparisons and contrasts with their own values. By hearing and observing what their peers say and reflect, students engage in the synthetic activity of developing their own ideas, leading to growth in their perceptions of their own world and their interactions with it.

ANALYSIS OF THE PEDAGOGICAL BENEFITS OF THE PRE-MAPPING TEACHER TALK

Let us examine what is going on pedagogically in this example of the idea-based approach to language development:

- ◆ The principal motivation in this approach is that it lets students focus on ideas so the acquisition of language is faster and the retention longer. The language is rich with meaning since students are relating to the ideas rather than to discrete vocabulary and structure items, and the thematic aspects of the upcoming input text are pre-mapped.

- ◆ The teacher is generating the language, making meaning with the new vocabulary by linking it to the students' reality, as compared to the isolated "look, listen, and repeat"-type exercises often used to pre-map and present new vocabulary. In this highly contextualized format, the teacher can expand on the vocabulary far beyond what graphic input will allow.

- ◆ Linguistic aspects and terms that are to come up in the input text are pre-mapped here, with certain groups (like the automobile attributes) being introduced in antonym/synonym (or derivative) pairs to build semantic families.

- ◆ The teacher is generating the bases for the ideas and students have opportunities to manipulate the ideas, as they practice active listening.

- ◆ In this early stage of the lesson, students are not required to produce more complicated responses than simply the raising of hands, the names of familiar brands of automobiles, agreement or lack of agreement with yes/no and multiple-choice type answers using the attributes presented in antonym/synonym pairs, and with high-recognition and/or cognate one-word descriptors already modeled with high repetition in the teacher talk and written on the "interactive" chalkboard as they arise in the discussion.

♦ These responses serve as comprehension checks while the teacher elicits active and personalized participation from the students.

♦ Students have constant visual verification of their own comprehension available to them by means of the grid, serving as a graphic organizer, being developed on the board in response to their active, yet non-pressured, non-stressed participation.

♦ The teacher can give many samples of lexicalized grammar structure in short bits so that students can recognize that meaning changes when syntax changes, such as the difference in the forms of the verb "to have" when used with singular and plural subjects, or the different forms of the adjectives being frequently repeated as they describe different nouns.

♦ With the focus on meaning, grammar is placed in its functional role of being a *tool* for communication rather than a *reason* for communication.

♦ Students are guided to the examination of key attributes contributing to the choice of different types of automobiles in their own culture, and thus are sensitized to considering how these same attributes might be evaluated by people in the target culture (as revealed in the upcoming input document to be studied).

♦ The inference of the relative concepts, such as those of size and economy, serves to pre-map issues discussed in the upcoming input text.

THE "PROCESSING," OR ACTIVE READING/LISTENING/VIEWING PHASE

After helping students identify the purpose and organization of the authentic text, having them draw meaning from visual cues, text layout, section titles, charts, graphs, images, introductory and summary statements, the teacher can proceed to the active reading/listening/viewing phase. Essential to successful student access to the input is the use of deliberate L2 teacher talk, the asking of guiding questions along the way, the stopping frequently and at short intervals, the replaying or rereading, the reiterating of key vocabulary, and the helping of students focus on key ideas. Particularly in the case of an authentic audio or video text, student comprehension will be significantly heightened since some of the key vocabulary was "worked" thoroughly in advance in the developmental pre-mapping teacher talk. This is because students can hear more clearly if they can say the words, as they have done in their earlier multiple-choice type responses. This gives them grounding, allowing them to confirm that they are understanding.

> " . . . (A)sking guiding questions throughout the active processing of the text encourages students to see each other as valid sources of information and insight and it decentralizes instruction."

By asking guiding questions along the way, students get to demonstrate their comprehension and are encouraged to support their assertions from the text by being asked frequently the question, *"How do you know?"* The stronger students, at least, will be able to respond at this point with one- and two-word answers by drawing from the specific vocabulary developed in the pre-mapping discussions. This technique will also help the weaker students "come on board" and soon be able to imitate the pattern modeled. Moreover, it encourages students to see each other as valid sources of information and insight and it decentralizes instruction. At the same time, they are modeling processing skills when they answer "How do you know?" questions and have to document their responses from the text. If the processing has been done well, the students will be able to support their assertions. Again, if they feel hesitant, they can be offered multiple-choice options to express their rationale.

THE "SYNTHESIZING," OR POST-READING/ LISTENING/VIEWING PHASE

Let us consider once again Rebecca Valette's comment on the concern that "it takes us so long to get the students to understand the vocabulary and grammar in the authentic texts that there is usually no time left to deal with the ideas in the texts." Perhaps by starting with the ideas and developing the language around the ideas, rather than beginning with language used merely as labels, students will be able to reach that often unaccomplished idea stage. Post-reading/listening/viewing activities should include synthesis, taking what the text has to offer and reshaping it into a new text for a new situation, using concepts, vocabulary, and phrasing that are familiar and comfortable for the students. After having looked analytically in the processing phase at the discrete parts and at the main ideas, the students can now be guided to make associations between the ideas, the mode of presentation or the language, and any related experiences in the students' backgrounds.

An example of this kind of synthesis might be a follow-up activity to the car advertisement exercise. Students could be asked to conjecture on the reactions to the car ad by different people they know, with a dialogue that might sound as follows:

Is this the kind of car you would like to have? Why (not)?

It's economical, sporty, beautiful, expensive, fast, etc./It's too large, small, ugly, expensive, high in gas consumption.

Whom do you know who would select this car?

My parents/my girlfriend/Uncle George

What attributes about this car would appeal to that person?

It's safe, economical, and large./It's small, it has a luxurious interior, and it is foreign./It's fast, it has a big engine, and it is red.

What can you tell us about that person's personality that might support your opinion? (if the students have studied personality traits)

My parents are old and conservative./My girlfriend likes to be sophisticated and likes exotic things./Uncle George is single, aggressive, and likes adventure.

In this way, the students anticipate or evaluate responses to the car ad by someone they know. They make an analysis based on personal perceptions and experience and they draw inferences about either the persons' priorities or their attitudes and the image they want to convey, especially in terms of how attitudes and perceptions are reflected in the language and paralinguistic communication. In this type of extension discussion, well-directed teacher talk can help students integrate the text and its meaning into their existing knowledge and experiences, help them grow intellectually, and then go beyond, synthesizing the new information with what they already know in order to gain and articulate new insights.

The purpose of doing post-activities is to consider different kinds of possible outcomes. If an ad for a vacation getaway were to be studied, students could think about how they could advertise their own area and what image they would choose to represent it, what "slogan" and captions they would write for it, how they would convince a visitor that the place is fun, interesting, beautiful, and how they could succinctly say what it has to offer.

USING TEACHER TALK AS LANGUAGE DEVELOPMENT IN ITSELF

As pointed out by Terry Ballman in her article in this volume (p. 100), teacher talk plays a key role in the first two segments of a lesson's instructional sequence, those of *setting the stage* and *providing input*. She states that "the teacher is the source of presentation of all new and recycled information" and that "only after students have gained enough linguistic experience through teacher-centered activities are they asked to carry out student-centered activities," in the *guided participation* and *extension* segments. The teacher talk presenting new information for language development might consist of a series of descriptions of visuals (pictures, drawings, posters, maps, charts) central to the lesson's theme and thematically related manipulatives and props.

Continuing under the rubric of the unit on transportation, for example, one might consider the presentation of descriptions of several different modes of transportation through a progression of compare/ contrast statements, cycling and recycling the targeted linguistic features while adding new elements. The visuals and specific elements being referred to in the visuals would be constantly pointed out during the teacher talk so that students could understand new vocabulary either from rich cognates, when juxtaposed with previously learned vocabulary, or by seeing what in the visual the teacher was pointing to. Thus, when the teacher talk takes on an interactive nature, focusing on ideas, it becomes even more effective in engaging the student. That presentation (Harper and Lively, 1989), in L2, might sound like:

Taxis are good for traveling within the city.

We often take a taxi from the airport to a hotel.

They usually carry a maximum of three passengers.

We always tip the driver. (*Mime "tip" by reaching in pocket and handing money to fictitious driver.*)

Taxis are more expensive than buses. (*Mime "expensive" by rubbing thumb and two fingers together in the gesture for money.*)

Airplanes are good for taking long trips. Taxis are good for traveling within the city.

Airplanes have wings, (*Point out wings in visual.*) but taxis have wheels. (*Point out wheels in visual.*) How many wheels do taxis have? (*Student response: four*)

Do airplanes have wheels? (*Exaggerate:*) I hope so!

Airplanes fly in the sky. (*Mime "fly".*) Taxis roll on the ground.

Commercial airplanes carry many passengers; How many passengers can taxis carry? (*Student response: three*)

Airplanes have a pilot.

We do not tip the pilot.

Airplanes are more expensive than taxis.

We wear seat belts in airplanes. (*Mime attaching a seat belt.*)

I traveled to Denver in July in an airplane. Who has recently traveled in an airplane? Jimmy, where did you go? (*Student response: Los Angeles, not even aware that a past-tense verb has been thrown at him*) Who else? Amy? You went to Seattle? Did you take a taxi in Seattle?

A sailboat is propelled by the wind. (*Mime blowing wind and having difficulty walking against the wind.*)

A sailboat is very quiet because it has no motor. The engine of an airplane is very noisy.

We ride in a sailboat on a lake. It goes on the water. An airplane flies in the sky. They are both dependent on the wind.

We use a sailboat for pleasure, not to go to work.

We travel in an airplane for pleasure. Can we use it to go to work, too?

Do you know someone who takes business trips?

Is a taxi used for both pleasure and work?

What about a sailboat? (*Student response: No, not for work. Teacher: That would be rare!*)

A sailboat does not have wheels. What has wheels? (*Student response: a taxi*)

Does a sailboat have wings? No? What has wings? (*Student response: an airplane*)

For safety we wear life jackets on a sailboat. But in an airplane we buckle up a seatbelt for safety. What do we use in a taxi? (*silence*)

In a taxi, do we wear a helmet, a life jacket, or a seatbelt for safety? (*a seatbelt*)

My uncle has a sailboat. Who knows someone who owns a sailboat? Brad? Whom do you know who has a sailboat? (*my friend*) Your friend? How many passengers can go on it?

Interactive teacher talk might resurface throughout the various phases of a lesson to provide cohesion among the many elements of the language development (vocabulary/grammar/cultural information) and to model the language needed for the discussion of concepts. This technique encourages students to manipulate concepts and to explore their own perceptions while it provides them the linguistic means to do so in L2. In short, it helps them to bring (L2) speech to their thoughts.

SUPPORT OF THE DEVELOPMENT OF MULTIPLE INTELLIGENCES

Gahala and Lange (1997) emphasize the importance of moving from ideas to speech in the development of Multiple Intelligences in the foreign language classroom. They advocate starting a lesson with thought-provoking types of presentational activities and then moving to the speech-producing activities: "When lesson planning begins with 'self *smart'* and works in reverse order up Howard Gardner's list of Intelligences (1993) to *'word smart,'* . . . learners will succeed more often," (Gahala and Lange, 30). Many of the instructional practices in the models of teacher talk for mediating authentic input and also for language development (see below) can help teachers systematically incorporate the development of Multiple Intelligences into their classroom. "When teachers incorporate the concepts of Multiple Intelligences into lessons, all learners have more entry points into the content they are learning" (Gahala and Lange, 29–30).

> Intrapersonal/Introspective intelligence, or "self smart," means understanding oneself and taking responsibility. Persons high in this intelligence like to daydream, reflect, and think for themselves. They need a learning environment that gives them time to think and that shows off their work, accomplishments, and unique identity (Gahala and Lange, 30).

By organizing rich activities which nurture understanding of self, responsibility, and reflection in an idea-based curriculum, the foreign language teacher can help promote the development of the intrapersonal/introspective intelligence in students. Several of the instructional practices present in the teacher talk models provide effective support mechanisms for the accommodation of Multiple Intelligences, such as the following examples:

1. For the *intrapersonal/introspective intelligence,* "self smart": opportunities for open-ended expression, and use of surveys that give and get feedback, personal priorities and goals;

2. For the *verbal/linguistic intelligence,* or "word smart": use of graphic organizers (grids on "interactive chalkboard") to promote brainstorming and the generating of ideas, and personal expressions (opinions, reactions, experiences);

3. For the *visual/spatial intelligence,* "picture smart": use of the overhead projector, chalkboard, video, concepts explained graphically, drawing of analogies (how something is like something else—visually), flowcharts and graphs, and teaching/learning experiences using drawings, charts, props, posters, paintings, photographs, and sketches; and

4. For the *logical/mathematical intelligence,* or "number smart": use of graphic organizers that show patterns and relationships (diagrams, charts, matrices, outlines, maps, etc.) and the exploration of patterns and relationships.

Gahala and Lange say that "it is impossible to overemphasize the effectiveness of open-ended personal expression in expanding linguistic proficiency, cultural understanding, and the development of brain power." (p. 32) Teaching to the intrapersonal/introspective intelligence has a triple payoff: (1) The actual experience of using this new language to express personal reality builds self-confidence; (2) personalizing the learning experience motivates learners far more than talking about the anonymous textbook characters that inhabit most textbooks (and many authentic input texts); and (3) divergent personal expression involving both target language and culture enriches the total classroom experience for all (p. 30).

CONCLUSION

This article has looked at various ways that teacher talk can provide opportunities for students to construct their own knowledge and to develop and express their own ideas. It has examined how, in the presentation portions of the lesson, the teacher can provide a catalyst for the students' development of ideas, guiding them to critical thinking rather than allowing them to passively listen and watch as the teacher performs. Suggestions have been provided for meaningful and effective presentational input, where the teacher takes responsibility for providing good samples of authentic texts, for modeling language, for supplying the initial ideas, and for organizing the interaction of the students. The underlying principle for the techniques described in this article is that these techniques guide students to process meaning, reflect on the ideas, and respond appropriately to stimuli while acquiring their own personal stock of linguistic expressions.

NOTES

1. See Alfred N. Smith's article, "Using Video and Newspaper Texts to Provide Topic Schemata in the Composition Class," *The French Review*, Vol. 70, No. 2, December 1996, for ideas on presenting a multiphase developmental lesson leading up to a composition assignment on the topic of the automobile.

REFERENCES

Ballman, Terry. "From Teacher-Centered to Learner-Centered: Guidelines for Sequencing and Presenting the Elements of a Foreign Language Lesson." In Harper, Lively, Williams, *The Coming of Age of the Profession: Issues and Emerging Ideas in the Teaching of Foreign Languages*. Boston: Heinle & Heinle ITP, 1998, 97.

Gahala, Estella M., and Dale L. Lange. "Multiple Intelligences: Multiple Ways to Help Students Learn Foreign Languages," *Northeast Conference Newsletter*, #41, Winter 1997, 29–34.

Gardner, Howard. *Multiple Intelligences: The Theory in Practice: A Reader*. New York: Basic Books, 1993.

Galloway, Vicki. "Constructing Cultural Realities: 'Facts' and Frameworks of Association." In Harper, Lively, Williams, *The Coming of Age of the Profession:*

Issues and Emerging Ideas in the Teaching of Foreign Languages. Boston: Heinle & Heinle ITP, 1998, 129.

Harper, Jane and Madeleine Lively. *HOTStuff for Teachers of Second Languages: A Manual of Units of Instruction Incorporating Higher Order Thinking Skills.* Arlington, TX: The Color Connection, 1989, 44–46.

Tschirner, Erwin. "From Lexicon to Grammar." In Harper, Lively, Williams, *The Coming of Age of the Profession: Issues and Emerging Ideas in the Teaching of Foreign Languages.* Boston: Heinle & Heinle ITP, 1998, 129.

Valette, Rebecca. "French Isn't Just for Majors Any More!" Session at SWCOLT/TFLA Joint Conference. Dallas, TX, 18 April 1997.

From Teacher-Centered to Learner-Centered: Guidelines for Sequencing and Presenting the Elements of a FL Lesson

Terry L. Ballman, *University of Northern Colorado*

Terry L. Ballman is Associate Professor of Spanish at the University of Northern Colorado (UNC) where she teaches undergraduate and graduate courses in Spanish language and linguistics, as well as methods courses for foreign language, ESL, and bilingual teachers. She also coordinates the elementary language program and supervises student teachers. Professor Ballman was recently honored in Who's Who Among America's Teachers, *has received two outstanding teaching awards from UNC, and another from the University of Texas where she earned her Ph.D. She has presented numerous papers and workshops, and has published articles in research volumes and journals such as* Foreign Language Annals *and* Hispania.

INTRODUCTION

"I attended a great presentation at the recent foreign language teachers' conference, and tried to use one of the activities I'd learned with my own students. Well, I tried the activity, and it was a disaster! The students were not only inattentive, but they were outright rowdy. It makes me wonder whether the so-called 'experts' really practice what they preach . . ." And so goes the lament of many foreign language teachers who try out new things, only to find that they do not work well. This unfortunate phenomenon may be due to one or more of the following decisions facing foreign language teachers regarding lesson planning: (1) Is the activity purposeful? i.e., Do students have a reason for doing the activity?; (2) Is the activity sequenced in the proper place within the lesson?; and (3) Do students have enough language or "linguistic support" (Lee, 1995) to carry out the activity?

This article will focus on these issues involved in lesson planning and will suggest criteria for designing lessons in such a way that they progress from being teacher-centered to learner-centered.

> " . . . (S)tudents need to be active participants in their own learning. . . (in) order for students to be active participants, they need to be given ample opportunity to use language and to use it with some autonomy."

BENEFITS OF LEARNER-CENTERED INSTRUCTION

Much has been written in recent years about the need to involve the learner in the learning process (see, for example, Kagan, 1989; Krashen and Terrell, 1983; Lee and VanPatten, 1995; Nunan, 1988; Savignon, 1983 and 1991; and Scarcella and Oxford, 1992). The philosophy expressed is that students need to be active participants in their own learning. And in order for students to be active participants, they need to be given ample opportunity to use language and to use it with some autonomy.

The popular work of Vygotsky (1978) lends support to the importance of social interaction. Vygotsky asserts that there is a developmental area called the Zone of Proximal Development which denotes the area between the learner's actual language level and his or her potential level. The learner can only achieve his or her potential through interaction with others. "Vygotsky's theory implies that . . . acquisition may be contingent on cooperative, meaningful interaction" (Shrum and Glisan, 1994: 11). One such avenue for learner interaction is through pair and small-group work. Long and Porter (1985), in their review of the literature, offer pedagogical arguments for the use of pair/group work, citing that it increases students' language practice opportunities, improves the quality of student talk, helps to individualize instruction, promotes a positive affective climate, and motivates learners (pp. 207–212).

Several empirical studies (Doughty and Pica, 1986; Porter, 1986; Rulon and McCreary, 1986) offer additional support for using pair/small-group work. In these studies individual students engaged in pair/small-group work on meaning-based tasks had more opportunities to use language communicatively than in teacher-led activities. In addition, these studies showed that students exhibited an increased number of negotiation behaviors when engaged in pair/small-group activity.[1]

CONCERNS AND SOLUTIONS SURROUNDING LEARNER-CENTERED INSTRUCTION

> "Pair/group activities are unlikely to increase learner language use if the teacher stresses form-focused drill over meaning-focused communication"

The potential benefits of pair/small-group work notwithstanding, teachers must keep in mind that pair/small-group work is not a panacea. The type of activity carried out during pair/group work is critical, as merely working in groups on a common task does not guarantee increased learning (e.g., Ballman, 1988). Pair/group activities are unlikely to increase learner language use if the teacher stresses form-focused drill over meaning-focused communication (e.g., Guthrie, 1984; Kinginger, 1990). In a study by Brooks (1990), for example, involving pair work in which each partner was asked to use adjectives to describe several fictitious people in Spanish, the researcher found that students exhibited more concern with using and correcting for the correct form of the adjective than with actually engaging in more open-ended language use. Brooks also found that this focus on form was what was stressed by the teacher, suggesting that students imitate teacher behavior. Activity types found to elicit more student participation and language use are those that actively require all students to participate (Brooks, 1992). Asking students to "interview a partner and ask him or her to describe his or her room (house/apartment)" will neither elicit as much language nor negotiation behavior as asking students to "interview a partner and ask him or her to describe his or her room (house/apartment) and draw the room (house/apartment) as he or she describes it." The latter activity assigns both students in the pair activity specific duties to carry out, for in order to complete the task, one student must ask questions, the other student must answer questions and describe, and both must work together so that the drawing task can be completed.[2] It is recommended that learners be assigned tasks that are concrete, such as drawing as in the above-mentioned activity, or filling out charts or questionnaires.

In addition to being cognizant of quality task type, teachers need to ensure that students use the target language and stay on-task during learner-centered activities. Just as it should be expected that students use the target language as much as possible, so should the teacher consistently model target language use.[3] The language teacher needs to be explicit about expected learner target language use, and these expectations should be reflected in evaluation. (Evaluation is addressed later in this paper.) The teacher also needs to make clear the purposefulness of the activities in which students are engaged. The purposefulness of activities is articulated in two ways: (1) what students are asked to do is meaning-based, and the information they share about themselves is treated with respect by the teacher and classmates; and (2) activities are designed in such a way that they are incremental, in that they build one upon the other to enable students to become more expressive with the language. Activities are thematic links in a well-developed chain leading to student-centered outcomes. (Activity types and lesson planning are discussed in the Lesson Planning section of this paper.)

> "Students who are expected to use the target language and to carry out a specific, purposeful task for which they have the necessary language, and who have a strict time limit, are much more likely to stay on-task."

Another way to help ensure that students use the target language is to determine that students have the language or linguistic support necessary to carry out student-centered activities. For example, a group activity in which students are asked to identify their group members' favorite/least favorite holidays will be more successful if the vocabulary of holidays is first introduced or reviewed. If students are 'warmed-up' to the vocabulary and structures needed to carry out a particular task, they will be much better prepared to use them in a learner-centered framework. A technique for encouraging students to stay on-task, in addition to assigning concrete tasks (e.g., to draw, fill out charts or questionnaires), is to implement strict time limits. Students who are expected to use the target language and to carry out a specific, purposeful task for which they have the necessary language, and who have a strict time limit, are much more likely to stay on-task.

THE ROLE OF THE TEACHER

> "The teacher is the source of presentation of all new and recycled information . . . Only after students have gained enough linguistic experience through teacher-centered activities are they asked to carry out student-centered activities."

Although most of the above-mentioned discussion has dealt with learner-centered activities, many classroom activities remain teacher-centered. The teacher is the source of presentation of all new and recycled information (i.e., vocabulary, grammar, culture). Only after students have gained enough linguistic experience through teacher-centered activities are they asked to carry out student-centered activities. This consists of a shift in responsibility from the teacher leading whole-class activities, to students engaging in pair or small-group work.

For learner-centered activities, the teacher's role is that of facilitator. By facilitator it is meant that the teacher sets up and models each student-centered activity. If during a lesson on the topic of family students are asked to work in pairs, for example, with Student A drawing Student B's family tree, the teacher would briefly explain what each student is to do. The teacher would also model the beginning of the activity with a student in the class. In the target language, the teacher could say: "Imagine that I am Student A and Laura is Student B. I will ask Laura questions about her family so I can draw and label Laura's family tree. Laura, what are your parents' names?. . . [The teacher would 'draw' this family tree information on the board.] How many brothers and sisters do you have? And what are their names? . . . [The teacher would again draw and label this information, thus modeling the activity.]"

During a student-centered activity, the teacher walks through the classroom, monitoring student work, and answering any questions. And immediately following a student-centered activity, the focus of the class goes back on the teacher as he or she must lead the class in a follow-up or synthesis activity. A follow-up to the above-mentioned family tree pair activity could be to ask a student to share with the class the family tree that he or she drew.[4] This could be repeated with two or three more students. To complete the follow-up, the teacher might then want to ask the class questions (in the target language, of course) based on information culled from the follow-up: "Whose family trees did we hear about? Who comes from the largest family? the smallest?" The main point to be made here is that the focus of teacher-centered activities, as well as the beginning of and follow-up to all learner-centered activities, is on the teacher.

LESSON PLANNING: THE INSTRUCTIONAL SEQUENCE

The determination of whether an activity is teacher-centered or learner-centered is dependent upon careful lesson planning. The roles and responsibilities of the teacher and learners become clear when the following instructional sequence is adhered to, consisting of four segments. Two segments of the instructional sequence, *Setting the stage* and *Providing input* are teacher-centered; and the other two segments, *Guided participation* and *Extension*, are learner-centered.

Setting the stage occurs at the beginning of every class period and focuses student attention on the topic, prompting students to access existing knowledge about the topic and the lesson. Existing knowledge is used to give meaning to new knowledge, and vice versa.[5] For a lesson on professions, for example, the teacher might display a series of pictures of numerous occupations. After establishing the obvious topic of the lesson, the teacher can point out the pictures that depict professions with vocabulary items with which the students are already familiar (e.g., teacher, doctor), and ask the class to identify them.

After drawing student attention to the topic and reviewing existing knowledge, the teacher could introduce new vocabulary (e.g., accountant, plumber) in the Providing input segment of the instructional sequence. *Providing input* consists of the presentation of target language vocabulary, grammar, or content (e.g., cultural information). Input is presented orally by the teacher, with visual support in the form of pictures, gestures, and/or written language; and student comprehension is consistently monitored by the teacher using comprehension check techniques common to the Natural Approach (Krashen & Terrell, 1983), such as yes/no and either/or questions. The input segment underscores the language acquisition principle that comprehension precedes production (e.g., Krashen, 1981).

Guided participation provides students with specific tasks in which students usually work together in pairs or small groups. The initial activities in this segment require students to attend to both the meaning and form of the new linguistic features (i.e., vocabulary or grammar) presented during the preceding Providing input phase, but without having to produce these features. The activities found later in this Guided participation segment require students to produce the new features.

Extension requires students to participate in a culminating activity in which much, if not all, the lesson's target vocabulary, grammar, and content are used. The language produced by students is more open-ended and creative, with spontaneous language use a likely phenomenon. It is during the Extension segment where most learner/learner interaction occurs, and where learners take on the most responsibility for their participation. These Extension activities are likely to be found at the midpoint of a lesson, and they are always found at the end of a lesson. Whereas Extension is by essence a review, the other segments of the instructional sequence—Setting the stage, Providing input, and Guided participation—may serve the dual function of review.

Sample activities for each of the four segments of the instructional sequence are provided in Table 1 (see below). It is necessary to note that the activities listed first under each category are more 'input' related, requiring that students understand new features of the language but do little, if any, production of the new features. These more 'input' activities, therefore, take place earlier in the lesson. Activities listed later under each category are more 'output' related, requiring more learner production, and would be done after the 'input' related ones. All activities are to be carried out in the target language (L2) by the teacher and students. The list of activities in Table 1 is not exhaustive but is offered to help clarify for the reader the kinds of activities which can be found in the instructional sequence, with those in the Setting the stage and Providing input segments teacher-centered, and those in the Guided participation and Extension segments learner-centered.

Table 1: Sample Activities for Each Segment of the Instructional Sequence

Setting the stage

- The teacher displays visuals (i.e., pictures, drawings, posters, maps, charts) central to the lesson's theme. The teacher describes each visual, emphasizing target linguistic features.

- The teacher brings in thematically-related props (e.g., clothing, foods, stuffed animals), and identifies and describes each.

- The teacher engages students in a word game, puzzle, matching, or unscramble activity related to the topic, preferably presented on an overhead transparency, for the purpose of review.

  For a matching activity, the teacher could present two columns, one column with a list of several target vocabulary or grammatical items to be matched with the appropriate definitions or associations presented in the second column.

  For an unscramble activity, the teacher could present several L2 vocabulary words presented earlier in the lesson and ask students to unscramble them. For a lesson on the community in a French class, for example, students could be asked to unscramble several theme-related words such as *el rbuuae ed toesp*→ (*le bureau de poste* [post office]).

Continued on p. 103

Providing input

- The teacher uses visuals or props presented in *Setting the stage* to introduce new vocabulary, grammar, or content (i.e., cultural information).

- The teacher leads class in TPR (Total Physical Response) activity in which target vocabulary or grammar is presented and practiced.

- The teacher reads a series of statements containing the target vocabulary or grammar, and students respond by indicating yes/no, *agree/disagree*, matching, or selecting an appropriate picture.

- Students are provided with a list of L2 vocabulary or grammatical items presented in random order. Students are asked to order them or to categorize them. Students could be asked to order a list of days of the week, various activities comprising daily routine (e.g., *He wakes up* would precede *He goes to bed*), or historical events. Students could be asked to categorize a list of recreational activities according to the logical place or season with which they are most closely associated.

Guided participation

- Students would be given a series of questions to ask of classmates. The questions would contain target vocabulary or grammar. The activity would require students to secure a different signature, representing an affirmative response, for each of the questions provided. If the lesson covered the Spanish simple past (preterite) tense, the questions could contain all preterite forms, e.g., *¿Fuiste al cine anoche?* (Did you go to the movies last night?) and *¿Desayunaste esta mañana?* (Did you eat breakfast this morning?).

- In pairs, students are provided with true/false written statements in the L2 that partners read to each other. The partner being read to must determine if each statement is true or false. Partner A reads to Partner B; then the partners switch roles.

- The above-mentioned pair activity can be replicated, but with students writing their own true/false statements in the L2.

- In pairs, Partner A describes a picture that Partner B draws; partners can later switch roles.

- Working in small groups, students are asked to find out specific information of their group members and to summarize this information. Specific information could include identifying and giving reasons for each student's favorite/least favorite leisure activities, holidays, vacations spots, traditions, political or historical figures, celebrities, movies, etc.

Continued on p. 104

Extension

- Students are divided into small group or teams. Teams of students alternate asking yes/no questions of a volunteer student who has been given a secret identity by the teacher. Questions are asked until the secret identity (e.g., famous person living or dead, current or historical event) is revealed. This 'twenty questions' game is played for several rounds, with the team with the highest number of correct guesses winning.

- Each student must interview a classmate and elicit information needed to be able to fill out the table, chart, paragraph, or questionnaire provided by the teacher. For a lesson on health and exercise, for example, a student could interview a classmate about his or her exercise habits, filling in a chart listing what the classmate's physical activities are for each weekday. The interviewer would later complete a paragraph in which he or she would state whether the classmate should/should not alter his or her exercise habits and why, and offer recommendations for change.

- Students, working in pairs or small groups, present a student-generated project. These projects could include such activities as a narrated fashion show after a lesson on clothing, a commercial after a lesson on driving and responsibility, or a brochure describing a city and the best places to visit after a lesson on travel.

The types of activities and their frequency over the course of a five-day lesson in the instructional sequence might look like this:

Day 1	Day 2	Day 3	Day 4	Day 5
Setting the Stage	Setting the Stage	Setting the Stage	Setting the Stage	Setting the Stage
Providing Input	Providing Input	Providing Input and Review	Providing Input	Providing Input and Review
Providing Input	Providing Input	Guided Participation	Guided Participation	Extension
Providing Input	Providing Input	Providing Input and Review	Providing Input	
Guided Participation	Guided Participation	Guided Participation	Guided Participation	
Guided Participation	Guided Participation	Extension		

An example of Day 1 as illustrated above would be for the teacher to introduce the lesson's theme during the Setting the stage segment. In the Providing input segment, the teacher would introduce new vocabulary or grammar related to the lesson's theme. During this segment the teacher would lead the class in three input activities using the new vocabulary or grammar. During the Guided participation segment, learners would work together in pairs or small groups using the vocabulary or grammar just presented in Providing input segment on two activities. As stated above, the teacher always sets up and models Guided participation activities, and he or she always does a follow-up to each of these activities. The follow-up to the second Guided participation activity would serve as the review for Day 1.

Day 2 would be similar to Day 1. When Setting the stage on Day 2, the teacher would reintroduce the lesson's theme and do a brief review of Day 1 content. The teacher would introduce a new linguistic feature in Providing input and would direct the class in three input activities. Students would then work on a new linguistic feature in the Guided participation activities, with the follow-up to the last activity providing a review of what was presented in Day 2.

On Day 3 the teacher would provide the Setting the stage and Providing input segments as reviews, and students would do a Guided participation activity after each Providing input presentation. After receiving modeling from the teacher, learners would engage in an Extension activity which requires them to use what they had learned so far in the lesson. At the end of the Extension activity, the teacher then would lead the class in a follow-up based on the Extension activity.

Day 4 would find the teacher presenting a new linguistic feature and/or cultural information during both Providing input segments, with students engaged in Guided participation activities. The teacher-led follow-up to the second Guided participation activity would serve as a review for Day 4 material.

For Day 5, the last day of the lesson, the teacher would lead students in a Providing input and Review activity which would serve to summarize the lesson's content. After, learners would be engaged in a lengthy Extension activity. The follow-up to the Extension would, of course, serve as a review of the activity and of the lesson's content.[6]

EVALUATION

An important concern for teachers is the issue of evaluation. Knowing how to evaluate student participation helps teachers feel more confident about structuring lessons so that students have the opportunity to work in learner-centered activities. Before exploring and implementing any approach to evaluation, every language teacher should answer the following questions:

1. What criteria will I use in the evaluation?
2. What system of grading will I implement? How will it be weighted?

3. Will I assign each student working in a pair or small group an individual grade, or will I assign students in each pair or small group the same grade?

4. Will teacher evaluation be combined with student peer evaluation? and/or with student self-evaluation?

5. How often will student participation be evaluated?

The first step a language teacher should take is to establish the criteria for which students will be accountable. These criteria might include: staying on-task, exclusive use of the L2, effort shown, completion of task, and/or quality of the completed task. The teacher may want to divide the evaluation into two parts: process, referring to when students are working together on an activity; and product, referring to what students produce as a result of working together. The products can include such tasks as filling out a table, chart, paragraph, or question-naire, doing a commercial, or writing a report or a travel brochure.

The second step is for a teacher to identify a system of grading and how it will be weighted. Some teachers may choose a point system, with students assigned a participation grade based on the number of total points earned, e.g., points earned/points possible. The point value of each criterion can vary, depending on the criterion's relative importance. A teacher may, for example, assign more value to being cooperative with classmates than, say, with using the L2 exclusively. Another system some teachers prefer is using a rubric with criteria whose answers have varying values, e.g., *The student/pair/small group stays on-task* Yes = 5 , Somewhat = 3, No = 0. Another possible system is the use of symbols. Symbols usually represent holistic evaluation, (i.e., one overall grade whose criteria may or may not be explicit). Symbols can also have point value. One set of examples of symbols is: + = exceeds expectations, √ = meets expectations, and − = does not meet expectations. Examples of the above-mentioned systems of grading are provided below:

EXAMPLE A.
Point System Evaluation Examining Process and Product

Process (when students are working together)　　　　Pts. Earned/Pts. Possible

- Uses only L2 (Does not use English)　　　　　　　　____/10
- Stays on-task　　　　　　　　　　　　　　　　　　____/10
- Cooperates with classmate(s)　　　　　　　　　　　____/5
- Demonstrates effort　　　　　　　　　　　　　　　____/5

Product (the task the students produce as a result of working together)

- Completeness of product or task　　　　　　　　　　____/10
- Quality of product or task (appropriate L2 use/accuracy)　____/10

　　　　　　　　　　　　　　　TOTAL　　____/50

　　　　　　　　　　　　　　(x 2 =____/100%)

In Example A a point and percentage system is used. Individual criteria carry different weight, with the criteria of *using only the L2* worth 10 possible points, and *cooperation between classmates* worth 5 points possible. This point value can easily be modified by a teacher based on what he or she judges to be the most or least important criteria. For example, the teacher may judge *quality of product or task* as the most important criterion, worth 20 possible points. Teachers have the option of tabulating the total number of points earned during an evaluation period (a quarter or semester) against the total number of possible points, or of tabulating the percentage earned for each activity evaluated. (The total points possible in Example A is a round number [50], which can easily be multiplied [in this case, by 2] to give a total percentage in evaluating one activity.)

EXAMPLE B. Rubric System of Evaluation Examining Process and Product			
Process (when students are working together)	Yes	Somewhat	No
• Uses only L2 (Does not use English)	10	6	0
• Stays on-task	10	6	0
• Is cooperative with classmate(s)	5	3	0
• Demonstrates effort	5	3	0
Product (the task the students produce as a result of working together)			
• Product or task is complete	10	6	0
• Quality of product or task is superior (L2 used is appropriate in vocabulary, grammar and accuracy)	10	6	0
TOTAL 50/EARNED ____			

Example B is a modification of Example A, with a rubric used in which teachers determine if each criterion is realized (*Yes*), somewhat realized (*Somewhat*), or not realized at all (*No*). Each answer (e.g., *Yes/Somewhat/No*) carries a different weight (e.g., 5/3/0 points, respectively). An option for teachers is to simplify the rubric by allowing only two answers: *Yes* or *No*, with *Yes* answers worth maximum points, and *No* answers worth zero points.

As with Example A, Example B allows teachers to tabulate points earned by the end of an evaluation term and calculate a percentage, or to calculate the percentage of total points earned per activity evaluated.

EXAMPLE C. Use of Symbols for Holistic Scoring		
Symbols	*Meaning*	(*Optional: Point Value*)
+	Exceeds expectations	(10)
√	Meets expectations	(5)
–	Does not meet expectations	(0)

For Example C, the teacher can simplify evaluation by assigning a series of symbols such as +, √, and –. These symbols can be representative of the criteria constituting the teacher's expectations. Although it is important with any system of evaluation, it is essential with a symbols system that the teacher communicate clearly what his or her expectations for student participation are. The teacher can opt to convert symbols into points (e.g., +, √, and – can be worth 10, 5, and 0 points, respectively), or can use the symbols only. In the latter case, the teacher would convert the number of +, √, or – into a grade or percentage at the end of an evaluation term.

The third question every language teacher must explore is whether each student working in a pair or small group will receive an individual grade or whether students in each pair or small group will receive the same grade. An advantage to assigning each pair or small group the same grade is that it encourages student cooperation and accountability. Students expecting to receive the same pair or small-group grade may be more apt to encourage their partners or group members to do their best.

The fourth question begging attention deals with whether teacher evaluation will be joined with student peer evaluation and/or student self-evaluation. Provided with grading instruments similar to those presented in Examples A, B, and C previously, students can be asked to evaluate the participation of their peers, namely of their partners or group members. In turn, a student can be asked to evaluate his or her own participation. Teachers using student peer and/or student self-evaluation may feel that they are getting valuable feedback from students and that they are giving students more ownership over the evaluation process.

The fifth and final question a language teacher must answer is how often to evaluate student participation. Although it may be ideal to evaluate student participation whenever students work in a learner-centered format, it is impractical to expect a teacher to evaluate each pair or small group when each is engaged in a pair or small-group activity. In response to this classroom reality, many teachers opt for "random" evaluation in which specific pairs or small groups are pre-chosen to be evaluated. In his or her role as facilitator, a teacher circulates through the entire class but evaluates the participation of only two or three partners or small groups. Teachers may choose to keep the identity of those being evaluated anonymous, as it may be better for all students to think that it is they who may be being evaluated at any given time.

CONCLUSION

This paper began with a quote by a disgruntled foreign language teacher who had used a learner-centered activity in his or her class that turned out to be a 'disaster.' One of the purposes of the article was to highlight the benefits of learner-centered activities, as well as to outline ways to ensure that these kinds of activities are, indeed, successful.

One way to help ensure successful student-centered work is for the teacher to consistently model meaningful target language (L2) use, and to ask students to engage in meaning-based activities. As VanPatten (1991) asserts: "If instructors themselves use language meaningfully and are constantly attempting to communicate with learners, then the learners in turn will attempt to communicate with each other when tasks with clear information goals are set up for them" (p. 70). The type of classroom activity to be performed should be determined through careful lesson planning. The Instructional Sequence outlined in the paper offers four kinds of classroom activities, with *Setting the stage* and *Providing input* being teacher-centered, and *Guided participation* and *Extension* student-centered. This Instructional Sequence sees the teacher's role changing from the center of attention during teacher-centered activities to being the facilitator and monitor of student participation during student-centered activities. This approach to lesson planning is purposeful in that one activity leads to the next, and student responsibility gradually increases. Students are asked to perform tasks only when they are sufficiently prepared (i.e., have the linguistic support) to do so. In this way, students are more likely to stay on-task and use the L2.

Evaluation is, of course, an important issue for language teachers. This paper offers teachers questions to explore, as well as a variety of evaluation approaches for assessing student participation.

The overall objective of the paper is to encourage teachers to implement learner-centered activities. It is hoped that by following the suggestions offered, language teachers will embrace student-centered instruction as a regular, systematic part of their classrooms. In so doing, it is likely they will be providing their students with a more enriching learning experience.

NOTES

1. Negotiation behaviors include prompts that cause the speaker to modify his or her language, such as being asked to repeat, rephrase, or clarify. Savignon (1983) and others view negotiation as a necessary requisite for developing communicative competence.

2. Lee (1995) provides an excellent discussion and several examples of task-based activities. Similarly, Walz (1996) delineates one type of task-based instruction, the information-gap activity.

3. A study by Wing (1987) of the teacher talk of 15 self-selected secondary teachers of second-year Spanish revealed that the teachers used the target language (i.e., Spanish) slightly more than half the time.

4. Ideally, the family-tree drawing activity would be done on an overhead transparency, making it easier for students to visually share their family trees with the class.

5. The role of existing knowledge is well documented in schema theory research (e.g., Bransford, 1979), which posits that comprehension and memory are enhanced when learners make associations between existing and new knowledge.

6. For detailed, step-by-step lesson plans, the reader is referred to Ballman, 1996, and 1997.

REFERENCES

Ballman, Terry L. 1988. "Is Group Work Better Than Individual Work for Learning Spanish?: The Findings of One Study." *Hispania* 71 (March): 180–85.

_____. 1996. "Integrating Vocabulary, Grammar, and Culture: A Model Five-Day Communicative Lesson Plan." *Foreign Language Annals,* 29 1: 37–44.

_____. 1997. "Enhancing Beginning Language Courses Through Content-Enriched Instruction." *Foreign Language Annals* 30, 2: 173–186.

Bransford, John D. 1979. *Human Cognition: Learning, Understanding, and Remembering.* Belmont, CA: Wadsworth Publishing Company.

Brooks, Frank B. 1990. "Foreign Language Learning: A Social Interaction Perspective." In Bill VanPatten and James F. Lee, eds., *Second Language Acquisition— Foreign Language Learning.* Clevedon, U.K.: Multilingual Matters, 153–169.

_____. 1992. "Can We Talk?" *Foreign Language Annals* 25, 1: 59–71.

Doughty, Catherine, and Teresa Pica. 1986. "Information Gap Tasks: Do They Facilitate Acquisition?" *TESOL Quarterly* 20, 2: 305–26.

Guthrie, Elizabeth Leemann. 1984. "Intake, Communication, and Second-Language Teaching." In Sandra J. Savignon and Margie S. Berns, eds., *Initiatives in Communicative Language Teaching.* Reading, MA: Addison-Wesley, 35–54.

Kagan, Spencer. 1989. *Cooperative Learning: Resources for Teachers.* San Juan Capistrano, CA: Resources for Teachers.

Kinginger, Celeste. 1990. *Task Variation and Classroom Learner Discourse.* Unpublished doctoral dissertation. Urbana, IL: University of Illinois, Urbana-Champaign.

Krashen, Stephen D. 1981. *Second Language Acquisition and Second Language Learners.* Oxford: Pergamon.

Krashen, Stephen D., and Tracy D. Terrell. 1983. *The Natural Approach.* Hayward, CA: Alemany Press.

Lee, James F. 1995. "Using Task-Based Activities to Restructure Class Discussions." *Foreign Language Annals* 28, 3: 437–46.

Lee, James F., and Bill VanPatten. 1995. *Making Communicative Language Teaching Happen.* New York: McGraw-Hill.

Long, Michael H., and Patricia A. Porter. 1985. "Group Work, Interlanguage Talk, and Second Language Acquisition." *TESOL Quarterly* 19, 2: 207–28.

Nunan, David. 1988. *The Learner-Centered Curriculum.* Cambridge: Cambridge University Press.

Porter, Patricia A. 1986. "How Learners Talk to Each Other: Input and Interaction in Task-Centered Discussions." In Richard R. Day, ed., *Talking to Learn: Conversation in Second Language Acquisition.* Rowley, MA: Newbury House, 200–228.

Rulon, Kathryn A., and Jan McCreary. 1986. "Negotiation of Content: Teacher-Fronted and Small-Group Interaction." In Richard R. Day, ed., *Talking to Learn: Conversation in Second Language Acquisition.* Rowley, MA: Newbury House, 182–99.

Savignon, Sandra J. 1983. *Communicative Competence: Theory and Classroom Practice.* Reading, MA: Addison-Wesley.

_____. 1991. "Communicative Language Teaching: State of the Art." *TESOL Quarterly* 25, 2: 261–277.

Scarcella, Robin C., and Rebecca L. Oxford. 1992. *The Tapestry of Language Learning: The Individual in the Communicative Classroom.* Boston, MA: Heinle & Heinle.

Shrum, Judith L., and Eileen W. Glisan. 1994. *Teacher's Handbook: Contextualized Language Instruction.* Boston, MA: Heinle & Heinle.

VanPatten, Bill. 1991. "The Foreign Language Classroom as a Place to Communicate." In Barbara F. Freed, ed., *Foreign Language Acquisition Research and the Classroom.* Boston, MA: D. C. Heath, 54–73.

Vygotsky, Lev S. 1978. *Mind in Society: The Development of Higher Psychological Processes.* Cambridge, MA: Harvard University Press.

Walz, Joel. 1996. "The Classroom Dynamics of Information Gap Activities." *Foreign Language Annals* 29, 3: 481–494.

Wing, Barbara H. 1987. "The Linguistic and Communicative Functions of Foreign Language Teacher Talk." In Bill VanPatten, Trisha R. Dvorak, and James F. Lee, eds. *Foreign Language Learning: A Research Perspective.* Cambridge, MA: Newbury House, 158–173.

From Lexicon
To Grammar

Erwin Tschirner, *The University of Iowa*

Erwin Tschirner (Ph.D University of California, Berkeley) is an Associate Professor of German at the University of Iowa, where he teaches courses in German, in Germanic linguistics, and applied linguistics. Professor Tschirner has coauthored two college-level German textbooks, Kontakte: A Communicative Approach and Assoziationen: Deutsch für die Mittelstufe. *His articles on second language acquisition and foreign language teaching methodologies have appeared among others in* Modern Language Journal, Die Unterrichtspraxis: Teaching German, Foreign Language Annals, Deutsch als Fremdsprache, Fremdsprachen Lehren und Lernen.

INTRODUCTION

In recent years, the study and teaching of grammar has experienced a renaissance (see, e.g., Bygate, Tonkyn, and Williams, 1994). Particularly, the notions of grammar awareness (Schmidt, 1992) and input enhancement (Sharwood Smith, 1993) have been widely discussed and are slowly entering mainstream teaching materials and teacher education programs. There is a real danger, however, in assuming that modern theories of grammar and grammar teaching are simply providing new justification for traditional notions of grammar and grammar teaching, which may have been shunned in theory but in practice may be just as widespread today as they were 20 years ago.

It is commonly understood that the word grammar has a number of very different meanings. Tonkyn (1994), for example, distinguishes between a descriptive grammar—as represented in the work of linguists—a pedagogical grammar—as represented in foreign language textbooks—and a psycholinguistic grammar—as represented in the head of the language user. In this article, I am mostly concerned with the psycholinguistic grammar in the heads of language users, specifically, how it grows and develops, what kinds of influences help it develop, and what constrains its development.

One important question we need to deal with in this context is what kind of relationship exists between a pedagogical grammar and a psycholinguistic one. It may be that both are very similar and that an explicit teaching of the pedagogical grammar has direct impact on the development of the psycholinguistic one. It may be that both are very dissimilar and an explicit teaching of the pedagogical grammar has little or no influence on the growth of the psycholinguistic grammar. Or, it may be that our mind can make use of the information provided by a pedagogical grammar for mental grammaticalization processes despite the essential difference of the two kinds of grammars. In the following, I will argue for a cautious interpretation of the last possibility.

I will also argue that the use learners can make of pedagogical grammar explanations is unevenly distributed across skill areas and across levels of instruction. For example, it seems unlikely that learners profit much from a cognitive understanding of grammar in listening comprehension, whereas they may profit considerably from such an approach in reading. It also seems unlikely that learners profit much from an explicit understanding and knowledge of a pedagogical grammar at early levels of instruction, while they may profit a great deal at higher levels.

GRAMMAR NEEDS VARY ACCORDING TO SKILL AREA

Grammar explanations found in foreign language textbooks in North America are commonly based on grammatical descriptions of the written language. It is assumed that these descriptions apply to oral language as well. However, there are a number of differences between written and oral language such as utterance length and choice of words and structures. These differences are mainly due to two reasons: a psycholinguistic one and a sociolinguistic one. On one hand, psycholinguistic processing constraints, i.e., how much language can be in a person's head at one point in time, limit the length, eloquence, and smoothness of oral texts. On the other hand, the presence or absence of an interlocutor influences the degree of explicitness and referential precision required. For these two reasons, the frequency of use of particular grammatical structures varies considerably between speaking and writing, which, in turn, should have an effect on what should be taught in what modality and in what sequence. For instance, Chafe and Danielewicz (1987) find that:

♦ Spoken utterances are considerably shorter (6.2 words on average) than written ones (9.3 words).

♦ Spoken utterances are usually linked by coordination, whereas written clauses are joined together in complex ways using subordination and coordination.

♦ Written clauses are frequently expanded with a variety of devices such as prepositional phrases, nominalizations, and attributive adjectives and nouns, which are considerably less frequent in oral conversations.

♦ Some grammatical structures, such as passive constructions, are infrequent in spoken conversations but frequent in non-casual writing because of differences in audience involvement and degree of abstractness.

Moreover, there are structures that are almost exclusively used in writing such as the French and German simple past tense (*passé simple* and *Präteritum*), while others such as the German flavoring particles are used primarily in oral conversations.

In addition to disparities between the spoken and the written language, there are major differences between the way language is processed in understanding and between the processes involved in producing language. Efficiency and effectiveness in comprehending spoken and written utterances is primarily due to an efficient use of top-down strategies with which listeners derive meaning by attending to the linguistic and situational context of a sentence or utterance and by applying world and common sense knowledge. In listening comprehension, in particular, syntactic (bottom-up) and semantic (top-down) processing are inextricably linked, while in production one may deliberately focus on either component (Garnham, 1994). Top-down strategies are particularly important in listening comprehension because the auditory stimulus is often impoverished and may even be inadequate (Aitchison, 1994).

The verb is of major importance as it establishes a cognitive framework that creates slots that need to be filled. A "hitting" scenario, for example, usually involves a "hitter," someone who gets hit, something used to hit with, some degree of violence, a location in which the hitting occurs, and so on (Brown, 1994). As people, things, and locations get mentioned in the course of an utterance they are assigned the above roles according to what appears to be "logical" without much attention to grammatical detail.

GRAMMAR NEEDS VARY ACCORDING TO SKILL LEVEL

One of the observable phenomena of second language acquisition (SLA) is the fact that there is staged development of second language acquisition, that is, second language learners go through stages of development towards the target language. At each stage, some grammatical structures or parts thereof are acquired while others remain unacquired. In addition, some structures build on other structures and cannot be acquired before these other structures are acquired (Pienemann, 1989). Elsewhere, I have argued (Tschirner, 1996) that the ACTFL Oral Proficiency Interview (OPI) may serve as a useful framework to develop hypotheses about such sequences and to test them empirically. It appears that the intermediate levels (novice high, intermediate low, and mid) are associated with sentence-level features such as subject-verb agreement and basic word order in simple sentences, while the advanced levels (intermediate high and advanced) are associated with paragraph-level features such as subordinate clauses and, for languages that have a case system, the case system. For German, I have proposed the following grammatical features to be controlled at various oral proficiency levels.

Novice	*essentially no grammar*
Intermediate	*present tense*
	subject-verb agreement
	word order in simple sentences
Advanced	*perfect tense*
	case system
	word order in complex sentences

One reasonable approach would be to introduce at each level the grammar structures that generally are, at least partially, controlled at the next higher level. That means, if first-semester students are generally at the novice level with respect to their oral proficiency, the focus of instruction should be on structures that are controlled, at least partially, at the intermediate level. If second-, third-, and fourth-semester students are generally at the intermediate level, the focus of instruction should be on structures that are controlled, at least partially, at the advanced level. And, finally, if students in their third and fourth college years are still by and large at the intermediate (high) level, the focus in these years—as far as speaking is concerned—should still be structures generally controlled at the advanced level and perhaps some that are generally controlled at the superior level.

CONVERSATIONAL LANGUAGE IS HIGHLY ROUTINIZED

One of the reasons why spoken and written language are so different is the fact that speaking is a behavior that takes place in real time and under severe processing constraints, i.e., short-term memory limitations. Pawley and Syder (1983) maintain that speakers are not free to concentrate on the grammatical content of their production because they must invest considerable energy into making their contributions coherent, sensitive to what has gone on before and what might happen later, and sensitive to audience knowledge and other features of the social situation. In addition, their talk should be native-like and in an appropriate register and meet other requirements such as being accurate, logical, witty, or modest.

Speakers can do all this and speak more or less grammatically correct because they have recourse to hundreds of thousands of memorized phrases, partial sentences, and complete sentences. Many of these prefabricated sentences and parts of sentences accumulated over a lifetime are accessed and used as wholes as they have been on previous occasions. Complete sentences (e.g., How are you going to do that? Once you've done that the rest is easy. There's nothing you can do about it now. Tell me what happened. And I'm just dying to hear all the gossip.) are not created from scratch every time a person wants to express these or other meanings but are simply accessed and used in their entirety.

This method of redundantly storing words and combinations of words appears to make good use of human memory resources which consist of a short-term or working memory that is very limited in size and a large, capacious, and redundantly structured long-term memory system. To make optimum use of their memory resources, speakers essentially follow two strategies when engaging in conversation: They focus on one clause at a time and they use a clause-chaining style, that is, they string clauses together consisting of from four to ten words, many of which may have been fully or partially preassembled.

> " . . . (A) significant amount of conversational language is highly routinized as prefabricated utterances. . . "

Nattinger and DeCarrico (1992) argue that many of these routinized formulas and other kinds of prefabricated language chunks carry a pragmatic meaning. They call these prefabricated patterns lexical phrases (which may, nonetheless, consist of entire sentences) and divide them into three groups: (1) social interactions, which are used for conversational maintenance such as summoning and nominating a topic and conversational purposes or speech acts such as questioning and complimenting; (2) necessary topics in daily conversations such as quantity, time, weather, and likes; and (3) discourse devices that connect the meaning and structure of the discourse such as logical or temporal connectors, fluency devices, exemplifiers, and evaluators. Nattinger and DeCarrico claim that a significant amount of conversational language is highly routinized as prefabricated utterances and argue for a new teaching approach that puts these lexical phrases at the center of classroom learning.

THE ACQUISITION OF THE LEXICON IS PRIMARY AND LEXICAL ACQUISITION DRIVES GRAMMAR ACQUISITION

Beginning language learning, especially, appears to be for the most part a question of learning vocabulary and lexical phrases. Hakuta (1974) and Wong-Fillmore (1976) investigated how children learn a second language and found that prefabricated language constituted a major part of their speech behavior. Children use these lexical phrases not only to communicate but also as raw material for later segmentation and analysis in developing the rules of syntax. Thus, routines and patterns learned in the language acquisition process evolve directly into creative language.

Ellis (1996) emphasizes the significance of lexical learning from a psycholinguistic, empiricist perspective. He argues that learning discourse structures largely involves learning particular sequences of words in stock phrases and collocations. Learners store complete clauses and sentences, which are then analyzed syntactically. However, this syntactic analysis does not take place consciously but rather unconsciously (implicitly) and automatically. Ellis also argues that very large numbers of lexical sequences need to be stored before the mind can start to build a grammar. He, thus, supports the position by Nattinger and DeCarrico (1992) who also maintain that the acquisition of a great many lexical phrases is a prerequisite for the development of grammar.

GRAMMAR IS ACQUIRED WHEN FORM AND MEANING ARE PROCESSED AT THE SAME TIME

Input may be processed for meaning alone (the default situation), in which case the form of the message, i.e., the actual words being used, are discarded after meaning has been extracted and only the meaning is stored. Although the input was comprehensible and was actually comprehended, no new language was learned. Sharwood Smith (1993) argues that both form and meaning must be perceived and processed at the same time for the interlanguage to develop. One technique he suggests for teachers to use is "input enhancement," that is, to draw students' attention explicitly to form features of the input. As students understand the meaning of a particular sentence while focusing on the form of that sentence, they process both meaning and form and, thus, further develop their growing grammatical system.

> "Grammar is acquired when form and meaning are processed at the same time."

Such "attention to form" may be one of the central advantages classroom learning has over "natural" learning environments. As Clark and Clark (1977) find, language users do not rely on a linguistic model when they are comprehending in authentic language use situations but rather are more likely to use comprehension strategies, i.e., they rely on syntactic and semantic clues, or background, or world knowledge. This strategy use may, in fact, prevent the input from being processed in linguistic ways with the resulting consequence that although comprehension was achieved no actual language was learned. The fact that language classrooms enable and invite teachers and learners to focus on formal aspects of the language is conducive to process input linguistically, which seems to be a prerequisite for further grammatical development.

OUTPUT DOES NOT EMERGE BUT NEEDS TO BE ACQUIRED TOO

While much research has focused on the comprehension side of language, i.e., on the input necessary to build up the grammar of a language, it is an important question to ask how comprehension is related to production.

Krashen (1981), for example, argues that comprehensible input alone drives the language acquisition process and that production will slowly "emerge" by itself as the grammar develops and matures on the basis of input. However, this view has been and continues to be very controversial because it does not seem to take into account the essential differences between comprehension and production processes. Swain (1985), for example, showed that immersion-educated children achieve high levels of comprehension performance, equivalent, in fact, to that attained by native-speaker children of comparable age. However, the children do not achieve the same level productively, casting considerable doubt on Krashen's claim that comprehensible input is the sole driving force for language development and that gains achieved in comprehension are transferred to production.

Keenan and MacWhinney (1983) looked in detail at the relationship between comprehension and production in L1 learning. They distinguish between six different learning tasks involved when learning to understand and produce language. Children acquiring their first language need to learn receptive forms for comprehension, receptive functions (concepts), and mappings between these receptive forms and functions. In addition, they need to learn expressive forms for production, expressive functions (communicative intents), and, again, mappings between these expressive forms and functions. In both, the acquisition of function and form, reception is primary. The sets of expressive functions and forms commonly derive from and are subsets of the receptive ones.

It is easy to see how receptive forms must be different from expressive forms when looking at pronunciation. The receptive forms must be stored together with auditive information, i.e., interpretation of sound waves, while the expressive forms must be stored with articulatory information, i.e., audiomotor commands to produce sounds in the vocal tract. In learning to speak, receptive forms (auditive) need to be converted into expressive forms (articulatory), which is not an automatic process. Rather, the child must devise an articulatory program in each new case, that is, for each new word or string of words. The most important point Keenan and MacWhinney make is that there is no carryover from receptive mappings to expressive mappings, that is, the ability to speak does not "emerge" but rather needs be acquired separately while engaging in conversation.

The task L2 learners face is somewhat different from that of the L1 learners above because they have already acquired their sets of receptive and expressive functions while learning their native language. First, they need to learn receptive forms (words, grammatical morphemes) and they need to map these forms to their receptive functions (meaning) already established in their L1 acquisition. From the set of receptive forms, L2 learners need to derive expressive forms. And crucially, they need to map their expressive functions (communicative intents) to these expressive forms because, as said previously, there is no carryover from receptive mappings to expressive mappings. In other words, the ability to use a word or grammatical form productively does not emerge from exposure to comprehensible input but rather is acquired when the item in question is used productively, i.e., while speaking, while trying to communicate.

IMPLICATIONS FOR TEACHING

> " . . . (L)exical learning drives grammatical learning . . ."

Grammar needs vary with respect to the skill being used and at various proficiency levels. Before offering some suggestions as to curricular implications of this postulate, I would like to focus on four main issues as derived from the previous discussion and their implications for foreign language teaching: (1) lexical learning drives grammatical learning; (2) grammar learning takes place when meaning and form are processed at the same time; (3) while input is primary, output does not simply emerge but needs to be learned and practiced separately; and (4) bias for accuracy is helpful in the acquisition of the productive skills.

☐ FROM LEXICAL SEQUENCES TO GRAMMAR

In general, grammar building appears to be an unconscious process, taking place on the basis of memorized sequences of words (phrases, partial sentences, and full sentences). These memorized sequences of words serve two purposes: (1) they allow learners to communicate even at beginning stages of language learning, and (2) they are used by learners to build up their psycholinguistic grammar. Being able to communicate from early on helps learners to start the language acquisition process by allowing them to engage in real communicative situations. After having stored a great number of such memorized phrases, learners will start to analyze them syntactically. The crucial point here is that very large numbers of lexical sequences need to be stored before the mind can start to build a grammar.

> "Rather than focusing on detailed grammatical development, beginning language instruction should help students to acquire a large and capacious vocabulary learned in context and stored as sequences of words and phrases."

This appears to argue for a complete reversal of the customary approach of introducing the "complete" grammar of a foreign language in the first college year and of restricting the vocabulary to be learned to a minimum of 1,200 or so words. Rather than focusing on detailed grammatical development, beginning language instruction should help students to acquire a large and capacious vocabulary learned in context and stored as sequences of words and phrases. Only when words are stored as syntagmas, i.e., as phrases, partial and complete sentences, do they incorporate grammatical information, which can later be analyzed and used to build up the learner's grammatical competence. Although this grammatical information is "frozen" as it were at the time of storage, it continues to be present in the mind as lexicalized grammar or as grammar in context until it can be used.

On the basis of this hypothesis, the following recommendations for foreign language teaching might be offered:

♦   Emphasize vocabulary learning over grammar learning.

♦   Present and practice vocabulary in context.

♦   Help students memorize and store partial and complete phrases and sentences within a meaningful context.

□ ATTENTION TO MEANING AND FORM

Learners are helped to store grammatically correct sequences of words which can later be used to build up correct grammars when the following conditions apply:

1. the input is optimal in the sense that it consists of relatively short sentences that are grammatical and that are easy to understand (at the level of the learner);

2. the formal features of the input are clearly perceived by the learner because the input is enunciated clearly and slowly enough for the learner to be able to hear individual words together with their linguistic context; and

3. the formal features of the input are processed in depth because the attention of the learners has been focused on these formal features so the learner can process both form and meaning at the same time.

Such "attention to form," however, does not imply that grammar needs to be explained using metalinguistic terminology. Rather, this expression is used here in the sense of pointing out grammatical regularities and helping learners to store "correct" and deeply processed language examples which they can use to develop their psycholinguistic grammar.

Since meaning is primary and essential for language acquisition to take place, the shift in classroom behavior towards imitating immersion conditions was a good one. In natural conversations, however, meaning is foregrounded anyway and very little attention may be given to form. Due to the overwhelming importance of top-down strategies, i.e., the use of scripts, world knowledge, and the context of the situation itself, a great deal of the grammatical information of a particular text may not be processed. For example, as soon as one hears the verb to give the first object mentioned will be interpreted as the object being given and the first person mentioned (after the verb) will be interpreted as the person receiving the object. In languages that have case markings to distinguish between direct and indirect objects, the listener does not normally need to listen to and process case markings to interpret semantic roles correctly and does not normally do so. In fact, the listener will probably understand that the object was given to the person, even if the speaker actually said it the other way. In such cases, the listener is likely to assume he or she misunderstood or that the speaker misspoke.

Most, if not all, listening strategies, in fact, are shortcuts aimed at helping the listener develop and further refine his or her top-down strategies, thus bypassing more syntactic processing modes. The positive side is that learners develop the ability to understand foreign language texts, which is an important teaching goal in its own right. The negative side is that by using top-down strategies learners do not learn any new language. To learn, students need to "break the code" of the foreign language, to figure out how forms are related to meaning. This requires a focus on form on top of the focus on meaning.

On the basis of this hypothesis, the following suggestions may be offered:

♦ Start with and emphasize the meaning of sentences and texts.

♦ Highlight selected formal features of these sentences and texts after meaning has been established.

♦ Allow for deep processing of these formal features, e.g., by asking students to write down phrases and sentences that contain these features.

♦ Combine strategy training in listening and reading comprehension with focused language learning.

☐ PRODUCTION ACTIVITIES

In addition to form-focused listening and reading experiences, learners' grammaticalization efforts profit a great deal from output experiences. First, output requires much more focused syntactic processing than input. In fact, the default mode in input processing is a focus on meaning, whereas speaking and writing focus the learner on the form his or her communicative intents require. Second, only in speaking (and writing) do learners map expressive functions with expressive forms, which is a prerequisite for the acquisition of productive competence.

How then is productive competence acquired? When students repeat and imitate what the instructor says without knowing what these words or sentences mean, students acquire receptive forms and productive forms. When students repeat and imitate what the instructor says while at the same time understanding and processing the meaning the words or sentences carry, they acquire receptive forms and receptive mappings between forms and functions, and they acquire expressive forms. However, they do not acquire expressive mappings. In order to do that, students need to start with a communicative intent. By using the expressive form to express that intent, students map the expressive function to the expressive form. In other words, learners need to use a particular word or grammatical morpheme productively within a communicative context in order to acquire it.

To learn words and structures for productive use, an expressive function, i.e., a communicative intent, has to be mapped to an expressive form. It is unclear how effective "suggested" communicative intents are, for example, in the form of task descriptions such as: Write five sentences about some of the things you did yesterday, using some or all of the following verbs. However, it seems reasonable to assume that the closer these task descriptions are to things students might want to say or write about in real communicative situations the greater the chances are that mappings between expressive functions and forms take place.

From this hypothesis the following guidelines might be drawn:

♦ Provide students with ample speaking and writing opportunities in addition to listening and reading experiences.

♦ Set up production activities in a way that allows students to start with their own communicative intents.

□ BIAS FOR ACCURACY

An important element of success in production tasks is how easy it is for students to think of the correct forms. Traditional grammar production tasks operated under the assumption that what students needed to learn was the ability to manipulate sentences consciously. Therefore, the stimulus sentences or texts were usually incomplete in such a way that the correct application of a particular grammar rule was needed to turn these incomplete sentences or texts into grammatically complete entities. Depending on the difficulty of the rule in question, the difficulty of the task, and the conscientiousness and intellectual abilities of the learner, students were just as likely to produce incorrect sentences or texts as they were to produce correct ones. This was unfortunate. The more incorrect strings of words are stored (and later analyzed), the less likely it is that learners are able to synthesize rules from these stored sentences that lead to native-like language production.

> " . . . (S)tudents should be provided with preassembled and accurate examples of the particular structure to be learned and that the actual task would be to express their own personal meanings with these preassembled phrases or clauses."

In my view, it is not the task of learners to consciously learn and apply rules but rather to correctly map meaning to form, or map specific communicative intents to correctly phrased words, phrases, and sentences. For this reason, it must be easy for students to generate correct sentences and texts. In particular, I would like to argue that students should be provided with preassembled and accurate examples of the particular structure to be learned and that the actual task would be to express their own personal meanings with these preassembled phrases or clauses. For example, rather than providing students with infinitives when they have to write five sentences about five things they did the day before, I would suggest providing students with the correct first-person singular past tense forms of the verbs together with the pronoun "I." The students' task is to expand these sentences with objects, adverbs, and prepositional phrases to express what they actually did. In this way, students will learn to use the new structure correctly while providing their own communicative intents.

Based on this hypothesis, the following recommendation may be made:

♦ Make it easy for students to use the structures to be learned correctly in communicative situations by providing them with preassembled phrases and sentences.

SUGGESTIONS FOR CURRICULUM PLANNING

In this final section, I will focus on grammar needs for the various skills during the first two years of college or four years of high school, i.e., the beginning and intermediate levels, while offering a few suggestions for the more advanced levels.

What are grammar needs for speaking purposes? Let us distinguish between explicit grammar and implicit grammar. Explicit grammar refers to conscious introduction and practice of grammatical structures in the traditional sense using metalinguistic terminology. Implicit grammar refers to the fact that there is an underlying grammatical syllabus which is reflected in the choice of phrases and sentences used in classroom activities and that there is a focus on form, i.e., the clear perception and processing of grammatical form as it is related to meaning. As learners move from beginning and intermediate levels to advanced levels of oral proficiency, the amount of explicit grammar increases.

At the early levels, there may be very little need for explicit grammar because learners cannot yet make any use of it. They have not yet stored sufficient examples of grammatical structures in context to be able to start any significant grammaticalization processes. At these early levels, the focus should be on working with language at the syntagmatic level, that is, helping students to learn words, phrases, and partial and complete sentences with which to express their meanings. As learners move into the second and third year of college level instruction and as their metalinguistic knowledge increases due to the use of metalinguistic terminology for reading and writing purposes (see below), they may very well profit from a conscious knowledge and application of grammar rules for speaking purposes as well. Without reducing the amount of implicit grammar and the learning of lexical phrases and other syntagmas, the amount of explicit grammar could then increase considerably.

As for listening comprehension, it is useful to distinguish between two kinds of listening behaviors: decoding vs. code-breaking. The aim of decoding is to understand the message. The aim of code-breaking is to learn the foreign language, to figure out how forms are related to meaning. The latter requires a focus on form in conjunction with the focus on meaning. As for listening comprehension proper, vocabulary development and the development of top-down listening strategies is of tantamount importance, perhaps throughout one's learning career. The attention to form in listening comprehension builds up the psycholinguistic grammar for both comprehension and production. However, this process does not appear to be aided significantly by any explicit discussion of grammatical features. For this reason, there does not seem to be much use, if any, for explicit grammar instruction in listening comprehension.

While it is probably unrealistic to expect learners to use conscious bottom-up strategies in listening comprehension (except when there is the possibility of repeated listening to the same text), it may make good sense to teach bottom-up strategies such as looking for grammatical cues in reading in addition to top-down strategies such as thinking of and applying appropriate scripts and schemata. In other words, it may be very useful to teach a reading grammar, that is, a grammar that starts with formal features in context and derives meaning from these features.

What should the scope of such a reading grammar be? Many learners (and many teachers) find it useful to learn about grammar in its traditional sense in foreign language courses. A reading grammar that focuses on how grammatical form is used to create meaning might go a long way towards satisfying these general grammar needs foreign language learners may have. It is likely that such a receptive focus will entail major changes in the order and presentation of the grammar topics and certainly in the way grammar will be practiced.

Although writing appears to be the skill most easily associated with a conscious, metalinguistic understanding of grammar rules, modern notions of writing as a creative process with a focus on ideas, information flow, and audience involvement do not lend themselves easily to a traditional bottom-up concept of applying grammar rules to construct sentences. I suggest distinguishing between writing as writing down and as composing. For the latter, sentence grammar rules are but one of a number of important structural features of compositions students need to know about, and, arguably, of lesser importance than those features that focus on information flow and the organization of ideas. Nattinger and DeCarrico (1992) argue convincingly that the use of lexical phrases abounds in this area, too, and that these phrases should be in the center of classroom teaching and not traditional sentence-based grammar.

While it may be too early to introduce composition tasks in the first (and perhaps the second) college year, there should be no lack of writing activities at the beginning levels. Writing as writing down may have a major effect on grammaticalization processes because there is a clear focus on form and, in contrast to speaking, there is sufficient time to process and apply grammar rules, and there are no conflicting demands on the attention of learners such as pronunciation requirements. Writing down allows the learner to focus both receptively and productively on grammatical detail and, even more importantly, encourages deep processing because of the length of time involved in writing down and the clear focus on form.

One way of thinking about a writing grammar is to make explicit what has been introduced and practiced implicitly in speaking. Thus, the writing grammar would essentially cover those grammar topics underlying the listening and speaking activities focusing on form while discussing these topics explicitly using the same metalinguistic terminology as in the reading grammar. Based on the arguments I presented previously (Tschirner, 1996), I would suggest that the scope of the writing grammar should be largely limited by what students can do at any particular point in their learning careers, that is, only a small portion of grammar topics found in first-year textbooks would actually be introduced and practiced for productive purposes. As with speaking, a large part of what traditionally has been considered grammar might be more effectively introduced as collocations and lexical phrases, therefore obviating the need for detailed grammar explanations at early levels of language learning.

At higher levels, starting at the latest in the third year of college language instruction, explicit grammar instruction could increase significantly to introduce topics that are more germane to planned formal speech and writing. It is conceivable that the great increase in grammaticalization that lies at the heart of the move from the intermediate to the advanced level of oral proficiency may be enhanced considerably by a conscious study and written practice of grammatical structures such as subordination, case, aspect and tense, which are essential at the advanced level.

CONCLUSION

In this paper, I argued that an explicit, metalinguistic knowledge of grammar does not appear to be of much use for learners at the beginning and intermediate levels as far as speaking and listening are concerned but that it may be of considerable use for reading and writing. I also argued that attention to form, i.e., a focus on grammatically accurate strings of words (phrases, clauses, and sentences) appears to be one of the most important contributions classroom-based instruction can make if done judiciously and in addition to providing students with the essential communicative and authentic language tasks and environments which are typical of today's communicative language classrooms.

One of the reasons why a rather traditional grammatical focus has survived in many foreign language classrooms despite the push for proficiency and content- and culture-based learning may be the fact that the study of grammar is expected and that it may be satisfying for some learners, particularly the more intellectually curious ones. However, we also know that many students simply sank during the swim-or-sink days of the cognitive method with its focus on explicit grammar instruction and the ability to manipulate linguistic form without much attention to meaning. One approach, therefore, might be to take the frustrating elements such as early production, comprehensiveness of coverage, and steep learning curves out of the teaching of grammar and to retain the satisfying elements such as the understanding of how languages work and how the foreign language contrasts with the native language. A purely receptive approach to the explicit teaching of grammatical structure may go a long way towards retaining the satisfying elements of grammar teaching without frustrating or overwhelming the less metalinguistically inclined.

In addition, I argued that we should teach grammar implicitly by focusing on the formal characteristics of words in context, i.e., of syntagmas both in listening and reading comprehension and in spoken and written production. However, this attention on form needs to remain clearly focused on concrete examples rather than turning into more abstract grammar discussions. While form-based feedback seems to be important in the learning of individual items, it appears to have little effect on a learner's ability to generalize this information to new items (Carroll, Roberge, and Swain, 1992).

My final comment deals with the scope of grammar instruction. Since the idiom principle appears to govern much of language used in context, the actual domain of grammar may not go far beyond the most basic structural features such as word order, verb conjugation, and case. It may be the case that precisely in this area, the domain of grammar proper that is not governed by idiomatic principles, there is not a lot teachers can do and learners can learn (other than learning the language holistically) because these grammatical developments are governed by psycholinguistic processes with their own timetables, both of which are still only poorly understood. The good news may be that more and more of what has been considered grammar is more appropriately considered to be part of the lexicon, which means that it can and should be consciously introduced, studied, practiced, and learned.

REFERENCES

Aitchison, Jean. (1994). "Understanding Words." In G. Brown, K. Malmkjær, A. Pollitt, and J. Williams (Eds.), *Language and Understanding* (81–96). Oxford: Oxford University Press.

Brown, Keith. (1994). "Syntactic Clues to Understanding." In G. Brown, K. Malmkjær, A. Pollitt, and J. Williams (Eds.), *Language and Understanding* (59–80). Oxford: Oxford University Press.

Bygate, M., A. Tonkyn, and E. Williams. (Eds.) (1994). *Grammar and the Language Teacher*. Hemel Hempstead, UK: Prentice-Hall International.

Carroll, Suzanne, Yves Roberge, and Merrill Swain. (1992). "The Role of Feedback in Adult Second Language Acquisition, Error Correction, and Morphological Generalizations." *Applied Psycholinguistic* 13, 2, 173–98.

Chafe, Wallace, and Jane Danielewicz. (1987). "Properties of Spoken and Written Language." In Rosalind Horowitz and S. Jay Samuels (Eds.), *Comprehending Oral and Written Language*, 83–113. Orlando: Academic Press.

Clark, H., and E. Clark. (1977). *Psychology and Language: An Introduction to Psycholinguistics*. New York. Harcourt, Brace, Jovanovich.

Ellis, Nick. (1996). "Sequencing in SLA: Phonological Memory, Chunking, and Points of Order." *Studies in Second Language Acquisition* 18, 91–126.

Garnham, Alan. (1994). "Psychological Processes and Understanding." In G. Brown, K. Malmkjær, A. Pollitt, and J. Williams (Eds.), *Language and Understanding*, 97–114). Oxford: Oxford University Press.

Hakuta, K. (1974). "Prefabricated Patterns and the Emergence of Structure in Second Language Acquisition." *Language Learning* 24, 287–97.

Keenan, J., and B. MacWhinney. (1987). "Understanding the Relationship Between Comprehension and Production." In H. Dechert and M. Raupach (Eds.), *Psycholinguistic Models of Production*, 149–155. Norwood, NJ: Ablex.

Nattinger, James, and Jeanette DeCarrico. (1992). *Lexical Phrases and Language Teaching*. Oxford: Oxford University Press.

Pawley, A., and F. Syder. (1983). "Two Puzzles for Linguistic Theory: Native-like Selection and Native-like Fluency." In Jack Richards and Richard Schmidt (Eds.), *Language and Communication*, 191–226. London: Longman.

Pienemann, Manfred. (1989). "Is Language Teachable? Psycholinguistic Experiments and Hypotheses." *Applied Linguistics* 10, 52–79.

Schmidt, Richard. (1992). "Awareness and Second Language Acquisition." *Annual Review of Applied Linguistics* 13, 206–226.

Sharwood Smith, Michael. (1993). "Input Enhancement in Instructed SLA: Theoretical Bases." *Studies in Second Language Acquisition* 15, 165–179.

Tonkyn, Alan. (1994). "Introduction: Grammar and the Language Teacher." In Martin Bygate, Alan Tonkyn, and Eddie Williams (Eds.), *Grammar and the Language Teacher*, 1–14. Hemel Hempstead, UK: Prentice-Hall International.

Tschirner, Erwin. (1996). "Scope and Sequence: Rethinking Beginning Foreign Language Instruction." *Modern Language Journal* 80, 1–14.

Wong-Fillmore, Lucy. (1976). "The Second Time Around: Cognitive and Social Strategies in Second Language Acquisition." Unpublished doctoral dissertation, Stanford University.

Constructing Cultural Realities: "Facts" and Frameworks of Association

Vicki Galloway, *Georgia Institute of Technology*

Vicki Galloway is Professor of Spanish at the Georgia Institute of Technology where she teaches language, literature, and culture courses and codirects the institute's intensive program in Spanish for business and technology. She is coauthor of the high-school textbook program Acción, *the college textbook* Visión voz, *and an intermediate college program in Spanish for business,* Saldo a favor. *She has served as project director at ACTFL and editor of* Foreign Language Annals *and has written articles on a variety of topics in language and culture learning for the* Modern Language Journal, *the* Northeast Conference Reports, *the* ACTFL Foreign Language Education Series, *and publications of the AATSP and the American Educational Research Association.*

> "I don't know what you mean by 'glory'" Alice said. Humpty Dumpty smiled contemptuously, "Of course you don't—till I tell you. When I use a word," Humpty Dumpty said, in rather a scornful tone, "it means just what I choose it to mean—neither more nor less."
>
> *Through the Looking Glass* (Carroll, p. 269)

INTRODUCTION

A century of readers has delighted in Lewis Carroll's tale of a young girl at once captivated and discomfited by the apparent randomness and absurdity of life in the "Looking-Glass" world. Equipped with her own assumptions, her own expectations, her own *reality*, she enters a different sense-making system in which "facts" do not "speak for themselves" and in which the familiar is often no more than a seductive illusion. Alice's real adventure lies in discovering, and ultimately functioning in, a different network of form-meaning associations. To understand—indeed, to survive—she must learn to construct a new cultural framework, one that allows her to interpret the actions and words of this world according to its own frame of reference. She must make sense of the culture *on its own terms*.

For our foreign language learners, the consequences of cultural misunderstanding are more subtle than the "offing of heads." Yet, each time the door of judgment is shut on "different," the separation is no less penetrating, the loss no less profound. One's culture is, in essence, one's *unquestioned reality*. To the bearers of a culture, the "insiders," their loosely shared ways of perceiving and interpreting the world appear logical, consistent, and cohesive; to the bearer of another, the "outsider," they may seem arbitrary, strange, or even "inferior." How do we guide foreign language learners to avoid the judgment trap in their study of other cultures? What can we do to help C1 learners connect the threads of evidence to construct a new and ever-expanding C2 framework, to make sense of another culture on its own terms? Perhaps our first message should be that "deep down, we are *not* all alike." It is an important one, for if sameness is assumed, difference becomes a lighted fuse.

SHARED FORM-MEANING FRAMEWORKS

> "to her great surprise, they all thought in chorus"
> (Carroll, p. 217)

Crucial to cross-cultural understanding is the recognition that in every culture there are *forms*, or outward manifestations, and there are functions, or *meanings*. The myriad forms of a culture—its words, behaviors, events, organizational patterns, objects and artifacts, and so on, are merely the symbols of message-packaging systems that communities of people saturate with their own sense. Therefore, although one may observe the same or similar form between two cultures, a unique environment of meaning must be assumed for each. This environment of meaning is complex, its relationships characterized by tension and flux. Since cultures are dynamic, open, and fluid systems, forms and meanings do not align themselves in static patterns, but in infinite constellations, establishing loosely identifiable norms that accommodate variability and idiosyncrasy within ranges, flexibility within boundaries. Forms change, meanings change, and form-meaning relationships reconstruct and reposition themselves in value hierarchies.

> "Forms change, meanings change, and form-meaning relationships reconstruct and reposition themselves in value hierarchies."

One "form" easily observed in the United States, for example, is that of the car. Its most obvious and universal meaning is that of transport. However, in U.S. culture, this form is linked to other meanings which, in turn, are linked to still others in an intricate network of associations. In the United States, the car is entwined in the culture's investment in what it considers high-ranking values and priorities, as *it* perceives and defines them: autonomy, ownership, privacy, space, freedom, control, mobility, time management, power, speed—even prestige, competition, conformity, acceptance. These values may exist in another culture. They also may not exist. If present, they may not only rank differently but, indeed, be perceived and defined differently, as well as realized through different forms.

Since the U.S. car is deeply embedded in high-level U.S. constructs, we may observe other "forms" not only accommodating it but also supporting it to ensure its integration and perpetuation. Indeed, such forms are evident in the design of U.S. cities, in the popularity of suburbs, shopping malls, drive-in banks and dry cleaners, fast-food restaurants, the morning "run" or Sunday afternoon carwash. Yet, the very stature of the values with which this form is vested also pushes and pressures the culture to create internal tensions: eroding municipal tax structures and deterioration of cities; stress, gridlock, traffic fatalities, pollution; distance, separation, isolation. Within U.S. culture, there are also ranges and variations in this form-meaning network. The meaning of a car is quite different in New York City than in Los Angeles, and it is certainly different for the middle-aged family man than for the teenager, for whom getting a driver's license has become the most prominent rite of passage.

The U.S. student, then, who innocently asks someone from another culture: "But where's your car?" or "How many cars do you have?" or "What kind of car do you have?" would be acting on normal assumptions derived from his own cultural reality. Yet, in transferring his own cultural coordinates, he would likely be quite unaware of the possibility of form-meaning *mismatch*. The following is the reaction of a Spaniard repeatedly posed a question by college students during a visit to the U.S.: *¿No echas de menos tu coche?* (Don't you miss your car?)

> Eso es lo que me dicen, tal cual suena. No preguntan si echo de menos mi país, o mis amigos, o mi familia, o mi lengua. Tampoco preguntan si poseo coche en España: dan por asumido que lo tengo. La primera vez no supe qué contestar: ...atribuí la cuestión a un interlocutor exéntrico. Pero... empecé a pensar que quizá el coche sea para ellos la medida de su cotidianeidad o de la ausencia de ella. Sí, [aquí] todo el mundo tiene coche. Es una espléndida manera de... impedir visitas indeseables. (Estampas bostonianas/1; Rosa Montero, *El país*, martes 13 de agosto de 1985.)

While the interrelations of form-meaning networks allow for a meeting of minds within a culture, they also powerfully bind perceptions and limit options, not only for assigning meaning to observations outside one's culture but, indeed, for selecting what to observe at all. In the effort to derive sense from another culture, one's own frame of reference, being the only one available, is projected onto it with the result that "our way of seeing is also our way of not seeing" (Burke, p. 70).

"FACTS" AND OTHER REALITIES

> That's a great deal to make one word mean," Alice
> said in a thoughtful tone.   (Carroll, p. 269)

Our cultural mind's eye will not allow us not to assign meaning. Yet, without the coordinates and connecting structure of *another* reality, it is often the seemingly familiar that produces the most tempting traps. The Spanish word *familia*, for example, is easily translated as "family." However, do Hispanics *mean* the same thing by *familia* as our U.S. students *mean* by "family?" When U.S. students see, hear, or use the word *familia*, are they possibly superimposing on this word their own cultural template, their own culture's environment of form-meaning associations? The following are transcripts of audiotaped reactions of beginning-level college students as they read and discussed in groups a "description" of the Hispanic *familia*, taken from a contemporary basal textbook:

> La familia hispana incluye a padres e hijos y también a abuelos, tíos y primos. Los hijos generalmente viven con los padres hasta que se casan. En muchas familias, los abuelos viven con sus hijos y nietos y ayudan a criar a los niños.

Student 1: "It's just saying they believe in the extended family, which really doesn't exist anymore these days."

Student 2: "*Tíos primos!*... I don't even know one of my uncles, and I can't stand my cousins. . . So they actually all live in the same house? I'd go crazy!"

Student 3: "Kids actually live with their parents until they get married? What babies!"

Student 4: "Do they get married really young, or what? I couldn't wait to leave home. And if I hadn't left, my parents would have kicked me out!" [laughter]

Student 5: "My brother doesn't have a job yet—I mean a *real* job—so he's living at home, but he has to pay rent and do his own laundry."

♦ Student #1 searches for sense and posits the description in his own associational network where he finds explanation only in a construct he must dredge up from *his culture's past*. The result is that *familia* is rejected as outmoded, antiquated, "backward."

♦ Student #2 simultaneously applies the U.S. reality of mobility, separation, and distance, and presumes the U.S. meaning of family as "being under one roof," an association that pulls up conflicts with her values of space and privacy. The other-culture reality is, therefore, "crazy."

♦ Students #3, #4, and #5 all present versions of *familia* as pushed through the sieve of a high-ranking U.S. equation: *self sufficiency = maturity*. The other-culture reality, now distorted, is judged as immature, irresponsible, wrong.

In all these cases, learners have tried to take in data using the only sense-making system they have available. What they have produced, however, is an imaginary hybrid—an artificial culture constructed *through* the coordinates of another.

The "facts" of culture as presented through sanitized textbook notes simply do not speak for themselves, for attempts to capture and encapsulate the C2 *for* learners necessarily contaminate it, sacrificing C2 authenticity to expose not another reality but a *two-culture relativism*. In trying to build bridges for our students through the blueprint of compromise, with the materials of sameness, we neither allow learners to distance themselves from their own culture nor enter another. What we end up with is only a bridge, a fabrication. Since static, simplistic, and invariable chunks of information cannot be endowed with the same realness, the same integrity, the same intricacy as the students' own C1 construct, such C2 "facts" may, at best, appear uninteresting and lie inert; at worst, they may be rejected as weird or unbelievable—the negative to a C1 positive.

> "For learners to construct a new reality *unblended with their own*, they will need to hear the 'voices' of the culture's own systemicness as it coheres within itself, requiring no justification for its own validity."

For learners to construct a new reality *unblended with their own*, they will need to hear the "voices" of the culture's own systemicness as it coheres within itself, requiring no justification for its own validity. When a culture communicates with its own, it reflects its own dynamism, its own loosely generalizable norm and range of acceptable variation, its own tensions and energy. As learners eavesdrop on these voices, they will require guidance to reflect, seek, sort, interpret, and connect the threads of sense into a C2 tapestry.

THE VOICES OF A CULTURE

> The first thing she heard was a general chorus . . . then the Rabbit's voice alone . . . then silence, and then another confusion of voices.   (Carroll, p. 62)

The past two decades have generated a great deal of enthusiasm regarding the classroom benefits afforded by "authentic texts"—those written and oral communications produced *by* members of a language and culture group *for* members of the same language and culture group. Authentic texts, as total communicative events, invite observation of a culture talking to *itself*, not to outsiders; in its own context; through its own language; where forms are referenced to its own people, who *mean* through their own framework of associations; and whose voices show dynamic interplay of individuals and groupings of individuals within the loose general consensus that is the culture's reality.

> "Authentic texts, as total communicative events, invite observation of a culture talking to *itself*, not to outsiders; in its own context; through its own language; where forms are referenced to its own people, who *mean* through their own framework of associations; and whose voices show dynamic interplay of individuals and groupings of individuals within the loose general consensus that is the culture's reality."

It has been only relatively recently, however, that such an astounding array of authentic texts has become so universally and quickly accessible to teachers and students through the Internet where, from advertisements to "chat box" letters to literature, the cultural voices transmitted are rich in substance and variety.

A visit to an authentic text is much like a visit to the country itself, where not only will one's understanding of the voices heard depend on one's experience in the culture, but the very type of voices heard will often depend on whether one's visit is that of an inexperienced tourist sheltered by tour guides, bilingual waiters, and hotel operators, or that of a temporary resident interacting on a deeper level. In other words, it will depend on whether one scratches the surface of the sanitized buffer zones of the culture or immerses himself in its more complex interior. To access the culture through any given text, C1 students will need guidance not only to *hear* these voices correctly, but to sort out their owners, to separate the voice of the masses from that of the individual, and to attend not only to the loudest shout but also to the soft and subtle whispers.

Although discussion here focuses on written texts, no attempt to diminish the role of *authentic* oral texts should be inferred. Rather, while the latter are characterized by pressure for quick message retrieval, the former invite revisitation and reflection *without* recourse to memory. Issues of oral text availability aside, for the purposes of deep cultural analysis, written texts allow classroom learners not only to hold messages for examination but to explore different *voices* and their messages across time. The following grid employs *figurative* use of the familiar labels *imperative, declarative, interrogative,* and *exclamatory* to illustrate the types of voices that may be identified in a given authentic text.

Voices of Culture

Imperative	Declarative	Interrogative	Exclamatory
organizing structure	meaning ranges	issues, questions	individual projection
rituals and routines	connotations	tension, flux	idosyncratic reflection
conventions, formulae	roles and ranges	instability, discomfort	revelation
artifacts	norms/values	repair	external alliance, special interest
indicators, indices	priorities	portents of change	challenge of iconoclast
symbols	associations	emotional investment	insider with outsider perspective

□ THE IMPERATIVE VOICE

Growing up in a culture, it is the *imperative voice* that we first hear: "Don't touch," "Be quiet," "Don't be late." This is the behavior-structuring voice, the "official" voice of accepted convention and ritual. In terms of the writings of a culture, this official voice, regardless of its source, will reflect the most established and shared norm or codified custom, the most general organizing parameters by which a culture conducts its quotidian affairs. In some texts, one will hear this voice clearly, though it may be of no certain source. It will simply say "This is what is done here," or "This is how it is done"—a business card: "this is how we name ourselves," "these are the titles we use"; a train schedule: "this is how we organize time for transport"; a sign on a restaurant: "this is when we eat meals"; a calendar: "these are the days that hold special importance for us." In some texts, this will be the only voice we hear. In other texts, this voice may be so subsumed and drowned out by others as to make it barely audible.

□ THE DECLARATIVE VOICE

Beyond this behavior-structuring voice, some authentic texts will also allow us to eavesdrop on the *declarative voice*, the voice of a people of the culture as they group and regroup in interaction. These voices give meaning to the imperative voice or organizational framework of the society, supplementing the how's and what's with the why's, exposing some of the complexity and dynamism of the culture through evidence of its connotations and networks, its form-meaning interweavings, its values hierarchies. These voices, if heard, may not only indirectly explain the culture's more official voice but, in representing the mass, may serve as the foundation for subsequent understanding of the separate voices of individuals. This declarative voice is often the prominent, though not the only, voice of such texts as surveys, many newspaper and magazine articles, feature stories and general reports of events, and advertisements. *It will be implicit in all other voices.*

□ THE INTERROGATIVE VOICE

As people interact in a culture, we also hear the *interrogative voice* of a society reflecting on, reacting to, and questioning itself: "Why is this the way it is?" "Why must it be this way?" These voices convey the general nature of *internally* perceived tensions—conflict, instability, flux. As the voices of "inside" or participatory assessment, they may be portents of change, expressed through heavy groans or self-mocking laughter. Sometimes these voices reflect the culture consoling and repairing itself—bridging discord or soothing discomfort as it "settles" from transitions. While this is still the voice of the mass, it will address more directly the *ranges of variation*; therefore, understanding the message of this voice will depend not only on attention to its source, but on one's understanding of the imperative and declarative voices that provide its foundation and context. The interrogative voice will often be the loudest (though *not* the only) voice of many editorials, social and political cartoons, and literary pieces.

☐ THE EXCLAMATORY VOICE

And sometimes in a text, as in the culture itself, the shout of *one* is louder than the chorus of the many. In some texts, we may only hear the *exclamatory voice*— the "No!" or "Yes!" of the iconoclast, intoned in shout or whisper. This is the voice that speaks to the center from the rim. It may be the lonely exhortation of an individual distancing himself from and projecting himself on the mass that is his culture. It may be the voice of a group seeking integration and acceptance into the whole, rejecting such integration altogether, or distancing itself from its common culture to seek truer union or compatibility through a special interest or agenda that cuts across cultural boundaries. Since the exclamatory voice assumes listeners who share the true "insides" of the culture, its message may be either inaccessible to or severely distorted by those not equipped with its shared connotative framework. Even given the sharing of this framework, attention to source is crucial to assignment of meaning.

Authentic texts provide access to the full array of cultural voices. However, planning for and guiding learners' understanding of these voices will require both prudence in selection of texts and care in designing experiences for learner interaction with them. The C1 learner approaching C2 texts whose exclamatory and interrogative voices on a particular theme are much louder or more prominent than the declarative or imperative voices will require the coordinates of a fairly well developed C2 background in the particular construct, for this reader will have to be able to distinguish the idiosyncratic from the more generalizable, the individual projection on society from the society itself, the solo from the concert of the mass. Without the framework of another reality to interpret the interrogative and exclamatory voices surrounding a given construct, two equally perilous paths await the C1 reader trying to "make sense": (1) His own culture's framework, being the only one available, may be implanted as their backdrop; the C2 message, once blended with the C1 culture, must then be interpreted and assessed through C1 criteria. (2) Lacking a coherent C2 perspective that allows for distinguishing the trunk from its branches or the multihued foliage from the color of a leaf, in the mind's eye the C1 reader, the words of the iconoclast may assume the stature of convention, producing distortions no less severe. In the same way, however, limiting exposure merely to the voices of the most routine customs and patterns of behavior leeches the culture of its vitality and integrity, for the true meaning of a culture's statements cannot be grasped without its questions. In all cases, it will be difficult to hear the voices of another culture while one's own is talking. Moreover, it will be difficult to appreciate the complexity of another cultural framework without some reflection on the complexity of one's own.

In an effort to help learners "hear" the voices of their own form-meaning system, the following task was conducted in an intermediate-level class of 25 college Spanish students.[1] An assortment of some 25 authentic texts from "mainstream" U.S. sources (ads, schedules, surveys, magazine and newspaper articles, essays and editorials, fragments of literature) was distributed among small groups of students with each group receiving three pieces. Over the course of two class sessions, their task was to uncover U.S. form-meaning associations using theses texts as their data. They were instructed to comment to each other as they read and to mark up the texts (highlighting, circling, drawing arrows, etc.) to display both obvious and subtle associations as conveyed through the texts' voices. As each group reported its findings, data was recorded on a class transparency with arrows inserted to depict those relationships observed. Though barely an atom of the vastness that is a culture's associational framework, a glimpse at the intricate connections that form a culture began to emerge. Extremely primitive in its representational value, unbalanced in its address of cultural constructs and therefore unqualified for any cultural weighting, this mapping of identified associations nevertheless produced a network distinctly recognizable as U.S. culture-colored. Areas where multiple arrows converged displayed themselves as "hot spots"—concepts so highly charged with value that explosion appeared imminent. The concept of "time," for example, revealed itself in this exercise as a central axis for the form-meaning relationships of constructs that filtered through it both to give it definition and be defined by it: work, play, youth and aging, friendship, health and eating habits, body image, technology. And scattered throughout the environments of these relationships were the indicators of fallout, the voices of the social "tensions": stress, fear, stimulation, pressure, guilt, control, memories. These were identified as the voices that not only question the culture, but energize it and direct the nature of change.

The intricacy and connectedness that characterize one culture characterize all cultures. While, obviously, our foreign language learners are not equipped to perform a task such as that just outlined with *another* culture, they can be guided to understand the C2 intricacy on a smaller scale. For, indeed, if all things are connected, we can choose one construct as a starting point in the construction process and, by exploring the complexity of this construct through the vast array of voices that give it meaning, help learners see its connections throughout the culture to ultimately expose "hot spots"—the C2's own center of gravitational pull.

Guiding students to hear the voices, contextualize their message, and connect the threads of meaning to construct a new and dynamic reality will require that we attend at least as much to the *how* as to the *what* of discovery. The process of *how* learners select for observation is as important as the observation itself; how learners resolve conflicts is as important as their own awareness of the conflict; the search for evidence, indeed, the search for lack of evidence, is as important as the hypothesis that gave rise to it. And the process of identifying, analyzing, and reflecting on one's own cultural assumptions is perhaps the most important all. To hear another's voice, we must be willing to hush our own for the moment and listen.

C2 TEXTS AND C1 LEARNERS

> Now we come to the passage . . . it's very like our passage as far as you can see, only you know it may be quite different on beyond.
>
> (Carroll, p. 181)

In selecting authentic texts for C2 encounters, some direct reflection on the C1 is crucial, for we will have to find learner entry points, either through the existing C1 or through the C2 under construction. Since all true learning must begin with where the learner is, use of these texts in the classroom will require that we keep in mind two coordinates and the logical consequences of their interaction: the C2 text itself and the C1 learner-reader.

For all learners, the primary consideration relates to the amount and type of relevant information they will be able to feed into the text as readers in order to decrease their distance from the author's frame of reference. For the novice learner encountering the authentic culture for the first time (and with limited linguistic tools), the C1 frame of reference will be the only one available. Yet, while the beginning learner's own culture will allow him to step into another and gain a foothold on this new ground, it should not set his pace or direction once inside. Pre-reading tasks can "prime" learners to approach a theme by guiding them to "pull up" their own form-meaning associations for a given construct, to hear their own version of their cultural voice, examine it, identify its solo, or expand its chorus through group interaction. However, to avoid the bleeding of their own framework into that of the culture they are about to encounter, learners must then be guided to claim *ownership* of their "own" and *put it aside*. By reflecting on and sharing one's "own," recognizing the internal variability, recording these reflections *in writing* through individual or class lists, grids, etc., then labeling the written inventory "my culture," learners can close their C1 notebook, for they have gained their foothold. They own culture, kept secure in their minds and on their papers, maintains its validity and integrity— unthreatened, unjudged, unquestioned—as *one* reality. By physically setting it aside, they have equipped themselves to begin formulation of a new list, a different grid—one that enables them to break ground in the construction of another *reality*. Thus, a *new* foothold is acquired—a C2 foothold—that, though still weak with uncertainty, provides its own point of departure. And as one discovery connects to, clarifies, broadens, and deepens another, as the C2 foundation becomes more sturdy, our "builders" will have to rely less and less on their own C1 scaffolding to access meaning, for they will be able to attribute "sense" within a new framework of meaning. As the architects of the construction process, our responsibility as teachers is to plan opportunities for *connection* as learners experience another culture through the life voices of its authentic texts.

The second crucial factor in text selection is that of maintaining the integrity of the C2 itself. The learner beginning the framework-construction process will require authentic texts that focus insight development on the broad, superordinate value themes of the culture—those value themes that weave their way in direct or indirect fashion into other prominent value themes and thus represent the forces that both push and pull the wheels of the society. These are the deep concepts and dominant constructs whose understanding will be crucial to understanding other aspects of the C2 reality. We will want to use authentic texts that cluster themselves in organized fashion with other texts so that the sense-making threads may connect to form networks, so forms and meanings begin to expose their natural constellations with each other and with other forms and meanings of the C2 system of values.

The network of connections that filters through the supercharged construct of *familia* in Hispanic cultures, for example, cannot be communicated through lifeless and static textbook "culture notes" that address its form but not its meaning; rather, it must be experienced through the culture's own voices—not merely the behavior structuring voices of its traditions, rituals, and conventions, but the voices of its connotations, associations, and ranges; the voices of its issues, questions, conflicts as it meets with other existing or emerging values or situations of change; and as it connects with and colors other constructs. Neither will we be able to explore the concept of *familia* through its own voices simply by looking for authentic texts that "describe" *familia*—real life does not conveniently separate into the neat compartments textbooks often impose.

The real threads of this concept will be found in other constructs for, if *familia* is a "hot spot," we will see it weaving its way throughout the culture, expanding, broadening, and deepening its coordinates. And indeed we do: The voices of *familia* echo throughout authentic texts of the Hispanic world, from the most lowly piece of "realia" to the most lofty literary creation. And the connections are infinite: from the most basic theme of individual identity; through themes of friendship, leisure, food, shelter; through concepts of youth, aging, death; through the structures, motivations, expectations, and hierarchies of the business world; through the systems of social and economic organization; through government policies and institutions.

Just as with each connection the array of voices exposes complex associations, with each connection, a foothold is made via one construct for the exploration of another. Through the learner's process of interaction with "clustered" texts, a reality slowly begins to construct itself, one that is no longer limited to the original construct, but that spirals through its entwined form-meaning relationships into others, each time not only refining the initial construct, but gaining a new baseline-access level for subsequent discovery. Each new level of C2 foundation, with constant attention to its sturdiness, can thus create a new scaffolding for learning, one that allows learners to become less dependent on their C1 as a point of entry, one that allows entrance into the culture on its own terms.

V. CONCLUSION

> She suddenly came upon a little three-legged table
> . . . there was nothing on it but a tiny golden key.
> (Carroll, p. 29)

It has been said that one cannot "teach" culture (Medley). Indeed, the culture of a people cannot be boxed, exported, and delivered in a classroom. The real-life story of intricate connections, interacting perspectives, and internal sense-making cannot be told. It must be *entered* and experienced with respect for its own validity and regard for its own integrity. While we cannot "teach" a culture, we can help learners find the right combinations to unlock the doors to a new reality, plan their itineraries, and serve as their guides. And as expert tour guides in this territory, our aim is not to have them visit through collections of trivial and isolated facts, but to undertake a long, even lifelong, journey—to guide them to hear, listen to, reflect on, and interpret the concert and cacophony of the culture's voices, to connect the message of a sense-making system.

> ". . . (T)he culture of a people cannot be boxed, exported, and delivered in a classroom. The real-life story of intricate connections, interacting perspectives, and internal sense-making cannot be told. It must be *entered* and experienced with respect for its own validity and regard for its own integrity."

Although we might begin with the voices of those artifacts that reflect the conventions of the "mass," the imperative or behavior-structuring voices will be incomplete without the undergirding conceptual framework that gives them meaning; they will ill inform without their culture's own voice of reflection and critique. As guides, our efforts in assisting C1 learners to construct a C2 reality may well require that we first rid ourselves of our own artificial barriers— specifically those that have led to the unhealthy separation of the cultural body from the imagination of the cultural mind. The culture's voices of question, exclamation, individual perspective, and creative solution beckon exploration through literature. To isolate or distance even the novice learner from these voices is to depict a culture that does not breathe.

NOTES

1. In this intermediate class, aside from U.S., the following nationalities were represented: India (2), South Korea (1), Jamaica (1), France (1), China (1). All had lived in the U.S. at least eight years and each was assigned to a different group for the purposes of this task.

REFERENCES

Burke, Kenneth. *Permanence and Change.* New York: New Republic, 1935.

Carroll, Lewis. *The Annotated Alice: Alice's Adventures in Wonderland and Through the Looking Glass.* New York, Bramhall House, 1960.

Medley, Frank W., Jr. "Authentic Texts and the Teaching of Culture." Paper delivered at the annual conference of the AATSP, San Diego, August 11, 1995.

Challenges and Opportunities: Curriculum Pressures in the Technological Present

Ana Martínez, *Middlebury College*; **David Herren,** *Center for Education Technology, Middlebury College*

Ana Martínez-Lage, Assistant Professor of Spanish (Language Pedagogy and Methodology) at Middlebury College, teaches courses in Spanish language at all levels. She has developed and taught a number of methodology courses for graduate students in the Spanish language Summer School at Middlebury College. She has created a variety of teaching materials at all levels of language instruction and has coauthored an introductory Spanish language textbook, ¡Tú dirás!, *and a CD-ROM for beginning Spanish,* Mundos Hispanos. *She is the recipient of a two-year Mellon Grant for the development of computer-based teaching materials. Her research interests include reading instruction and the application of hypermedia technology to the teaching of reading and culture.*

===== ||| =====

David Herren, Associate Director for Technology and Instruction, Center for Educational Technology, Middlebury College is the author of the xMediaEngine Template series—an integrated package of applications designed to facilitate the production of hypermedia-based curricular materials for the teaching of the world's languages. Formerly an instructor of Spanish at the university level, he has conducted dozens of workshops and presentations worldwide promoting the use of hypermedia technologies to enhance the foreign language curriculum.

INTRODUCTION

Advances in technology and the increase in faculty investigating the use of technology in the language curriculum are the two-part focus of this article. In the first part we examine the incorporation of technology as it applies to the different language skills as well as to the presentation of culture in the foreign language curriculum. We have given particular attention to the use of authoring tools which allow teachers to develop their own personally-relevant technology-based lessons that are flexible enough to meet changing needs through time.

In the second part of the article our focus is on the advances in technology which have already begun to have an impact on the language curriculum, or which are expected to be significant to foreign language instruction soon. As academic institutions and departments begin to plan for renovations of their language learning facilities, and to reexamine their curricula, this information may well serve to inform the process. Some advances, though ultimately applicable to the language curriculum, are of a rather technical nature, or are applicable at such a "low level" that any discussion of them might seem out of place in a volume of this type. Nonetheless, we believe them to be significant developments, and any educator involved in the use of, or planning for the expanded use of technology in the language curriculum should be at least passingly familiar with what is, and what is to be. We have summarized and simplified these topics wherever appropriate.

TECHNOLOGY AND THE FOREIGN LANGUAGE TEACHER

Technology, from the common television set and VCR to the more sophisticated personal multimedia computers, has become a part of our daily lives, both at the professional and at the personal level. The question is, however, what does the computer have to offer specifically to the FL teacher?

Using technology in the FL classroom is not a new idea. FL teachers have been using tape recorders, VCRs, transparencies, and slides in their classes for many years to provide students with authentic visual and oral input. What *is* relatively new is the capability of the computer to deliver all of these media in an integrated manner from a single source. Further, the computer brings a new dimension to the process: It allows students to be in control of the materials in such a way that they can manipulate them at their own pace and according to their own individual needs. The computer empowers the learner in ways that were simply not possible before.

> ". . . (T)he computer brings a new dimension to the [teaching/learning] process: It allows students to be in control of the materials in such a way they can manipulate them at their own pace and according to their own individual needs."

COMMERCIALLY AVAILABLE SOFTWARE AND AUTHORING TOOLS

How many teachers are content with the entirety of the textbooks that they use? Is it not common to replace some of the materials in our textbooks with others? Do we not supplant some materials? And have not most of us supplemented the texts with materials of our own? It is not our intention to review specific products, but to point out the advantages and disadvantages of using commercially available software packages vs. developing one's own materials. Commercially available software, like textbooks, are developed by individuals consonant with their personal views on language teaching, and those of the publishers. While some packages may be satisfactory for large numbers of faculty, many will discover deficiencies associated with the product: a lack of vocabulary that they want students to learn and use, limited feedback opportunities, and most of all, the final product cannot be modified, particularly if it is CD-ROM based.[1]

A distinct advantage of using these products despite any perceived deficiency is that one does not need to invest the time in creating similar materials. On the other hand, there is nothing more satisfying than being able to create one's own multimedia materials that are sufficiently flexible, which can be modified over time, and which address the specific needs and styles of the educator in question—needs which may not be addressed by any of the commercially available packages. A quick examination of the *CALICO Resource Guide for Computing and Language Learning*, (Borchardt, 1995) will show that there is a large selection of language oriented authoring tools from which to choose. In our discussion of authoring tools we note which ones seem to be particularly well suited to specific language skills, though some of the tools included are more generally applicable.[2]

For many instructors, the ultimate objective in the teaching of foreign languages is to provide students with opportunities to acquire and practice the target language in contextualized and meaningful communicative situations. Learning a language with the goal of communicating in that language requires that students develop both comprehension and production skills. Moreover, for this learning to be meaningful, it has to take place in a culturally rich environment and take into account the individual needs and interests of the learner.

On the one hand, the development of comprehension ability in a FL requires that the learner be exposed to comprehensible input (Krashen, 1985) both oral and written, preferably coming from authentic sources, that is, materials created by native speakers for native speakers. On the other hand, producing in a FL requires that students engage in communication with a *clear need* for negotiation of meaning (Swain, 1985) and for exchange of ideas. To be able to carry out a communicative task, learners need to have at least a basic knowledge of vocabulary, some understanding and control of the basic rules of grammar and syntax, and adequate pronunciation skills, as well as knowledge of the sociolinguistic rules of the target culture.

In the following section we will examine potential uses of technology as they might be applicable to the comprehension and production areas of language development.

□ COMPREHENSION SKILLS

1. Listening

The exposure to authentic oral language, as it is produced and used by native speakers, is no longer limited to the listening of audiotapes, nor to the viewing of videos either in or out of class. A multimedia computer facilitates the use and manipulation of both audio and video to expose students to the target language in order to develop their listening comprehension skills. Though conceptually identical to traditional audio and video, these media, once rendered on the computer, are typically referred to as "digital" audio and "digital" video. Commercially available packages for foreign languages integrate a variety of media to provide learners with opportunities for listening to and watching native speakers as they interact in the target language.

Access to digital audio and video does not have to be limited to what is available commercially, however. Teachers who are willing to undertake some basic training can create their own custom-developed lessons including digitally recorded audio and video materials. These lessons might include activities designed to help students develop listening comprehension strategies, ranging from listening for the main ideas to listening for details and specific words. There are a number of authoring tools available today that have been developed specifically with the foreign language professional in mind and which emphasize the listening skills required in the language learning process. A few of these include:[3]

♦ *Dasher*, developed at the University of Iowa, is designed to create a wide range of activities, from "traditional drill to multimedia-based activities for building listening comprehension and vocabulary acquisition" (Borchardt *et al*. 1996, 27). According to the authors, the learning curve is very low, and the time required to create lessons, very short. It works on both Macintosh and Intel-based platforms, and authors who develop lessons in one PC platform can deliver them on the other and vice versa.

♦ *Libra*, developed at Southwest Texas University, is a tool designed to develop listening comprehension activities using a videodisc as the primary source material. Libra is "a stand-alone application based on HyperCard's object-oriented, event-driven environment" (Borchardt *et al*. 1996, 43). This authoring system is organized into a series of templates which include four basic question formats: multiple choice, checklist questions, matching exercises, and icon sorting questions. There are several possible variants of these formats, such as true/false, scrambled words, and scramble sentences.

♦ *The xMediaEngine Template Series*, developed at Middlebury College, for the Macintosh platform, includes several templates[4] which focus upon the different skills of the language learning process. Three of the templates can be applied to listening skills. Of these three, CDictation, is a tool designed for developing dictation and/or cloze exercises using audio compact discs as the source material. QTDictation and VideoDictation function similarly to CDictation, the difference being the medium used— digital movies and videodiscs respectively. All three templates provide a mechanism for including pre-listening information and instructions, as well as open-ended post-listening activities.

A significant advantage of using the computer to develop and/or deliver listening comprehension activities concerns the rich environment in which they are delivered—the learner has access to a variety of textual and visual aids to decode the script. Learners may access a script in a variety of ways, depending upon the design of the tool selected. Occasionally, the script is available immediately, that is, at the same time students play the audio/video segment, even for the first time; in a different design they may only see the text after they have listened to the segment at least once (see, for example, Dominguez *et al. Mundos Hispanos*). To expand the learning options even further, scripts may be annotated with glosses or vocabulary explanations that assist the student in the understanding of the target language. There is little doubt that the combination of audio, video, and text addresses the variations in learning styles by satisfying the needs of both the visually oriented learner and the learner who performs best by focusing upon the oral or written aspects of the language alone.

> "There is little doubt that the combination of audio, video, and text addresses the variations in learning styles by satisfying the needs of both the visually oriented learner and the learner who performs best by focusing upon the oral or written aspects of the language alone."

Another significant advantage to using the computer for listening comprehension activities concerns the ease with which digital audio and/or video segments can be manipulated by the learner. Digitally rendered audio and video are more easily navigated than their respective analog counterparts: Audio and video tape are essentially linear media. While it is certainly possible to move forward and in reverse using tape, this not only takes more time but it is also more difficult to find the precise segment desired than when using the digital form of the medium. Time saved in accessing the desired segment of an audio or video recording increases the possible number of repetitions performed in a given time frame.

2. Reading

Interacting with written material in the target language is no longer limited to looking up words in a dictionary or looking for the familiar glosses which appear in the margin of so many foreign texts. Computer-based hypermedia texts can provide FL learners with a number of new ways of interacting with material written in the target language thus making it more accessible. It is now quite easy to create annotated texts which include sound (and virtually any other media type). This sound might be an oral introduction to the reading, the oral version of the complete text (see, for example, *Transparent Language*[5]), or the pronunciation of individual words or expressions. In hypermedia-annotated texts, words can be simply glossed and the gloss accessed immediately by clicking on the words themselves. Visual support might appear in the form of still images or digital video connected to the text to illustrate the meaning of unknown words and expressions.

Most commercial packages created for foreign language learners and which include reading materials incorporate some variety of hypermedia annotations of those texts. Teachers, accustomed to the modification of textbook-based materials, often find that they would like to use new or different texts, or to supplement their own computer-based activities for those texts. The following are some authoring tools available to help teachers develop hypermedia annotated versions of FL texts.[6]

- ◆ *Annotext*, a program for the Macintosh platform developed at Dartmouth College, is designed to create annotated reading lessons using a variety of media including videodisc, images, and sound. It allows teachers to use custom dictionary files created in a spreadsheet with intelligent capabilities with respect to word forms. Annotations appear as solid bars to the left of the text for the section concerned, and can be accessed by clicking the bars. It requires HyperCard or the HyperCard player to be used.

- ◆ *GALT* (Glossing Authentic Language Texts) is a tool developed at Pennsylvania State University. ToolBook-based, "GALT enables instructors to link pictures, sounds, graphs, definitions, pronunciation files, and notes to specific foreign language texts. It also allows for entire passages to be 'read' to students through the audio CD option" (Borchardt 1996, 41). The program currently works on the Intel-based PC platform, and the authors are working on a Macintosh version.

- ◆ *Guided Reading*, another of the xMediaEngine Template series for the Macintosh, is designed to assist the instructor in the preparation of media-based annotations and glossaries of texts. The instructor can annotate any pages and/or sentences of a text, in virtually any language, using digital audio, videodisc, virtual reality panoramas, images, digital video, and text. All xMediaEngine-based lessons can be linked to other lessons in the series, or to content located on the World Wide Web.

As noted elsewhere (Martínez-Lage, 1996), foreign language readers benefit in many ways when given the opportunity and the tools to explore a foreign language text that has been annotated with supporting materials such as glossaries, grammatical and cultural explanations, still images, sound, and video. Research on the use of hypermedia-annotated texts by foreign language readers has shown that having immediate access to on-line vocabulary explanations can result in greater vocabulary acquisition (Lyman-Hager *et al.* 1993; Chun and Plass, 1996). Further, access to visual information assists the learner in understanding the meaning of unknown words and unfamiliar concepts. A study conducted by Chun and Plass suggests that students better retain vocabulary that has been annotated with both text and images than vocabulary with only textual support (1996).

When we provide students with hypermedia-annotated foreign language texts, we are providing them with greater opportunities to interact with those texts outside of class on an individual basis. Students who have worked with such texts "come to class prepared to comment on the content and meaning of what they have read" (Martínez-Lage, 1996, 149). Thus, classroom time can be spent more efficiently getting students involved in meaningful discussions rather than having to dedicate time to vocabulary and other mechanical explanations. These technology-based annotated texts present us with new opportunities to assist our students in getting beyond the "mechanical" aspects of the reading process and to provide them with a means of developing good reading strategies. Careful, planned use of these tools will move student and teacher closer to a productive and cognitive relationship with the text in question.

☐ PRODUCTION SKILLS

1. Writing

Computers have become a nearly indispensable tool for writing classroom-related materials for both teachers and students. Certainly increasing numbers of foreign language educators and students are familiar with and feel at ease when using the computer for writing purposes. This section discusses several uses of computer applications in connection with foreign language student development of writing skills. These applications include word processing, commercial writing-assistants, electronic mail, and conferencing systems in the FL setting. Their use requires design and intervention on the part of the faculty member and typically cannot be productively used in an "off-the-shelf" manner.

♦ *Word processing.* Undeniably many educators have come to rely upon their word processing software rather than a typewriter to prepare professional papers, office memos, and classroom materials such as worksheets and transparencies.

The advantages that the word processor brings to us as FL professionals (spell checking, editing, saving, copying files, to mention just a few) also accrue to FL learners. According to Beauvois, "Equipped with a screen, a keyboard, and word processing software, students find themselves in a relatively stress-free writing situation in which correction and revision are made easy, and one that seems to encourage the flow of their thoughts" (1996, 165). When students prepare their assignments using a word processing application, they benefit enormously when the time comes to revise and correct their work. As we know all too well from our own experience, moving things around in a document, adding new ideas, or deleting those which do not work, is much easier when our work is conducted using a word processing application. As Scott points out, "the most obvious advantage of using word processing in FL composition instruction is rewriting" (1996, 76). It goes without saying, that the quality of the revision carried out by students will be only as effective as the feedback provided by the teacher.

Beyond the advantages of revision and rewriting, many word processors offer spell-checking capabilities in a FL.[7] We believe that it is critical to train students in the proper use of the spell-checking feature by demonstrating that a document may still contain a different type of error even after the mechanical check. (In Spanish for instance, the computer will accept as correct both *hable* and *hablé*, but only one of them will in fact be acceptable in a given sentence). This additional training can well serve to focus students' attention on form and content—time which might have otherwise been spent looking for typographical errors.

There are several factors not directly related to language learning that can affect student success in completing writing assignments, and one needs to keep them particularly in mind when requiring students to use computers for writing. First, one needs to consider the role of typing ability. Scott has indicated that "[G]ood typists may feel at ease composing at the computer because their fingers move rapidly enough to keep up with their thoughts. Poor typists may feel that the flow of their thoughts is interrupted by their clumsy hunt-and-peck typing skills" (1996, 82). Beyond typing skills, it is important to evaluate students' level of familiarity with word processing functions and to be ready to provide extra help to those who do not have enough background in the basic functions such as saving, deleting, formatting, etc. Finally, we need to be aware of the kind of access students will have to computers and computer facilities so that we remain flexible enough when the availability of equipment is limited (Scott, 1996). Though the personal computer is a nearly universal tool among our students, it is not entirely so.

◆ *Foreign language writing-assistants.* Writing-assistants such as *Système-D, Atajo,* and *Quelle*[8] are commercially available, language-specific programs designed to assist the FL writer. They include bilingual dictionaries (searches can be carried out from English to the target language and vice versa); a verb conjugator (any verb looked up in the dictionary can be conjugated in all tenses); a basic grammar of the language searchable in English by topics (e.g., personal pronouns, subjunctive, past tense); and, a lexical database divided into phrases (this includes samples of language necessary to carry out linguistic functions such as asking for information, describing an object, talking about the past, linking ideas, and sequencing events) and vocabulary (words and expressions are arranged by semantic categories such as sports, body, and automobile). The lexical databases are also searchable in English.

Scott has conducted several informal studies with university-level French students to determine the effect that using *Système-D* has upon their writing skills. According to Scott, this FL writing software "suggests a philosophy of learning based on the notion that FL students are naturally curious and want to engage in expressing themselves in the target language" (1996, 85). When students use *Système-D* or other writing assistants they can explore the databases which expose them to material with which they are not familiar but that they feel comfortable using because the program provides useful, contextualized examples. This exposure to new and contextualized material may explain some of the Scott's results. It appears that a writing assistant helps beginning students to generate more and better ideas than when they are asked to write with paper and pencil (Scott, 86). When comparing the amount of writing produced by students using the computer writing assistant with those students writing with paper and pencil alone, students in the first group produced twice as much (p. 86).

These preliminary results reported by Scott are clearly encouraging, however, there is still much more research needed in this area before we can determine not only the short-term but also the long-term effects of using FL writing assistants.

♦ *Electronic Mail and Conferencing.* Electronic communication has become part of our personal and professional daily lives. It is a similar situation for many college students who now have access to e-mail accounts through their academic institutions and at home.

E-mail communication is perhaps the technology that has most rapidly entered the foreign language classroom.[9] Teachers immediately realized the potential of this tool for expanding the range of writing assignments and for opening new paths to authentic communication with their students. Uses of e-mail in the FL classroom have been well documented in the volume edited by M. Warschauer (1995). According to Warschauer, "[T]here is little doubt that on-line communication is an important tool for language teaching. Students can now share documents, texts, and ideas with their teacher or classmates 24 hours a day, from school, work, or home" (p. XV).

Some possible uses of e-mail and electronic conferencing in the FL curriculum include:

a) *Individual authentic communication*:

Through e-mail students can communicate with one other, as well as with their instructors, and on an individual basis. This provides an ideal means for practicing informal writing in the target language similar to the writing most students do in their own language when communicating among peers.

E-mail is perfect for the production of dialogue journals, i.e., "written conversations between a student and a teacher [...]. Both partners write back and forth, frequently and over a period of time, about whatever interests them. Their goal is to communicate in writing, to exchange ideas and information free of the concern for form and correctness so often imposed on developing writers" (Jones, 1991, 3). The positive effects of using paper-based dialogue journals in writing development have been extensively studied through research in both ESL and FL (Gutstein 1987; Kreeft *et al.* 1984; Morroy 1984; Peyton *et al.* 1989; Staton *et al.* 1988). The ease with which writing can be conducted by means of the computer and electronic communications would predict similar, if not greater, benefits.

Many institutions are experimenting with the use of electronic communication in their FL curricula. Arizona State University has implemented this technology in several of their language programs with generally very positive results. According to Lafford and Lafford,[10] "the use of e-mail solely to communicate with the instructor and others in the class on any topic (e.g., homework, reactions to assignments, plans) was judged very favorably by two SPA [Spanish] 102 (second-semester) classes during the Spring 1996 semester. The students enjoyed being able to use e-mail to ask questions about assignments and get extra help on grammar (on-line tutorials)" (1996, 245). Some of the negative reactions that these investigators discovered in their implementation of e-mail in the FL classroom had no relation to the usefulness of the technology itself but with the difficulties imposed by limited access to the facilities. Our experiences would appear to confirm this. This is an issue we need to bear in mind whenever we plan to require our students to use tools that may not be readily available.

b)   *Participation in public electronic forums*:

There are approximately 14,000 newsgroups available and open to anyone who has access to the Internet and is willing to participate. Usenet Newsgroups are Internet standards-based "bulletin boards," which are topically organized in a hierarchical fashion. One serious drawback to many newsgroups is that they are generally unmoderated; messages are rarely reviewed prior to being posted to the list at large. On Listservers, in contrast, one must frequently be a subscriber to the list to post messages, and many listservs are carefully moderated by the list manager. Moreover, anyone can post messages to a newsgroup, even if their message has nothing to do with the topic.

A significant number of Usenet Newsgroups exist in which participants discuss issues related to the culture and current events of different countries and which may be of interest to FL learners and educators. Participation by students may be limited to just reading messages posted by others, or it may involve becoming active in replying to postings or even to sending original contributions. Newsgroups that are of interest to the FL teachers and learners are typically those found in the "soc.culture." hierarchy. The list names are followed by the name or language of country in question (e.g., soc.culture.spain, soc.culture.chile, soc.culture.german).

For the most part, the language used in the messages posted to the soc.culture newsgroups is the target language of the country of interest. Since the linguistic level required to follow these electronic discussions is rather high, we believe that advanced students will most benefit from participation in them. Frequently the postings include colloquial and very idiomatic expressions that may be otherwise difficult to understand. However, for the intermediate to advanced student, such messages may be ideal as they are exposed to informal written language not easily found in textbooks and which will be critical in their subsequent interactions with native speakers.

c)   *Conferencing systems*:

While Usenet newsgroups can be considered to be conferencing systems, a number of commercially available software packages such as Daedalus or the FirstClass Conferencing system expand upon the conferencing capabilities of Usenet. Typically, these systems are of the "client-server" variety, that is, software running on a larger central computer (the "server"), with dedicated "client" software running on the individual computers of students and faculty which connect exclusively to the central server.

These systems differ from Usenet in that they are typically much easier to administer and participation in the various discussions can be limited to just the members of a particular class. Further, it is typically quite easy to create new topically oriented conferences without the intervention of a UNIX systems administrator.

Still another advantage that such systems have over Usenet has to do with language capabilities. Though foreign language newsgroups do exist, it is rare that they support the extended characters required of even the European languages (resulting in orthographic anomalies such as "banno" or "banyo" for the Spanish *baño* to circumvent these limitations). Dedicated conferencing systems frequently use proprietary schemes such that conferencing is available in any of the world languages, complete with accents and other diacriticals, and the enormous character sets of the Asian languages. Further still, such conferencing systems frequently provide for "moderated" discussions. In other words, messages sent to the conference can, at the instructor's discretion, be made unavailable to the larger group until they are approved as topically relevant.

Several language courses at Middlebury College take advantage of this kind of electronic conferencing,[11] among which, fourth-semester Spanish students participate in an electronic conference to develop collaborative writing projects, exchange and generate ideas for papers, and discuss assigned topics. Students in second-semester Spanish use the conferencing environment to post personal announcements, react to movies, and write stories initiated by the instructor and developed gradually by individual postings from all students in the class.[12]

d) *Electronic exchange of documents*:

The ease with which fully formatted documents such as compositions can be sent electronically provides yet another tool to the foreign language instructor.

In composition courses where students' papers undergo several revisions, it is useful to have students submit their work electronically rather than on paper or disc. Thus students have more flexibility as to when to turn in their assignments, and teachers can return assignments to students when convenient.

Instructors can dramatically speed up the correction process by using macros or glossaries[13] for inserting standard comments in exchanged documents to assist students in revising their work. While comments related to content and ideas must be personalized and specific for each piece of writing, corrections related to form and language use are frequently repeated. Using a glossary or macro, the task of inserting corrections becomes much less time-consuming: one might insert comments such as "add a preposition," "use impersonal *se*," or "check agreement," wherever appropriate. By reducing the mechanical effort and the fatigue of correcting student papers, instructors have more time to focus upon the content rather than the form of the student work.

Like the authoring tools discussed in the previous section, one must be cautioned that merely implementing the use of these writing tools will not necessarily produce concomitant positive results. Assignments should be carefully planned with specific pedagogical goals in mind, and these goals should be made clear to the students themselves to be truly effective. Just as one would not attempt to implement a textbook with which one had no familiarity, educators should expect to have a better than average understanding of word processing and electronic communication before attempting to implement these tools in the foreign language curriculum. Halting and hesitancy on the part of the instructor will only serve to discourage students who may thus quickly lose sight of the intended benefits. It may well be advisable to implement these tools gradually into the existing curriculum rather than attempting a radical adoption of several simultaneously.

In many institutions the nature of access to and availability of public laboratories may in fact be the pivotal element in the gradual introduction of these new technologies. Only as students have ready access to the tools at convenient times will their potential be fully realized.

2. Speaking

Though clearly technology does offer some benefits in the area of speaking skills, such as discrete pronunciation practice, there really is very little additional benefit that technology in its present state of development has to offer the language learner.[14] Perhaps it is timely to remind ourselves at this point that technology, like any tool, is best applied where appropriate and avoided where inappropriate. It is unlikely that we will conduct realistic conversations with machines in the near future, or that attempts at simulating conversation with machines will prove to be particularly useful to the learner. Let us keep in mind, then, that by using technology where appropriate with respect to the other primary language skills, we may thus regain some portion of the class time previously spent on those activities, and which might best be applied to this critical language skill.

> "Let us keep in mind, then, that by using technology where appropriate with respect to the other primary language skills, we may thus regain some portion of the class time previously spent on those activities, and which might best be applied to this critical language skill."

☐ TECHNOLOGY FOR GRAMMAR AND VOCABULARY PRACTICE

We do not intend to engage in a discussion of the value of computer-based materials which focus upon grammar and/or vocabulary practice. Suffice to say that these kinds of tools were among the first computer-based materials to be created and introduced, and that many students and faculty find them to be useful. Studies demonstrate, moreover, that clear benefits may be accrued to students, particularly with respect to vocabulary acquisition (Lyman-Hager *et al.,* 1993; Chun and Plass, 1996).

Nearly all current language textbooks are accompanied by some type of electronic workbook designed to provide students with opportunities to practice the grammar concepts presented in the textbook in a controlled environment. These electronic workbooks generally introduce (or review, in case the concept is introduced in the book) grammatical concepts and rules and then follow with mechanical practice and feedback (positive or negative according to the learner performance).

For those teachers who wish to create their own grammar and vocabulary exercises, there are a number of tools available to them.[15] Among them:

♦ *Dasher*, which we introduced in the "Listening" section above, can also be used for developing lessons geared towards vocabulary and grammar practice.

♦ *SuperMacLang*, developed jointly at Harvard University and Dartmouth College, for the Macintosh platform, facilitates the creation of workbook type activities such as fill-ins, jumbles, column matching, and multiple choice, and which can be based on text and/or media. The materials created can be used in a "practice" mode as well as in a "test" mode.

♦ *WinCALIS* (Computer Assisted Language Instruction for Windows) was developed at Duke University. "It is a multilingual, multimedia, language learning and authoring system for Microsoft Windows 3.1 and Windows 95" (Borchardt, 1996, 30). It allows instructors to create lessons using different media (text, digital audio, digital video, animation). A lesson may begin with a text that includes hypertext aids. After reading the text students can answer content-related questions in the form of short answer, multiple choice, true-false, and cloze.

□ TECHNOLOGY AND CULTURE

Technology has certainly provided us with much broader access to authentic cultural materials. In the not too distant past, teachers were typically limited to their textbooks, outdated newspapers and magazines, slides and pictures taken during trips to the target country, and possibly to some videos, to provide students with general knowledge of the history and lifestyle of the country or countries in question.

The growing popularity and use of the World Wide Web, as chaotic as it may seem sometimes, has penetrated the FL curriculum very rapidly and is being used by FL professionals in many different ways (see M. Warschauer, 1995). The Web provides FL teachers with ample opportunities to access nearly unlimited authentic materials in the form of text, images, and sounds. It commonly serves as a reference resource for students' papers and projects. FL newspapers on-line provide an excellent source of authentic and current reading materials that assist both teachers and students to stay in touch with events in the target country or countries.[16]

Beyond its use as a source of authentic materials which can be used within the curriculum, the Web is a useful mechanism for the distribution of information created by the instructor and targeted at his or her own students as well. The number of college and university course syllabi and supplemental materials found on the Web grows daily.

The Web is not without its disadvantages, however. A frequent complaint concerns the speed, or lack thereof, of gaining access to popular materials. Large graphics (often commercial advertisements of little pedagogical value) slow access to the valuable content, and network traffic in general can bring activities planned for the classroom to a screeching halt. The international connections necessary to reach sites popular with the language instructor are occasionally unreliable and make access to those sites impossible during class time.

It is the inherent lack of structure to the Web, however, that is perhaps its most serious indictment. Those of you who have investigated the Web at all know that it is all too easy to become lost as we navigate from one link to another, quickly losing sight of the designated activity. Students are particularly susceptible to the temptation to follow links leading them away from planned activities and the task of keeping them on target is made all the more difficult for the instructor. We must stress again that the use of any material, technological or otherwise, must be well planned, and the well-prepared instructor should be ready with alternatives when planned activities fail.

Beyond the largely unstructured Web, a number of software tools facilitate the structured presentation of cultural information. These tools fall into two categories: general authoring "systems" (not to be confused with our use of the term authoring "tool")[17] offering nearly limitless capabilities, and which require a high level of competency on the part of the user, and tools which might be considered as "presentation packages." The more flexible authoring systems typically necessitate learning some variety of a programming, or scripting, language. HyperCard for the Macintosh and Toolbook for the Intel PC platform are excellent examples of this type, though certainly others exist as well. Macromind Director and Authorware are two more examples of this category, though perhaps even more demanding of their users. Though this type of tool is considerably more manageable than learning a programming language such as C or Pascal, they are not for the faint of heart. Their flexibility comes at a cost.

In the presentation package category, one might make mention of such commercial packages as Microsoft PowerPoint, and Aldus Persuasion. These packages are designed to present text, graphics, and even video together, and can be used to prepare materials rich in cultural content. Because they are not specifically designed for the language instructor, their language support may be limited (notably for the Asian and right-to-left languages). Typically these tools are much easier to learn than a more generic authoring system but more limited in their capabilities as well.

Though they do not fit precisely in the presentation software category, a number of authoring tools do exist which facilitate cultural materials presentation and which *are* directly targeted at the language educator. The primary distinction which one might raise between these tools and the presentation packages just discussed has to do with their world language support—a feature all to often ignored by the commercial software market. Among them are:

♦ *Guided Listening & Viewing*, also part of the xMediaEngine Template Series developed at Middlebury College. In addition to simplifying the presentation of rich cultural materials, this template provides a means to link structured lessons to pages on the World Wide Web and to other lessons in the xMediaEngine Series.

♦ *WinCALIS* (described above) supports texts in all of the world's languages, including Arabic and the Asian languages. WinCALIS offers many capabilities for mixing text, graphics, and sound in the presentation of cultural materials.

It is perhaps here in the context of presenting cultural information to students where technology will have its greatest impact on foreign language education. Of course we would like for our students to be able to experience the richness of the cultures they study directly but as we all know this can be impractical or impossible. New and newly simplified access to technologies provide the innovative and creative instructor with capabilities never before imagined. Rather than presenting aspects of the culture in discreet isolation, computer-based technologies have begun to allow us to create rich materials with unprecedented "dimensionality" and life impossible when limited to the individual media common in the classroom in years past.

> "It is perhaps . . . in the context of presenting cultural information to students where technology will have its greatest impact on foreign language education."

We must remember, however, that technology is a means and not a method. Flashy presentation will never compensate for poor pedagogy or lack of content. Indeed, the technologies themselves can become so seductive that we are all potentially at risk of losing sight of our objectives.

> ". . . (T)echnology is a means and not a method. Flashy presentation will never compensate for poor pedagogy or lack of content."

TECHNOLOGICAL ADVANCES: AN OVERVIEW

Advances in the basic technologies which might be applied to the language curriculum have been rapid and often unexpected in the past few years. In this section we will briefly outline the current technologies and suggest equally applicable technologies which are on the horizon. Our treatment should not be considered to be an exhaustive survey, however. Many new technologies now on the workbench behind the closed doors of research and development organizations are likely to burst upon the scene virtually out of the blue, or, as in the case of digital video technology, years ahead of the collective wisdom's predictions. These sudden turns of events make any predictions of the future difficult at best, and tarot-reading at its worst.

We have clustered related technologies together and suggested within their discussions the areas in which they might most logically be applied to the development of technology-based language materials.

SPEECH, ORAL COMPREHENSION, AND PRODUCTION

□ SPEECH RECOGNITION

Speech recognition is that technology whereby the user no longer needs to use a mouse or keyboard to manipulate a desktop computer. Speech recognition has been around for many years, but early efforts required considerable training of the recognition software and was speaker-dependent. Thus you might train your computer to perform simple tasks such as opening your word processing program, but your spouse would need to train the machine independently to achieve the same results. New developments by several manufacturers in the last two years have brought speaker-independent speech recognition to the commercial market. The current state of affairs does not mean that we shall be throwing out our mice and keyboards any time soon, however. Recognition software can still only recognize commands it expects and currently works only with standard American English or Mandarin Chinese, but commands do not have to be completely isolated from room noise and conversation, and the technology is now able to accept continuous speech input for a series of commands.

We are (probably) far from the point where we can do significant text input via the spoken word, but RISC-based machines[18] have the processing power to achieve far greater results than today's commonly available CISC-based machines,[19] and a breakthrough just might be on the horizon. Recent commercial software releases for speech input in Mandarin Chinese on the Macintosh are impressive but still require significant training by the speaker.

Potential applications to the foreign language curriculum are clear. As the technologies improve to allow recognition of foreign languages (potentially spoken without complete accuracy), students will be able to interact in a much more natural way with lessons prepared by their instructors. Simulations, or "stimulations" (Pusack and Otto, 1996, 23), will improve significantly if students are able to speak to the machine, rather than clicking on buttons or typing to respond to queries during a simulation. We do not intend to suggest that accurate conversations with a computer are looming on the horizon, or even that such conversations would be desirable, but unquestionably even limited control or interaction with the computer using human speech would bring entirely new capabilities to bear on foreign language software.

□ TEXT TO SPEECH

The inverse to speech recognition is commonly referred to as text to speech. This technology allows one's computer to speak back to the user, reading dialogs and longer texts. Most everyone has heard the machine-like voice of a computer at one point or another. This primitive technology has evolved significantly in the past year, however. Very human sounding voices are now possible on currently available computers with only a subtle difference in cadence indicating that the speech is being generated by a computer. Indeed, the voices are real human ones in many cases, the computer stringing together previously digitized syllables into sentences. Unknown words may still lead to pronunciation errors, and long numbers still sound like the telephone information system, but more improvements are inevitable. Commercially, we are aware of at least one word processing application that already includes text-to-speech in a selection of foreign languages, and it is inevitable that more will include this feature in the coming months and years.[20]

Clearly one area where this technology will be useful is with vision-impaired students of languages. Class notes could be read back to the student without necessitating a reader, resulting in greater independence on the part of the student. As the technologies improve, mainstream students will have their papers read to them as a form of proofreading, and applications will be able to provide detailed instructions in the target language.

□ AUDIO CD

Audio Compact Discs offer several distinct capabilities to the foreign language educator. Music is a very powerful tool in the hands of an innovative language educator, stimulating multiple senses and providing students with meaning and points of reference difficult to convey using traditional methods. Audio CDs consist of very high quality audio—far superior to any cassette tape available— and, if carefully selected, deliver unparalleled quality native speaker models to the student. An audio CD inserted into a CD-ROM drive can be manipulated to isolate discrete elements such as phrases, single words, or even syllables, and students can play those segments repeatedly. Each repetition is as high quality as the previous, with no damage to either the mechanism or the medium with each repetition. Significantly, we do not suffer the standards issue presented by video (an audio compact disc purchased anywhere in the world is playable on virtually any CD player). This enormous library of authentic materials remains largely untapped but more educators are beginning to become aware of the potential.

VISUALIZATION

□ VIRTUAL REALITY

One relatively new technology now available commercially shows just how quickly advances are being made; recent developments provide us with tools unthought of a year ago.

QuickTimeVR, a technology developed by Apple and available for both the Macintosh and Intel PC architecture machines running Microsoft Windows, was recently released to developers and consumers alike. QuickTimeVR will allow an educator to take a series of still images, such as those produced with a 35mm camera, and assemble them into a virtual walk-through of an area. Thus, one might place a camera on a tripod in the middle of the Puerta del Sol in Madrid and shoot a series of images in a 360° panorama. The resulting images are processed by QuickTimeVR developer tools producing a single file such that a user is able to "look around" the area at will, looking to the left or right, up or down within the full panorama. This differs significantly from a video tape segment of the same area. The linear nature of video makes user navigation impossible. Many of you may be familiar with the *À la rencontre de Philippe* videodisc package in which the student is able to navigate Paris and a variety of buildings. While the video clips allow a certain amount of exploration, the student cannot "turn his or her head" at will to change the perspective of their view. With QuickTimeVR, this act is quite simple—the users merely move the mouse in the direction they wish to look. The potential for even more realistic simulations in foreign languages is very exciting.[21]

□ KODAK PHOTOCD

Pioneered by Kodak, the PhotoCD is a special format CD-ROM designed specifically for the storage of near photographic quality images. Up to 100 images in five different sizes may be stored on a single disc. If used only to archive the many hundreds of photographs that most language educators have in their personal collections, this is a technology worth investigating. Since the images are easily indexed and referenced, it is quite possible to manipulate *ad hoc* a collection of images right in the classroom, taking the first steps towards the "fundamental changes in both presentation content and classroom dynamic" suggested by Pusack and Otto (1996, 9).

One of the significant features of the PhotoCD is that one does not have to fill the disc with all 100 images at once. It is completely conceivable to place 30–50 images to be used in a particular course on a disc, and to add additional images throughout the semester as they become available or relevant. Slides, prints, or negatives can be added to the disc by dropping off images and the disc at any Kodak developer.

STORAGE DEVICE IMPROVEMENTS

In 1985, a 20-megabyte hard drive for a desktop computer, approximately 3" wide, 8" tall, and 10" deep, cost approximately $1,000.00. Today a 1.2-gigabyte hard drive (1228 megabytes), which is 1/3" high, only 2 1/2" wide, and 3" deep, is approximately 1000 times faster than the 1985 drive—at two-thirds the cost and the cost is constantly dropping. As storage devices become larger in capacity, smaller in physical size, and less expensive, we will see increasingly complex applications for teaching of languages delivered which are far larger than anything we might have dreamed of ten years ago. Miniaturization proceeds at a rapid pace and changes will very likely be exponential in nature.

□ LARGE CAPACITY REMOVABLE MEDIA

The production of foreign language materials, particularly utilizing digital audio and video, is extremely demanding with regard to disc space requirements.

Fortunately the demands are greatest only during the capture, edit, and compression cycle, and the resulting files are much smaller than the raw audio or video materials when initially captured. Using large capacity removable storage mechanisms, a video production workstation is essentially unlimited in its disc capacity, and long term storage of raw video footage is quite viable.

□ RECORDABLE COMPACT DISC MEDIA

It is now possible and economically feasible to produce CD-ROM discs right on campus—indeed right in our own office. This ability would have cost over $20,000.00 in the early 1990s, though as we near the end of the decade, this capability is available for under $1,500.00. The practical impact of this will be far reaching. Instructors will be able to produce a full course's materials on a CD-ROM disc which is then commercially duplicated (for about $1.00 a disc) and made available in the college store. Students with their own CD-ROM equipped computers (virtually all desktop computers sold today) will be able to do a significant portion of their work in their rooms without impacting the campus network. Huge data sets can be delivered directly and will thus also relieve some of the burden of providing large numbers of media capable machines in public facilities.

□ DIGITAL VIDEO DISC OR DIGITAL VERSATILE DISC (DVD)

DVD is a new computer disc format. What makes it exciting is its potential capacity and speed. DVD discs look very similar to today's CD-ROM discs. However, a CD-ROM typically contains no more than 650–700 megabytes[22] of data, while even a single sided, single density DVD disc will be able to hold six to seven times that amount. Double-sided/double-density DVD discs will hold nearly 19 gigabytes of data on a single disc! This enormous capacity will allow discs to contain (and the format includes the specifications for) a full length film in multiple formats—the wide screen or "letterbox" format commonly viewed in theaters, and the "pan and scan" format commonly viewed on a television—all on a single disc. Furthermore, such discs can easily include sound tracks in several languages, and much more.

> "Whatever the number of global regions ultimately agreed upon, this segmentation is a *fait accompli*. We will have multiple, regionally incompatible DVD disc formats."

One serious drawback to the DVD format, which is frequently left out of discussions, is the fact that the format which has been agreed upon includes multiple, regional "standards." DVD discs will introduce regional variations such that DVD discs produced and sold in one country will not be compatible with players in other countries (Levine, 50). This revisits the video format problem of PAL, SECAM, and NTSC, only much worse. One proposal for dividing up the world had as many as eight regional formats, though the current discussions would suggest that we will end up with somewhere between three and eight global regions.[23] Whatever the number of global regions ultimately agreed upon, this segmentation is a *fait accompli*. We will have multiple, regionally incompatible DVD disc formats.

☐ COMPRESSION

This is a technology which will have a profound impact on language education, though it is quite unlikely that the average faculty member will even be aware of the changes. Since 1984, we have had analog to digital and digital to analog audio capabilities in an affordable desktop computer. The drawback to this capability has long been the size of the resulting files. As compression algorithms improve, longer and higher quality recordings fit into less disc space. Thus, we can produce more complete simulations containing greater quantities of authentic speech. The same is true of digital video, allowing us to fit longer and larger moving images into the same space.

While most faculty will not be aware of the advances in this area, the practical side of the equation will allow them to produce better and more complete materials, containing more and more richly created simulations. If we can fit two hours of video onto a single removable disc, we can produce a much more complete lesson than on a disc on which only ten minutes of video will fit. Advances in this area are being announced daily and are incorporated in commercial materials just as quickly.

NETWORK BANDWIDTH

As our networks grow and improve, becoming faster and capable of carrying even more information simultaneously, we will be able to bring many more current and larger data sets to our students. A simulation which "pulls" images nearly instantly from digital cameras in place around the world can be much more engaging than one in which the images are static or dated. A fascinating example of this technology in application brings hourly updated images from a central plaza in Berlin. This potential is limited only by the bandwidth of the network connections in between.

☐ FASTER NETWORK PROTOCOLS

Networking can be expected to become an increasingly important component of all language software for many years to come. This networking will be primarily of two types: the Internet type of networking which connects your institution to institutions and individuals worldwide, and the "intranet" variety—the connections among the individuals at your own institution as well as the machines located in computer-based learning laboratories. Certainly advances will be made in both areas, but in particular, increases in the speed and "bandwidth" on the local network will have a significant impact on the nature of language computing. Digital video and audio—the core components of language learning software—place huge demands upon a campus network.

☐ CHANGES IN NETWORKING ARCHITECTURES

In addition to basic speed increases, we can also look forward to changes in network architectures (such as increased use of switched-ethernet), which are themselves more efficiently designed and which will improve performance, particularly in the transmission of digital video.

PROCESSOR ADVANCES

☐ SPECIALIZED PROCESSORS

Computer processor designs will see significant advances in the near future. In particular, designs specifically engineered to improve the performance of digital audio and video such as the Intel MMX[24] will continue to be refined and released at a rapid pace in an attempt to keep up with the inherent media processing capabilities and raw speed increases in RISC architecture machines.

☐ PROCESSOR SPEEDS

When the computer's primary task was limited to the manipulation of text, the speed of the computer's central processing unit was certainly much less critical. Perfectly adequate computers dating to the late 1980s and early 1990s had processors measured at eight or sixteen megahertz (MHz).[25] Now in the middle 1990s, commercially available machines containing processors functioning at 200–500 MHz. are already available. Expect to see more advances in this area, but a word of caution is in order. As one plans to implement additional technology in the curriculum, or to redesign a language learning center, do not assume that one computer is necessarily faster than another merely because it has a faster processor. Processor speed is merely one of a number of variables which determine the overall speed of the machine.

☐ MULTIPROCESSING

Potentially even more important to language computing than individual processor speed is the increasingly common use of multiprocessing in desktop computers. As any consumer will have noticed when buying a computer, incremental increases in the speed of the central processor of desktop computers are often concomitant with logarithmic increases in the cost of the computer. As manufacturers produce faster and faster processors, however, the cost of the previous generation's processors falls significantly.

By using multiple processors in a single computer in conjunction with carefully designed software and operating systems, the performance of a computer, particularly when it comes to the multimedia so important to language materials, brings about significant increases. On a multiprocessor system tasks can be divided among the processors such that each has more time to devote to the several tasks of the computer as a whole. Multimedia computing of the type commonly employed in language materials benefits particularly from this technology.

FINAL REMARKS

Constant and rapid changes in technology may seem overwhelming. Though there is no going back to a technology-free educational environment, FL educators need to approach the incorporation of technology with very realistic expectations and a well designed plan. Technology by itself is just one more tool in the hands of the teacher and must be used in conjunction with a pedagogically sound approach to language instruction.

Finally, the information presented in this article is intended to be used as a point of departure for those FL teachers beginning to plan the implementation of technology in their curricula. Each academic institution has distinct needs, and its teachers and administration are responsible for deciding what is feasible within the context of the institution in question.

Though technology is not the panacea for magically improved language learning, there are a number of benefits accrued by both teachers and learners:

♦ *Better and more effective use of class time.* One of the more serious limitations placed upon teachers and students is one of contact time. Since academic language programs must make decisions regarding what material will be covered in order to maximize classroom opportunities to use the language communicatively, one clear advantage technology presents is that it allows us to remove many activities from the classroom which can be successfully performed outside of class using computerized materials. In so doing, we are free to devote more class time to communicative and task-based activities.

♦ *Individualized learning.* The nature of learning would suggest a carefully designed curriculum which attends to the needs of the individual learner. Clearly we cannot provide this level of individualization in the classroom, but through judicious use of technological tools we can implement such opportunities for students to work at their own pace in computer laboratories and at home.

♦ *Empowerment.* Though perceived as something to fear by many, the implementation of a technology-based FL curriculum enables a richer learning environment for both teachers and learners—an environment in which both are empowered in the attainment of their goals. Teachers can provide more authentic, current, and culturally rich materials to the learner. They can implement new opportunities for their students to interact with native speakers around the world. Furthermore, using increasingly accessible tools, they can exercise their instructional creativity to develop materials that address the individualized needs of their students.

> "The richness of the learning environment possible when utilizing the emerging technologies engages students in a manner heretofore impossible to achieve short of a study-abroad experience."

Students gain new control over their own learning, freed from the essentially linear nature of traditional materials, and "least common denominator" syndrome of those traditional materials. The richness of the learning environment possible when utilizing the emerging technologies engages students in a manner heretofore impossible to achieve short of a study-abroad experience. Engaging students in the use of and creating of their own projects utilizing these same technologies facilitates student use of linguistic skills and cognitive processes, further encouraging lifelong independent learning.

NOTES

1. CD-ROM stands for "Compact Disc Read Only Memory." In other words, the materials on a CD-ROM cannot be modified—they can only be "read" and not "written" or changed in that format. The CD-ROM technology really presents no new capabilities to the language instructor beyond the fact that it has a large capacity, and therefore is capable of storing more of the digital multimedia materials applicable to language instruction. Nothing which can be stored on a CD-ROM could not also be stored and/or delivered via a typical computer hard drive.

2. We feel it is important to remember that our discussion of particular authoring tools is not intended to be an exhaustive survey, nor an endorsement of particular applications. However, we do feel that many educators will profit through reference to specific packages as a point of departure for their own subsequent investigations. Readers interested in learning about other authoring tools not described herein can consult Frank Borchardt, Claire L. Bradin, Eleanor Johnson, and Laura Rhodes, eds., *Proceedings of the Computer Assisted Language Instruction Consortium. 1996 Annual Symposium "Distance Learning."* (Durham, NC: Duke University, CALICO.)

3. For more detailed information on these and other authoring tools for creating comprehension exercises, see Borchardt *et al.* (1996).

4. The dictation series includes: *CDictation, QTDictation, VideoDictation*, and the Guided series includes: *Guided Reading and Guided Listening & Viewing*.

5. Transparent Language Inc. (<http://www.transparent.com/>) offers software products for foreign languages. *LanguageNow*, a reading package, "enables users to begin understanding and enjoying articles, stories and conversational material from the first lesson in any of seven languages: Spanish, French, German, Italian, Latin, Russian, and English." <http://www.transparent.com/presskit/version5.htm>.

6. For more detailed information on these and other authoring tools for working with texts, see Borchardt *et al.* (1996).

7. NisusWriter, WordPerfect, MicrosoftWord, among others.

8. All three are published by Heinle & Heinle. *Système-D* is for French, *Atajo* is for Spanish, and *Quelle* is for German. These programs can be purchased either for individual or for institutional use. *Atajo* is also integrated within other computer-based materials such a *Mundos Hispanos*, a CD-ROM for beginning Spanish which incorporates writing in every lesson in the form of personal journals and more guided writing assignments.

9. An issue which is not fully addressed in all communications software regards the use of diacriticals and non-Roman alphabets or syllabaries. While many client/server packages support these capabilities, few server-based systems do. Educators should investigate the capabilities of their own systems, and when possible, push for the use of foreign language friendly systems.

10. In their article "Learning Language and Culture with Internet Technologies" these two authors report on their experience using e-mail with FL students and suggest several activities for different levels of language ability.

11. The software package used to set up the conferences is FirstClass Conferencing package from SoftArc, Inc.

12. Arizona State University has also experimented with the use of electronic conferencing with students in Spanish and Japanese classes. Lafford and Lafford (1996) give a report of the experience and provide some interesting possible activities for this type of communication.

13. Most word processors (NisusWriter, MicrosoftWord, etc.) allow one to create macros or glossaries of terms which can be assigned to a user-specified keyboard command.

14. Where students otherwise have no access to native speakers, video conferencing may offer some limited benefits in the development of speaking skills. However, considering the current status of the technology, the advantages may be far outweighed by technical limitations. Two-way video conferencing via satellite is extremely expensive to implement due to the high costs of satellite uplink technology. Internet-based video conferencing suffers from severe performance limitations, often reducing video frame rates to no more than 5–10 frames per second unless dedicated network services are provided. Dedicated services such as parallel ISDN lines (digital telephone network) or parallel virtual circuits are frequently very expensive and limited to the corporate boardroom, or completely unavailable as in many rural locations.

15. For more detailed information on these and other authoring tools, see Borchardt et al. (1996).

16. A good discussion and review of possible uses of the Web in a FL class is provided by Lafford and Lafford (1996).

17. We reserve the term authoring "tool" to refer to any software package designed and intentionally limited specifically to produce tightly focused lessons of a particular variety. An authoring "system" might be considered to consist of a number of "tools" or to be a means of producing new "tools" as defined herein.

18. Reduced Instruction Set Computer. RISC is a technology which was once found only in scientific workstation class computers, or supercomputers. Now they are commonly available in desktop computers from several manufacturers. The "brain" in a RISC computer understands fewer commands than the "brain," or "central processing unit," of a Complex Instruction Set Computer (CISC—see Note 19 below). Though they are capable of executing a smaller number of commands

within themselves, they execute these commands much faster than a CISC computer is capable of executing the same command. Rarely does a RISC processor require more than a single clock cycle to execute any instruction. To accomplish more complicated tasks, programmers break down the complicated tasks into smaller pieces to be executed by the RISC processor "in software" rather than "in hardware." This process of doing more "in software" rather than in hardware would result in slower operation on a CISC computer, but is much faster on a RISC machine. The real advantage is that it is much easier to update software than it is to update a chip.

19. Complex Instruction Set Computer. The "brain," or "central processing unit," of a CISC device is quite complex and it "understands" a large number of instructions, or commands which it can execute internally. Typically, executing one of these complex commands requires a number of "cycles," or "ticks" of the clock if you will. While the processor is involved in this execution, the rest of the computer is essentially forced to wait for the processor to complete the task before moving onto the next task. Most CISC processors, such as those from Intel or Cyrix, are beginning to adopt some characteristics of RISC (reduced instruction set computer) processing internally in an attempt to keep pace with the more rapid RISC development.

20. The 4.0 release and later of NisusWriter from Nisus Software is capable of reading text in English, Spanish, French, German, and Italian. Earlier text to speech technologies could read French, for example, but it was pronounced using English pronunciation guidelines and was for the most part unintelligible. Nisus' efforts have paid off, however. Foreign language texts read by NisusWriter follow the rules of the language concerned and pronunciation and cadence are quite good, though further improvement would be welcome.

21. At Middlebury College, we have begun to produce a number of QuickTime VR movies shot in Pamplona and Barcelona, Spain. These images will be made publicly available at our Flannet ftp (file transfer protocol) site for educators to use in their own materials once complete.

22. A "byte" can roughly be considered to be equivalent to a single character of the alphabet. Thus a kilobyte, or "K," is 1024 characters, a megabyte is 1,048,576 characters, and a gigabyte, 1,073,741,824 characters.

23. Major motion pictures produced in the United States are typically released first in the U.S. After the initial box office release here, films filter throughout the rest of the world into particular "markets" as determined by the motion picture production companies. Since a high quality digital film could easily be distributed worldwide within days of its release, the producers of films want to retain some of the staggered income generation they have become accustomed to as films are released into the European, Latin American, and Asian markets. It is for this reason that they are insisting upon—and have guaranteed—that this multiple standard will become a reality.

24. Specialized processors can potentially introduce undesirable results. The MMX in particular is known to have significant problems when switching from its specialized media functions back to mathematical functions. See Petreley, Nicolas. 1996. "Is Intel Keeping the MMX Under Wraps to Hide Real Flaws in the Chip's Design?" In *InfoWorld Online* (article dated November 18, 1996, site last verified January 12, 1997), http://www.infoworld.com/cgi-bin/displayNew.pl?/petrel/np111896.htm

25. Megahertz (MHz) is simply a measure of speed. Higher figures can roughly be associated with higher performance of the computer in question, though it is

patently false to believe that one computer will be faster than another simply because it has a higher measure. In reality there are so many variables which have an effect on the overall performance of a computer such as memory, disc speed, network speed, dedicated media processing, that one should consider megahertz as no more than one of a number of variables to consider.

REFERENCES

Asymetrix Corporation. 1994. *Multimedia ToolBook*. Belleview, WA.

Beauvois, Margaret. 1996. "Computer-Mediated Communication: Technology for Improving Speaking and Writing." In Michael D. Bush and Robert M. Terry (Eds.), *Technology Enhanced Language Learning*. ACTFL Foreign Language Series. Lincolnwood, IL: National Textbook. 165–84

Borchardt, Frank and Eleanor Johnson (Eds.). 1995. *CALICO Resource Guide for Computing and Language Learning*. Durham, NC: Duke University, CALICO

_____, Claire L. Bradin, Eleanor Johnson, and Laura Rhodes (Eds.). *Proceedings of the Computer Assisted Language Instruction Consortium. 1996 Annual Symposium "Distance Learning."* Durham, NC: Duke University, CALICO.

Chun, Dorothy M. and Jan L. Plass. 1996. "Effects of Multimedia Annotations on Vocabulary Acquisition." *Modern Language Journal* 80: 183–98.

Dominguez, Frank, Ana Martínez-Lage, and Jeff Morgenstein. 1997. *Mundos Hispanos, Level 1*. Boston: Heinle & Heinle Publishers.

Fischer, Robert, and Michael Farris. *Libra*. San Marcos, TX: Southwest Texas University.

Furstenberg, Gilberte and Stuart A. Malone. 1993. *À la rencontre de Philippe*. New Haven: Yale University Press.

Gutstein, Shelly. 1987. *Toward the Assessment of Communicative Competence in Writing: An Analysis of the Dialogue Journal Writing of Japanese Adult ESL Students*. Unpublished doctoral dissertation. Georgetown University.

Herren, David. *xMediaEngine Series*. Middlebury, VT: Green Mountain Mac.

Jones, Paul. 1991. "What are Dialogue Journals?" In Joy Kreeft Peyton and Jana Staton (Eds.) *Writing our lives. Reflections on Dialogue Journal Writing with Adults Learning English*. Englewood Cliffs, NJ: Prentice-Hall. 3–10.

Krashen, Stephen. 1985. *The Input Hypothesis: Issues and Implications*. London: Longman.

Kreeft, Joy, Roger Shuy, Jana Staton, and Leslee Reed. 1984. *Dialogue Writing: Analysis of Student-Teacher Interactive Writing in the Learning of English as a Second Language*. Final Report to the National Institute of Education. Grant No. NIE-G-83-0030. Washington, D.C.: The Center for Applied Linguistics.

Kunst, Richard, and Satsuki Scoville. *WinCALIS*. Durham, NC: Duke University.

Lafford, Barbara A. and Peter A. 1996. "Learning Language and Culture with Internet Technologies." In Michael D. Bush and Robert M. Terry (Eds.) *Technology Enhanced Language Learning*. ACTFL Foreign Language Series. Lincolnwood, IL: National Textbook Company. 215–62

Levine, Martin. "Spin Cycle", *Video*, June 1996: 47–50.

Lyman-Hager, Mary-Ann, James Davis, Joanne Burnett, and Ronald Chennault. 1993. "*Une Vie de Boy*: Interactive Reading in French." In Frank Borchardt and Eleanor Johnson, Eds., CALICO Proceedings. 93–97

Lyman-Hager, Mary-Ann, Marilynne Stout, and Morris Weinstock. 1995. *Glossing Authentic Language Texts*. State College, PA: Education Technology Services, The Pennsylvania State University.

Martínez-Lage, Ana. 1996. "Hypermedia Technology for Teaching Reading." In Michael D. Bush and Robert M. Terry (Eds.) *Technology-Enhanced Language Learning*, ACTFL Foreign Language Series. National Textbook Company. 121–64.

Morroy, Robby. 1984. "Teacher Strategies: Their Effect on Student Writing." In Joy Kreeft, Roger Shuy, Jana Staton, and Leslee Reed, *Dialogue Writing: Analysis of Student-Teacher Interactive Writing in the Learning of English as a Second Language*. Final Report NIE-G-83-0030. Washington, D.C.: Center for Applied Linguistics. 124–152.

Negroponte, Nicholas. 1995. *Being Digital*. New York: Vintage Books.

Foelsche, Otmar *et al. Annotext*. Hanover, NH: Dartmouth College

Foelsche, Otmar, Judith Frommer, and Greenfield. *SuperMacLang*. Hanover, NH: Dartmouth College and Cambridge, MA: Harvard University.

Otto, Sue K. and Pusack, James P. 1996. "Technological Choices to Meet the Challenges," in Barbara H Wing (Ed.) *Foreign Languages for All: Challenges and Choices*. Lincolnwood, IL: National Textbook Company. 141–186,

Peyton, Joy Kreeft. and Jana Staton. 1989. *Dialogue Journal Writing with Limited English Proficiency Students*. A Workshop Packet for Teachers. Alexandria, VA: TESOL.

Pusack, James P. and Otto, Sue K. 1996. "Taking Control of Multimedia," in Michael D. Bush and Robert M. Terry (Eds.) *Technology Enhanced Language Learning*. Lincolnwood, IL: National Textbook Company. 1–46

Scott M., Virginia. 1996. *Rethinking Foreign Language Writing*. Boston: Heinle & Heinle Publishers.

Staton, Jana, Roger Shuy, Joy Kreeft, and Leslee Reed. 1988. *Dialogue Journal Communication: Classroom, Linguistic, Social and Cognitive Views*. Norwood, NJ: Ablex Publishing Corporation.

Swain, Merrill. 1985. "Communicative Competence: Some Roles of Comprehensible Input and Comprehensible Output in its Development." In Susan Gass and Carl Madden (Eds.) *Input in Second Language Acquisition*. Rowley, MA: Newbury House. 235–53.

Warschauer, Mark. 1996. *Virtual Connections*. University of Hawaii Press.

APPLICATION OF IDEAS ON PRESENTATION

1. Lively/Williams/Harper list three phases in the treatment of input material—pre-mapping, processing, and synthesizing the texts. They indicate that meaningful, interactive L2 teacher talk, or mediation, is essential at each phase in order to provide the interface between the students and the authentic texts themselves.

   Create activities at the three levels of instruction (pre-mapping, processing, and synthesizing); then write possible supportive teacher talk for each of the three phases.

   (1) Pre-mapping phase

       a. Select an authentic text on a topic that fits into your curriculum.

       b. Identify a theme which lends itself to the development of ideas.

       c. Identify (by highlighting) cognates, synonyms and antonyms, vocabulary spiraled from earlier lessons, other key expressions, and specific cultural information and significance which will be useful in accessing the text.

       d. Decide on a theme (idea) which you want to develop with students. Find an angle from which you think your students can approach the topic, engaging them personally.

       e. Draft a potential interactive chalkboard result of the classroom discussion, including expected grids(s), web(s), or diagram(s) to be developed through the interaction. To minimize surprises in front of the class, consider a variety of possible directions that the discussion might follow.

       f. Write a series of guiding questions to lead you through the pre-mapping discussion.

   (2) Processing

       a. Decide on the major break points of the text.

       b. Make a list of possible questions to lead students through each section. Pay particular attention to the inclusion of questions that will set students up as sources of information for one another.

       c. Make a separate list of questions with multiple-choice answers (using the newly developed repertoire of terms from the interactive chalkboard). These questions will be used to help students vocalize their ideas and rationales.

(3) Synthesizing

Create an activity which will allow students to integrate the text and its meaning into their existing knowledge and experience as they develop and articulate new insights. The activity should encourage creativity; it should be open-ended, with no single expected or right answer.

2. Select another topic for which you want to present new vocabulary. Write possible interactive teacher talk to be used with visuals or manipulatives to develop the language in a meaningful, compare and contrast format.

3. Terry Ballman identifies the first segment of the instructional sequence, *setting the stage,* as teacher-centered. Prepare to "set the stage" on a topic for a class;

(1) Select a topic that you might be expected to teach during the next few weeks.

(2) Make a list of what you would expect students to be able to do at the end of the unit (functional outcomes).

(3) Determine the essential vocabulary for students to recognize and produce on the topic. Select a few of these items for your initial presentation.

(4) Determine two or three basic structural elements that students will need to be able to use. Plan to teach these generally as vocabulary and to use them frequently, making their meaning as transparent as possible.

(5) Identify, select, and prepare for presentation at least five visuals (e.g., photos, drawings, slides, manipulatives, actual objects, toy objects, video clips) representative of the essential vocabulary that you can use to introduce the topic.

(6) List prior knowledge that you can expect of your students to which you can make reference.

(7) Write a possible presentation of approximately three to five minutes (in the target language) to set the stage to teach your topic.

(8) Practice on your colleagues.

4. The second segment of the instructional sequence, *providing input,* is also teacher-centered, as noted by Ballman. On the same topic as above, add an input activity to your setting the stage segment.

(1) Assemble your visuals. Add a second set, either more of the same type to present additional vocabulary or another type to add variety of presentation and recycling of the same vocabulary.

(2) Determine three to six categories of contrasts or comparisons of traits that you can make between and among the items (e.g., size, color, use, benefit, preference, ease, speed, cost, location). Make a chart (for yourself) showing the attributes of each item.

(3) Plan your "teacher talk" for your presentation to the class, including comprehension checks and TPR activities. Provide at least one active response from students (e.g., moving to a corner of the classroom, holding up a picture/object/hand, identifying a fellow student, pointing at or moving a manipulative, making a mark on the chalkboard, voting) as well as examples of appropriate yes/no and either/or questions. Make notes to prompt your sequence of examples and activities.

(4) Practice on your colleagues.

5. As you observe the presentations of your colleagues, watch and listen for examples of each of the following:

(1) Key vocabulary presented

(2) Repetitions of key vocabulary

(3) Ways of identifying meaning of key vocabulary

(4) Main attributes of key vocabulary (points of contrast or comparison)

(5) Repetitions of main attributes

Design a method to help you note and evaluate these principal elements in the presentations in your group. For example, you might make a list of the key vocabulary presented and tabulate how many times each is repeated; you might list each different way that meaning is attached to each of the key vocabulary items; you might observe and tabulate how many times each "student" actively participates in some way. Brainstorm the design of your instrument (e.g., checklist, chart, tabulation) within your group and agree on several that you would like to implement in practice sessions among you. Use a variety of methods within your group or class in order to provide feedback on effectiveness to each presenter.

6. Keep a journal about the presentations that you observe. Determine which elements in each presentation you feel are most effective. Tell why you think that these activities or materials worked well. Would these activities or materials work as well for you? Why or why not? What adaptation of the style of presentation observed might enhance your presentation effectiveness? What extensions could you add to the activity to incorporate additional "Cs" of the National Standards (e.g.,

connections, comparisons)? How might you raise the level of the activity to incorporate more higher order thinking skills?

7. Tschirner explains that speakers usually focus on one clause at a time and chain fully- or partially-preassembled clauses together when engaged in conversation. If much of conversational language is highly routinized as prefabricated chunks of speech, then it appears that the teaching of high-frequency phrases for oral production may support language acquisition.

Give three to five expressions that you believe language learners could use frequently in constructing a conversation in each of the following categories or situations:

(1) To ask directions

(2) To indicate the time of day

(3) To express regret

(4) To request a favor

(5) To indicate enthusiasm

(6) To get someone's attention

(7) To solicit advice

(8) To offer an opinion

(9) To show lack of understanding

(10) To shower praise

8. Tschirner confirms that since "both form and meaning must be perceived and processed at the same time for interlanguage to develop," comprehension is only one of the goals of input. After comprehension has been achieved, students need to pay attention to a limited number of high-use structures to encourage their internalization.

For any four of the categories in Activity 1, isolate one structural element that you would call attention to with novice learners. Then write five examples of typical use of each structure that you could add to your teacher talk for your second presentation of the topic.

9. Vicki Galloway points out that "crucial to cross-cultural understanding is the recognition that in every culture there are *forms* or outward manifestations, and there are functions or *meanings*." She offers the example of the car in the U.S. culture.

Choose a form from a culture where the language that you teach is spoken and prepare to explore its meanings with students in your U.S. community:

(1) Select a form (e.g., word, behavior, event, organizational pattern, object, artifact).

(2) Describe its most obvious meaning.

(3) Create a web to map the linkages of this meaning to other meanings in the culture.

(4) Comment on the values and priorities of the culture that can be observed or inferred by these meanings. Rank the significance of these values in the culture as you perceive them.

(5) Tell what other cultural forms have developed in the culture to support or accommodate the form being studied.

(6) Analyze how the form-meaning network may vary within the culture.

(7) Select authentic texts that could help students to discover and/or you to explain some of the cultural meanings of the form.

(8) Design a presentation activity that will allow students to begin to explore the form and its meanings through the authentic texts.

(9) Make a list of other authentic materials to be used later with these students to reinforce these concepts.

10. Martínez-Lage and Herren briefly describe a number of software programs that can be used effectively in the teaching and learning of foreign languages.

Review several of the software programs in the following list. You may find them in your school media center or language center or library, in the information systems office/department of your institution, in a media communications program or a language technology program at a college or university, or at any number of retail merchandisers of computer products (Samples of *Système-D*, *Atajo*, and *Quelle* are on the compact disk accompanying this book. The transparencies designed to accompany each article in this text were created in PowerPoin*t*.):

Dasher
Libra
xMedia Engine Template Series
Annotext
GALT (Glossing Authentic Language Texts)
Système-D
Atajo
Quelle
Super MacLang
WinCALIS (Computer Assisted Language Instruction for Windows)
Hypercard
Toolbook
Macromind Director

Authorware
Microsoft PowerPoint
Aldus Persuasion

For each of the software packages that you study, answer the following questions:

(1) Can you use this program in your language, including diacritical markings?

(2) Will this program run on a computer available to you? available to your students? available in your classroom?

(3) What assistance or support will you have in learning to use this program (e.g., written manuals, experienced colleagues, workshops on campus, workshops or courses in area colleges or educational service centers, commercial courses)?

(4) How could the use of this program aid in the presentational aspects of your instruction (e.g., link visual and aural input, provide samples of accurate pronunciation, show body language with oral language, give access to authentic texts, allow multiple repetitions, permit flexible timing of use by students, provide access to meaning in a variety of ways, meet individual learning styles of students, add color for emphasis or categorizing, improve organization, hold student attention)?

(5) What specific texts, topics, or functions are you preparing to teach that you could use the program for to enhance the effectiveness of your presentation?

(6) How can you envision using your new instructional materials?

Part III

Activities

Including articles by:

Mary K. Williams/Jane Harper/
Madeleine G. Lively
Jeannette D. Bragger and Donald Rice
Michael Geisler
Frederick Toner

Designing Theme-Based Activities: Bringing Ideas to Speech

Mary K. Williams, Madeleine G. Lively, and Jane Harper,
Tarrant County Junior College, Fort Worth, Texas

INTRODUCTION

Developments in the teaching and learning of foreign and second languages have led educators to address the importance of communication in language learning as well as in language use. We all recognize that simply memorizing vocabulary and learning structures will not enable students speak a second language. They must communicate real information; they must endue the language with meaning. The National Standards suggest that the communication we practice in class must do more than produce personally meaningful utterances, that it should also promote the development of ideas. For this, we need to provide activities that encourage reflective processing and, that call upon students not only to tell about what they know and experience, but also to reflect on their knowledge and experiences, to compare what they know and do with what others know and do, and to enhance their awareness of how their own knowledge and experience fit into larger frames of reference. In an initial effort to label and qualify such activities, we will call them "thematic" in this article.

> ". . . (T)hematic activities encourage reflection; they ask students to work with ideas and explicitly to examine their knowledge . . ."

Here we cite the *American Heritage Dictionary*, which distinguishes "theme" from "subject" and "topic" in the following words: "*Theme* refers especially to a subject, an idea, a point of view, or a perception that is developed and expanded on in a work of art." We want to emphasize "an idea, a point of view, or a perception that is developed and expanded on . . ." Basically, thematic activities encourage reflection; they ask students to work with ideas and explicitly to examine their knowledge and their world view. In this sense, thematic activities are a natural development from work done over the past two decades in personalizing function-based activities, developing student-centered instruction geared to learner-centered learning, and encouraging critical thinking in classroom interaction.

In the following sections of this article, we will consider some elements in the design of activities that promote reflective processing.

MAKE THE TOPIC ENGAGING

Generally speaking, our curricula do not allow us to say that any topic is inherently too boring to teach. In many cases, it is we who make vocabulary or structures interesting by making them relevant to our students. Functionally organized materials have brought us much closer to this goal of relevance. Still, the fact that an exercise practices a valid linguistic or social function does not necessarily make it affectively or intellectually engaging to students. As Phillips notes, "Teachers will have to create the communicative tasks, the cultural investigations, and the community events that will motivate and intrigue students to persevere" (p. 11 in this volume).

One way to make activities relevant and engaging is to use them to link L2 to the notion of community service. For example, in a lesson on foods, authentic texts from an L2 community might discuss how citizens in that culture have organized to provide canned goods and nonperishables for hungry children abroad, to establish a food bank in their community, or to have a bake sale to benefit some cause. An activity based on these texts could use a Venn diagram to have students compare the food items mentioned in the text from the L2 culture with the kinds of items they would choose for such a project in their own community.

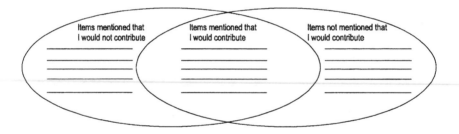

Depending on the content of the realia, students might be able to draw some initial inferences about different perceptions of food in the two cultures.

In an extension of this activity, the teacher could use supportive teacher talk to elicit a variety of features that would make foods inappropriate for the project (Lively, Harper, and Williams, pp. 81–95 in this volume). For example, if students were selecting items to send abroad, they would reject things that had the following attributes:

1. quickly become stale,
2. are not packaged well enough for shipping,
3. require preparation,
4. require refrigeration,
5. lack nutritional value.

Once several of these features have been written (in L2) on the board, students can work in small groups or in a plenary group to make lists of items that should be rejected on these grounds.

> ". . . (A)ctivities [can] bind concepts and language together in new insights . . ."

Since the minimal linguistic requirement[1] for these exercises is only to list vocabulary for food items, it can be done very early in a lesson. In spite of the simplicity of the language, however, the items provide meaningful practice of the vocabulary in contexts that relate it to decision-making in the world beyond the textbook. Equally important, such activities bind concepts and language together in new insights for those students who have not previously thought of foods in these terms.

ALLOW FOR PERSONALIZATION

Another way to make activities relevant and engaging is to provide a means for students to relate their own experiences. For example, to practice the preterit, an activity might be based on preparing résumés and interviewing for jobs. Preparing a résumé in L2 offers a meaningful context for writing a highly structured narrative about past events of particular significance to each student. Students who have no work experience are not excluded, for they can tell about the courses they have taken, their extracurricular activities, volunteer work they have done, summer camps, travels, and other experiences that demonstrate their qualifications. If the students are sufficiently advanced in their language skills, they can be specifically asked to identify the experiences that particularly qualify them for the positions they seek.

The résumé activity may also help students develop the habit of selective learning, since each student is apt to need particular vocabulary to discuss his or her own experiences. For example, some students may want to say they have served as volunteer tutors, while others may have done volunteer work with their church, some may want to say they have been to international camps or computer camps, and so on. Clearly, it will not be necessary for everyone in class to learn all of the same vocabulary for production.

The information developed in the résumé could be recycled in a follow-up activity based on a job interview, providing an opportunity to articulate those same ideas in another modality. This exercise might begin with a job application in L2 from an international company. An employer's questionnaire or a survey based on employee characteristics sought and those to be avoided enables students to role-play interviewer and applicant, giving insight into both perspectives of the interview process. (Documents of this sort often yield information for discussing perceptions of work-related values in different cultures.)

Both of these activities allow students to reflect on the value of their personal experiences for their future plans. For some—even at university level—the process of preparing a résumé will lend new insight into the significance of their choices of pastimes.

ENGAGE CRITICAL THINKING

When activities involve critical thinking, they provide a framework for students to use L2 to process information.

> "When activities involve critical thinking, they provide a framework for students to use L2 to process information."

Traditionally in pedagogy, we have used Bloom's taxonomy to define critical thinking skills: knowledge, comprehension, application, analysis, synthesis, and evaluation. However, rather than begin with knowledge, at the base of Bloom's pyramid, to organize activities, it is more productive to focus on the three higher-level skills, for they naturally entail those at the lower levels: Analysis requires knowledge of some information; synthesis requires comprehension of it; evaluation is dependent on application (Williams, Lively, and Harper, 1994).

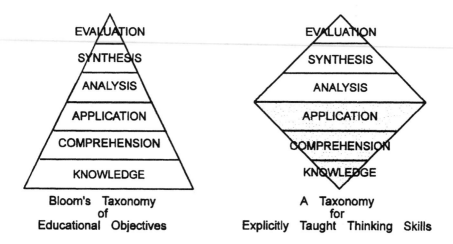

The higher-level thinking skills are even accessible even to students with novice language skills if there is extensive, well-contextualized input and if the concepts are kept on familiar ground.[2] One way to consider conceptual difficulty is in terms of two continua: (1) How concrete or abstract are the ideas involved? and (2) How subjective or objective are the judgments that students are asked to make?

Less difficult ⇨	⇨	⇨	⇨	More difficult
Ideas				
Concrete ⇨	⇨	⇨	⇨	Abstract
Judgments				
Subjective ⇨	⇨	⇨	⇨	Objective

For example, in a beginning lesson on foods, we would work with fairly concrete concepts and subjective judgments. Exercises might be developed around the following suggestions:

Analysis: Categorize the vocabulary items according to different attributes: basic food groups, edibles vs. potables, meals at which they are typically served, whether they are usually served hot, cold, or either way, etc. (Cultural comparisons and contrasts can be brought in here.)

Evaluation: Which foods are essential to your personal diet? Which do you avoid whenever possible? Tell which you consider healthy, which unhealthy. Which would you qualify as easy to prepare? Which do you think are time-consuming or difficult to prepare? Which do you prefer to eat at home? Which do you prefer to have at a restaurant? Which at the home of a friend or relative? (These are all very subjective judgments, allowing students to attend to ideas rather than "right" vs. "wrong" answers.)

Synthesis: Example 1: If you were organizing a party for the class/a family reunion, would it be a banquet, a formal dinner, a buffet, a picnic, a luau? What foods/dishes would you serve? Why?

Example 2: If you were going to open a restaurant, what would you name it? What clientele would you want to attract? What meals would you serve? What foods would you serve? What would your specialty be?

The second of these scenarios, while less "authentic" for most students, provides an opportunity for creativity, letting them play with an idea while keeping the concepts concrete and their judgments personal and subjective. In our experience, students enjoy giving free rein to their imaginations when they have been provided enough relevant input to express their ideas.

If foods come up in an intermediate-level lesson, we might ask students to work with more abstract concepts and to be more objective in their evaluations, that is to say, require that they offer valid arguments to support their evaluations.

Analysis: Categorize food products by the regions where they are produced. (Depending on the lesson, this may be regions of the United States [Connections], regions of the world, or the country or countries where L2 is spoken [Culture]). Name some foods that are tastier and less expensive "in season" but that can be bought year around. Associate food products with the types of weather and other geographical conditions required to produce them. Associate dishes and flavors with regions and cultures. Define the links between the food products of different regions and dishes that are associated with those places. (Here, for example, students would note that seafoods are generally associated with coastal regions, dairy products with areas that will support pasturing cattle or goats, rice with warm rainy areas, products like olives and dates from around the Mediterranean. Having surveyed—at least superficially—the effects of sun and soil, students are ready to note the ways that cultural heritages influence dishes, and the interplay between these factors.)

Evaluation/Synthesis: Example 1: Which foods do you consider luxury items? Why? If you had to decide which foodstuffs would be subject to a sales tax, which would you make taxable? Which nontaxable? Why?

Example 2: If you were planning the menus for a daycare center, which foods would you serve most often? Which would you never serve? Why?

Exercises such as these address, to some extent, the concern raised in Bragger and Rice (p. 195 in this volume): ". . . the teaching/learning of content is also designed to raise issues of importance on both an individual and a global scale."

Both of these sets of examples illustrate the benefits of grouping and sequencing activities to guide students through the process of idea development. The analysis stage serves to link words meaningfully to the reality they represent, and the evaluation and synthesis stages engage affective responses to information and concepts. Generally speaking, it is at the level of synthetic reasoning that we create new ideas.

> ". . . [We need to] group and sequence activities to guide students through the process of idea development . . . Generally speaking, it is at the level of synthetic reasoning that we create new ideas."

ESTABLISH A SUMMATIVE GOAL

Of course, every exercise has a pedagogical purpose, but we do something more when we give students a communicative objective. In giving an activity a summative goal, we imply that it involves meaningful communication of information and that something can be done with that information once it has been communicated. This is the essence of task-based activities.

Taking the broad outlines for the synthesizing activities on foods (p. 178), beginning students can work in pairs to decide on a menu and prepare a shopping list for their class party, or create an advertisement for their restaurant. At the intermediate level, they might work in small groups to reach a consensus on taxable and nontaxable items, as a legislator would. In a lesson on personality traits, working in pairs, they can identify the most remarkable traits of their favorite celebrities, giving examples of how those traits are manifested (e.g., "I think . . . [s/he] is generous because s/he does a lot of concerts for the homeless"), then decide together on which of the people they have discussed they will invite to a weekend retreat, basing their decisions on the personalities of their guests. More advanced students can be asked to come up with solutions to problems (Toner, pp. 247–248 in this volume), pool and analyze the data from their small group discussions, or explain the differences of opinion that blocked consensus in their small-group discussions.

In reality, the summative goal is a tool. It helps students stay focused on the task and provides for a sense of accomplishment and closure. Since it is the process that students work through to reach the goal that promotes reflection, the goal should be closely aligned with and—to the extent possible—dependent on the process.

USE GRIDS AND FORMS

Grids, forms, flow charts, and other schematic representations provide many benefits. First, they help students stay on task by serving as graphic organizers for instructions. This is particularly useful with multistep activities, where a grid delineates the steps and shows their relation to one another and to the goal of the task.

> ". . . (A) grid delineates the steps and shows their relation to one another and to the goal of the task."

For example, in the activity for which students discuss their favorite celebrities to decide whom they will invite to their weekend retreat, they might record a summary of their discussion on a grid like this (in L2):

Celebrity's Name	Remarkable trait	How the trait is manifested?	Invite? yes / no

Grids can also be used to provide opportunities to practice receptive processing of vocabulary and structures prior to production, as in the following example (adapted from Lively, Williams, and Harper, *Liens: En*

Paroles, p. 20), where students practice with expressions associated with environmental issues by checking the appropriate cell (presented in L2):

Suggestion:	No, it isn't practical.	No, but I've been intending to.	Yes, sometimes.	Yes, often.	Absolutely!
Buy recycled paper products					
Don't use disposable products					
Carpool					
Use public transportation					
Don't throw trash on the sidewalk					
Use rechargeable batteries					
Don't let the water run while brushing teeth					
Use warm, rather than hot water for bathing					
Avoid plastic products					
Avoid aerosols					
Don't use the dishwasher					
Sort recyclables from the trash					
??? (Add your own ideas.)					

It is important to note that grids and forms can also bring structure and organization to activities without imposing limits on students' creativity. For example, the culminating activity in a thematic group through which students work in teams to organize a community service project might have each team prepare a press release for their project. All of the teams will need to make the same kinds of decisions, but what each group decides to do is apt to span a broad range of choices. In previous activities students will have accomplished these tasks:

1. Agreed on a cause that you want to benefit;

2. Decided on a feasible goal;

3. Identified the talents and material resources at your disposal; and

4. Planned the event that you will organize to benefit your cause (e.g., a car wash, a book sale, a work day).

In their press release, they will need to convey outcomes of most of the discussions in steps one through four. They will also need to tell who they are, identify their sponsors or contributors, if they have any, and set a date and time for their event. (In some cases you may want them to decide in which media they want to publish their announcement, based on the audience they want to reach with it.)

A form to guide students through these instructions can simply list the key idea for each step (in L2), providing space to record the decisions. This sort of guide helps them follow the sequence of a complex activity, freeing them to focus their attention on ideas rather than "assignments."

Title of our project:

1. Who we are: _____

   _____

2. Community cause to benefit: _____

   _____

3. Goal: _____

   _____

4. Resources (sponsors, prizes, etc.): _____

   _____

5. Kind of event: _____

   _____

6. Who should come: _____

   _____

7. Place: _____

   _____

8. Date and time: _____

Here, again, the form simply provides a schematic representation of the directions; it serves as a checklist for the directions. Nevertheless, even though it offers step-by-step guidance, it is unlikely that any two teams will fill it out with the same information.[3]

Most importantly in terms of reflection, schematics such as these can be used to illustrate the relations among concepts. For example, Venn diagrams can be used to show contrasts and comparisons; tree structures show hierarchical relations; flow charts are useful for depicting cause and effect as well as sequence in decision-making; matrices help us to illustrate comparisons and contrasts among attributes.

> "Most importantly in terms of reflection, schematics . . . can be used to illustrate the relations among concepts."

EMPHASIZE TEAMWORK

Almost any exercise is improved when students work together. Even simple substitution drills allow peer tutoring. When students work together, they come up with more questions and more solutions; they learn to negotiate meaning in their communication and opinions in their decision-making; they learn to draw on the knowledge and experiences of their peers and to share their own knowledge. All of these make them more active and reflective learners.[4]

Generally speaking, the strongest interactive activities involve "cooperative learning." While the term is by now well established in pedagogy, it bears some discussion here. Interactivity alone does not make a truly cooperative activity. Cooperative activities usually involve an information gap, requiring that each student get information from the other(s) in their group in order to accomplish a particular task. These two features, the information gap and the task, assure that students engage in meaningful communication, that the listeners attend to the message (active listening), and they are the essence of reflective group work. If the task results in a product—which may be anything from a consensus or group decision to a team project—deliberation and persuasion are usually required to induce all members to subscribe to the decision made.

The more meaningful we make the task, the more engaged students become in its achievement. In their description of a large-scale team activity, Geisler and McArt (p. 223 in this volume) suggest the great satisfaction that students experience when the product of their teamwork can be put to practical use by others. And Ballman demonstrates in workshops that when students are strongly motivated to communicate they are less apt to be deterred by gaps in their skills. In these situations, students become committed to expressing themselves, and accuracy assumes its proper and significant role in communication, that of assuring the comprehensibility of the message.

USE THE DIRECTIONS TO STIMULATE IDEAS

Finally, we can provide "food for thought" in the directions we give for activities by suggesting multiple possibilities or perspectives for students to consider as they compose their ideas for the assignment. At the same time, we encourage them to use L2 well by giving examples of some of the expressions they may need, reminding them of vocabulary and structures they have already studied as well as supplying a few additional items of particular use in the assignment. In this, we take care to offer them the language in the terms that we expect them to use it.[5] The following example (given to students in L2) is a composition assignment to follow a unit on "describing personalities."

The Perfect Guest List:

You are planning the perfect dinner party. Given that there will be only you and three guests, (1) whom will you invite? (You may choose your guests from contemporaries, historical figures, or even fictitious characters from literature or films. The only criterion is that they be well-known.) (2) Describe each member of the party in terms of his or her personality. Don't forget to include yourself! (3) Mention two or three traits for each person. Is it someone friendly, charming, zany, talented, creative, intelligent, witty, inspiring, courageous? (4) Explain how those traits are manifested in the person's behavior. Is he or she famous for having many loyal friends, making people feel appreciated, making people laugh, playing a musical instrument superbly, winning prestigious awards for his or her work, writing beautiful music or fascinating books, being brave in difficult situations?

Basing your explanation solely on character traits, (5) tell your reason(s) for each choice. Explain what each member of the group will contribute to the ambience that you want for your party. For example, if you want an animated discussion, who in the group will be witty, original, imaginative, warm, enthusiastic, engaging, informed on a variety of topics? Who will articulate his or her ideas well? If you want a tranquil atmosphere, who in the group will lend serenity, calm, grace, or sensitivity to the evening? Who will be unaffected, open to others? How will the different personalities in the group complement each other?

Finally, (6) is there someone that you would not, under any imaginable circumstance, invite to your ideal party? Why? Is this person mean, cynical, boring, egotistic, gossipy?

In this composition activity (which can be adapted for different ages and levels), the linguistic challenge is fairly limited, having three principle elements: descriptive statements, future-time statements—which might be accomplished with a periphrastic structure—and causal dependent clauses. The simplicity of the language allows students to focus their attention on the complex ideas that they will treat. We use the directions to guide them through some of the thought processes. Through the rich vocabulary that we provide, we suggest a range of possibilities for them to consider. Rather than restricting their choices, the detailed instructions invite a breadth of values and encourage students to examine their own individual viewpoints.

> "Rather than restricting their choices, the detailed instructions invite a breadth of values and encourage students to examine their own individual viewpoints."

CONCLUSION

In this article we have sought to identify some of the ways that teachers can encourage students to examine their own knowledge and ideas. It is important to note that the ability to work with ideas is not confined to any particular age group; nor is it necessary that students be advanced in their L2 studies before they can reflect on the significance of their knowledge and experience in diverse situations. What is required is that teachers provide engaging activities in which complexity of language is balanced with conceptual challenge, allowing language and ideas to develop together, each giving substance to the other.

NOTES

1. A marginally expanded version might provide a model for conducting the discussion in L2:

   Student A: Shall we send ____?
   Student B: Yes, that's good./No, because ____.

   The reason provided would be one of those listed on the board.

2. See examples in Lively, Harper, and Williams, pp. 88–89 in this volume.

3. Although our primary concern here is with the benefits of grids and other schematics for promoting reflection, it is worth noting some of their other benefits for teachers. Forms such as this help us document how we maintain coherence in our approach to curricular goals even while promoting selective learning and learner-managed learning. In addition, forms and grids give teachers a document to mark for grades. This is not to suggest that grades should be based on the information or even the language on the forms or grids. But these documents can provide a frame for observations of how the teams discussed and reached their decisions.

4. See Terry Ballman's article in this volume, pp. 103–104, for further discussion of "student-centered" activities.

5. See Erwin Tschirner's article "From Lexicon to Grammar," p. 117, for more information about lexicalized grammar.

REFERENCES

Ballman, Terry. "Listening and Speaking: Integrated Skills Development." Workshop at SWCOLT/TFLA Joint Conference. Dallas, TX, 17 April 1997.

Bloom, Benjamin Samuel. *Taxonomy of Educational Objectives—The Classification of Educational Goals: Cognitive and Affective*. New York: David McKay Company, Inc., 1956.

Bragger, Jeannette, and Don Rice. "Connections: The National Standards and a New Paradigm for Content-Oriented Materials and Instruction." In Harper, Lively, and Williams, *The Coming of Age of the Profession: Issues and Emerging Ideas for the Teaching of Foreign Languages*. Boston: Heinle & Heinle Publishers, 1997.

Geisler, Michael and Linnéa McArt. "Creating Interactive Hypertext in German." In Harper, Lively, and Williams, *The Coming of Age of the Profession: Issues and Emerging Ideas for the Teaching of Foreign Languages*. Boston: Heinle & Heinle Publishers, 1997.

Lively, Madeleine G., Mary K. Williams, and Jane Harper. "Mediating Language with Teacher Talk: Bringing Speech to Thought." In Harper, Lively, and Williams, *The Coming of Age of the Profession: Issues and Emerging Ideas for the Teaching of Foreign Languages*. Boston: Heinle & Heinle Publishers, 1997.

_____. *Liens: En Paroles*. Boston: Heinle & Heinle Publishers, 1994.

Phillips, June K. "Changing Teacher/Learner Roles in Standards-Driven Contexts." In Harper, Lively, and Williams, *The Coming of Age of the Profession: Issues and Emerging Ideas for the Teaching of Foreign Languages*. Boston: Heinle & Heinle Publishers, 1997.

The American Heritage Talking Dictionary. Computer software. SoftKey International Inc., 1995. Win95 version 4.0, CD-ROM.

Toner, Fred. "Thinking Workshops: Developing New Skills for a Changing World." In Harper, Lively, and Williams, *The Coming of Age of the Profession: Issues and Emerging Ideas for the Teaching of Foreign Languages*. Boston: Heinle & Heinle Publishers, 1997.

Williams, Mary K., Madeleine G. Lively, and Jane Harper. "Higher Order Thinking Skills: Tools for Bridging the Gap." *Foreign Language Annals* 27.3 (1994): 401–426.

Connections: The National Standards and a New Paradigm for Content-Oriented Materials and Instruction

Jeannette D. Bragger, *The Pennsylvania University;*
Donald B. Rice, *Hamline University*

Jeannette D. Bragger (Ph.D, 1971, University of California, Santa Barbara) is professor of French and head of the Department of French at the Pennsylvania State University, University Park. In addition to articles on foreign language acquisition, she has coauthored, with Donald Rice, Du Tac au tac, Allons-y!, J'veux bien!, Quant à moi... !, On y va!, *and, with Delphine Chartier,* La France dans tous ses états.

===== ||| =====

Donald B. Rice (Ph.D, 1969, University of Wisconsin, Madison) is professor of French at Hamline University in St. Paul, Minnesota. He has coauthored, with Jeannette Bragger, Allons-y!, On y va! Du Tac au tac, J'veux bien!, Quant à moi... !, *and, with Peter Schofer,* Autour de la littérature.

> . . . the most effective way of teaching a second language is through teaching the content of ordinary subject lessons. In such cases, the interactions will be characterized by message-oriented goals. (Widdowson, 1978)

INTRODUCTION

The *Standards for Foreign Language Learning: Preparing for the 21st Century* introduces the "Connections" goal by stating that "Since the *content* of a foreign language course deals with history, geography, social studies, science, math, and the fine arts, it is easy for students to develop an interdisciplinary perspective at the same time they are gaining inter-cultural understanding" (1996). While this statement is no doubt a partial representation of the current reality in foreign language teaching and learning and while it may reflect a desired goal for the future, the term *easy* may oversimplify the integration of interdisciplinary content in the foreign language curriculum. Connections to interdisciplinary content, if they are to be established in meaningful ways, present particular challenges for materials developers, educators, and students. The "knowing how, when, and why, to say what to whom" of the Standards has yet to be addressed in terms of a systematic approach to interdisciplinarity.

191

It could be persuasively argued that content has always played an important role in foreign language courses. From the French Revolution to the lifestyles of adolescents in Mexico to German expressionist art to Japanese social interactions, culture and the resultant connections with other disciplines have always enriched the foreign language curriculum to one degree or another. Furthermore, the language itself is content, as any linguist would insist. How it works, how it reflects culture, how it facilitates or hinders communication are central both to the skills side of learning/acquisition as well as to the content orientation advocated by the national standards and the many guiding documents that preceded it. Interdisciplinarity, at least in an embryonic form, has therefore played a significant role in what have been traditionally called "skills" courses. However, to say that math, as an example, has been part of the foreign language curriculum because we teach numbers in the target language and have students reinforce them through a few simple additions and multiplications is a weak claim for interdisciplinarity. The complexities of "connections" to academic content, as espoused by the Standards, are therefore far from being realized in the current foreign language teaching and learning environment nor is it certain that we have clear ideas about how to implement a true content orientation as called for by the Standards.

To be sure, content-oriented teaching is not new. It is clearly present in many ESL courses, in foreign languages across the curriculum, in education abroad experiences, in language for special purposes, and in a variety of other contexts. With the exception of ESL, however, very little of this content orientation has touched the mainstream foreign language courses as they are currently designed and offered in K–12 or in college and university courses. In fact, as a profession, we unfortunately continue to reinforce the notion of "skills" versus "content" courses, concepts that have been picked up by students, teachers, administrators, parents, legislators, and other constituencies to argue that foreign language courses are not "really" part of the humanities curriculum. While the implications of the skills/content dichotomy are serious, it is not within the purview of this article to address them in any depth. Suffice it to say that the Standards suggests a newly-conceived paradigm that has, among other goals, the reintegration of skills and content for meaningful communication within the humanities.

Historically, foreign language teaching has come a long way in the United States. While we may still be on the conservative side as a profession (as is probably true for educational institutions in general), we have nevertheless demonstrated that we are willing to try new things and, for the sake of our students, to renew and improve our teaching strategies. We have lived through a number of methodologies, we have worked hard to move our curricula into a communicative (proficiency-oriented) mode, and we seem, again, to view the newly formulated Standards with enthusiasm. This is perhaps best demonstrated by the fact that, as of this writing, ACTFL has already sold 14,000 copies of the Standards and distributed 10,000 copies of the Executive Summary of the Standards, and that implementation workshops are being organized very rapidly. Many states and school districts are already hard at work revising foreign language curricular guidelines based on the Five Cs. Perhaps one reason for this overwhelmingly positive response is that the framers of the Standards have created a document that succeeds in integrating much of what we have learned about foreign language acquisition for the past several decades. They are clear in addressing the role of proficiency, they are not undoing the work that has been done, and they are not suggesting an exact blueprint of what curricula must look like. The very flexibility, inclusiveness, and concrete suggestions will appeal to all of us who acknowledge both our past successes and our continued need to improve. It can therefore be assumed that we will not suddenly be overcome by inertia and pessimism and that, therefore, change is indeed possible.

CONTENT-BASED INSTRUCTION: WHAT IT IS

Connections with other disciplines (i.e., interdisciplinarity) and content-orientation are concepts that have multiple definitions and can lead to a myriad of misconceptions (see the math example above). For purposes of this discussion, setting parameters and providing some definitions are therefore central to the development of the paradigm we will propose.

> "Content-based foreign language instruction uses learning objectives and activities drawn from the [...] school curriculum as a vehicle for teaching foreign language skills."

Brinton, Snow, and Wesche provide definitions of particular importance here. In the broadest terms, they define content-based second language instruction as "The integration of particular content with language-teaching aims" (1989). Somewhat more specifically, they continue the definition as ". . . the concurrent teaching of academic subject matter and second language teaching." In her article, "Learning Language Through Content: Learning Content Through Language," Met proposes the following definition: "Content-based foreign language instruction uses learning objectives and activities drawn from the [. . .] school curriculum as a vehicle for teaching foreign language skills" (1991). There is a clear consensus in these definitions that academic content, or content from the school curriculum, is concurrently present in the learning of foreign languages. Brinton *et al* state the case for integration even more strongly: ". . . content-based instruction aims at eliminating the artificial separation between language and subject matter classes which exists in most educational settings" (1989). A further assumption is that such content be presented through authentic materials, defined by Brinton *et al* as "written or oral texts which were created for a purpose other than language teaching. These provide in concrete form the structures, functions, and discourse features to be taught."

> "Authentic materials [are] 'written or oral texts which were created for a purpose other than language teaching. These provide in concrete form the structures, functions, and discourse features to be taught.'"

For purposes of this article, we will focus on what is called "theme-based" language instruction. Brinton *et al*, referring to theme-based courses, state that "the language class is structured around topics or themes, with the topics forming the backbone of the course curriculum." According to their definition, theme-based instruction:

- ♦ uses "target-language materials in a meaningful, contextualized form with primary focus on acquiring information";

- ♦ uses "authentic texts and materials";

- ♦ assumes that "materials are supplemented to make them comprehensible";

- ♦ has as its primary purpose "to help students develop second language competence";

- ♦ gives the language instructor "sole responsibility for language and content instruction"; and

- ♦ assumes that "students earn language credit and are evaluated primarily on the development of their second language skills."

CONTENT-BASED INSTRUCTION: WHAT IT IS NOT

As the National Standards are translated into materials and instruction, we run a very real risk of subverting the idea of content, either by giving it too much importance (i.e., it becomes the main goal of instruction) or by diluting it to the point where it becomes meaningless. To avoid misunderstandings, it is therefore useful to broaden the definition of content-based instruction to include not only what it is but also what it is not:

- ♦ It is not a shift from teaching/learning language to teaching/learning content; as Snow *et al* make very clear, the focus of the second language course is still to teach language.

- ♦ In a content-rich language course, it is not necessary that teachers be experts in the content. If content materials are presented coherently and clearly, we do not have to be science teachers to introduce basic scientific principles and we do not have to be Einstein to introduce math. Furthermore, it is entirely possible that, for some content areas, students know more about a topic because of its immediacy in the curriculum. Rather than seeing this as a disadvantage or a weakness, it should be viewed as an opportunity to empower students to teach the teacher.

♦ The purpose of academic/interdisciplinary content is not simply to teach vocabulary and grammar. For example, the focus of a presentation about the ecosystem is not just to teach (enumerate) words like "plastic container," "newspaper," "landfill," and "recycling." Nor do we talk about oceans just to teach the names of different fish and mammals. Were that to be the primary goal, it could just as easily have been realized with a series of decontextualized drawings. Instead, the teaching/learning of content is also designed to raise issues of importance on both an individual and a global scale.

This last point requires that we examine materials carefully as we consider adopting them for courses. In a rush to comply with the National Standards, material developers will be tempted to insert so-called content that, upon closer examination, is simply another way to acquire new vocabulary or grammar. While this may be an excellent strategy, it may also not deserve the "content" designation. Another example serves to illustrate the point. Paintings (art) are particularly useful to present a variety of vocabulary and functions (e.g., colors, describing people and places) and they can add considerable interest to such a presentation. However, unless the paintings are also viewed as art content (e.g., in a historical context, as part of an artistic movement, in terms of techniques), they have not fulfilled established criteria for interdisciplinarity in a meaningful way.

THE NATIONAL STANDARDS AND CONTENT-BASED INSTRUCTION

Just as preceding frameworks (e.g., communicative competency, proficiency guidelines), the National Standards are a stimulus for change. However, they are unique in the ever-evolving domain of language teaching/ learning in that they are clearly identified as "content standards" (1996) that integrate language skills, culture, and connections in the five goals (communication, cultures, connections, comparisons, communities). In fact, among the advantages of the Standards are the absence of compartmentalization (i.e., skills versus content) and the intertwining of all the facets of language and content. The Standards present five broad goals, yet no particular order of priority is dictated. They reflect the need to adapt to the new learner, teacher, and learning environments. They provide a flexible framework that does not inhibit individuality, future developments in language acquisition theory, or curricular flexibility. Perhaps most importantly, the developers of the National Standards recognize that any standards ". . . have to be subject to change. They cannot be conceived [of] as permanent and immutable.

The enterprise of developing standards is new for many and so what is learned in implementation must be brought back to change the Standards to make them better" (Lafayette, 1996).

In this article, we have chosen to focus on the goal called "Connections." We have done so because, in some respects, interdisciplinarity is perhaps one of the least elaborated and understood of the goals, particularly as it is currently implemented in school curricula. And, while there seems to be agreement that the introduction of content in the foreign language class is desirable, it is far from clear how this is to be accomplished in the typical, mainstream classroom environment.

The two Standards identified in "Connections" are as follows:

♦ Standard 3-1: Students reinforce and further their knowledge of other disciplines through the foreign language.

♦ Standard 3-2: Students acquire information and recognize the distinctive viewpoints that are only available through the foreign language and its cultures.

An elaboration of these two Standards yields the following principles:

1. There is a difference between academic and cultural content.

2. Students have a great deal of knowledge from other disciplines, knowledge that will be connected to the new language they are learning.

3. As they are learning this language for special purposes (i.e., science, art, geography, music, etc.), they are also enhancing their knowledge of that area.

4. Students are acquiring information through authentic documents, both oral and written, that were created "for a purpose other than language teaching" (Snow *et al*, 1989).

5. Students gain cultural insights while, at the same time, enhancing their general language proficiency.

A MAJOR PARADIGM SHIFT

Anyone examining learners, learning environments, teachers, and theoretical developments will no doubt concur that a major paradigm shift will occur in language teaching over the next few years (a comparison of a few of the projected changes are represented in the chart on the next page). It is not a question of "if" but rather a question of "when." To what extent the foreign language profession is prepared to benefit from the paradigm shift will largely depend on our willingness to change. To be closed-minded in a rapidly changing world will probably lead to extinction. An open-minded approach is not, however, necessarily sufficient for change to occur. The typical learning environment makes extraordinary demands on teachers who deal with complex issues that go far beyond the teaching of their subject matter. For example, few have the time or the inclination to develop materials that will reflect the goals in the National Standards. It is therefore logical that materials developers play a major role in precipitating and facilitating the projected paradigm shift.

PARADIGM SHIFT	
Old Paradigm	**New Paradigm**
Self-contained (content limited to target culture); bits and pieces of target culture (cultural notes); limited exposure to literature, history, art, geography. *Connections* = students to target culture	Interdisciplinary. *Connections* = students to any academic and cultural content
Students are the clones of the teacher. We want students to be like us; we reward students who are most like us; we're the ones who got "A"s in French; concept of student as empty vessel. *Connections* = students to teacher	Students have the opportunity to be different from us (within TL class) by developing their own interests. *Connections* = students to content
The audience for students is always the teacher; when students make presentations in class, the goal is to impress the teacher and to prove that the work was done. *Connections* = students to teacher	Student becomes teacher; cooperative learning; connections from student to student. *Connections* = students to peers and to the community
At college level: division between "skills courses" and "content courses." *Connections* = virtually absent	*Connections* = integration of language skills and content

A DEVELOPMENTAL MODEL FOR CONTENT-ORIENTED INSTRUCTION

On the basis of the definitions and principles elaborated on the preceding page, we propose a developmental model (on next page) for content-oriented instruction as a means for implementing the

"Connections" Standards 3.1 and 3.2. The stages of development are not associated with a particular time frame (i.e., each stage can represent one or several years of study depending on the curriculum) although they could correspond to language levels 1–4/5. The stages can be superimposed on any curricular levels, from kindergarten through college. It is assumed that the sooner learners reach Stage 4, the more the content orientation can be expanded. Therefore, it will always be preferable if learners begin their foreign language study in elementary school.

Stage 1 of the model is designed to prepare learners for the content connections that will become increasingly sophisticated as they advance in their study of the foreign language. In that sense, the content is presented in small, manageable "chunks" connected to specific structures and vocabulary being studied. The academic content is familiar and the cultural content may present new information. The language, however, is likely to be one step beyond the learner's productive proficiency. Since it is a stage primarily dependent on the receptive skills, learners may engage in discussions in English to demonstrate their comprehension (see below for discussion of the role of English). In terms of the National Standards (Standard 3.1 and 3.2), this stage corresponds to grade 4 of the sample progress indicators, which state that:

♦ Students demonstrate an understanding about concepts learned in other subject areas in the target language, including weather, math facts, measurements, animals, insects, or geographical concepts.

♦ Students read, listen, and talk about age-appropriate school content, folktales, short stories, poems, and songs written for native speakers of the target language.

Stages 2 and 3 of the model focus on the development of the content orientation, with progressive sophistication of the content and of the productive skills. Increasingly, learners use the target language to discuss and present content. Stages 2 and 3 correspond to grade 8 of the sample progress indicators in the National Standards (Standards 3.1 and 3.2). According to these progress indicators:

♦ Students discuss topics from other school subjects in the target language, including geographical terms and concepts, historical facts and concepts, mathematical terms and problems, and scientific information.

♦ Students comprehend articles or short videos in the target language on topics being studied in other classes.

♦ Students present reports in the target language, orally and/or in writing, on topics being studied in other classes.

Developmental Model for Content-Oriented Instruction			
	ACADEMIC CONTENT	OUTCOMES	CULTURAL CONTENT
	Standard 3.1: Students reinforce and further their knowledge of other disciplines through the foreign languages.		Standard 3.2: Students acquire information and recognize the distinctive viewpoints that are available only through the foreign language and its culture.
STAGE 1 (Preparing for content connections)	Links to content areas (e.g., math word problems, metric system)	RECOGNIZE UNDERSTAND	Links to cultural data (e.g., music, poems, folktales)
STAGE 2 (Developing the content orientation)	Familiar academic content (e.g., human biology, geography)	UNDERSTAND TALK ABOUT PRESENT (word/phrase/sentence level)	Familiar (Equivalent) cultural content (e.g., short novel, health)
STAGE 3	Less familiar academic content (e.g., art history, genetics)	PRESENT (sentence/ paragraph level) RESEARCH + PRESENT	Less familiar cultural content (e.g., short novel, history of film)
STAGE 4 (Expanding the content orientation)	Unfamiliar academic content (e.g., psychology, information theory)	RESEARCH + PRESENT	Unfamiliar cultural content (e.g., social structures, literature)

Familiar/Less familiar/Unfamiliar = varies on individual basis (age, place in school curriculum, home environment, experiences)
PRESENT = work with content provided
RESEARCH + PRESENT = discover new content

♦ Students use sources intended for same-age speakers of the target language to prepare reports on topics of personal interest, or those with which they have limited previous experience.

Stage 4 of the model expands the content into unfamiliar areas, particularly as other disciplines are dealt with in the target culture. While it is assumed that learners have touched upon aspects of the content in other courses (e.g., they have dealt with U.S. political issues in their social studies course), the perspectives of the target culture(s) are unfamiliar to them. In the optimal learning environment, this stage corresponds to the grade 12 sample progress indicators of the National Standards (Standards 3.1 and 3.2). According to these indicators:

♦ Students discuss topics from other school subjects in the target language, including political and historical concepts, worldwide health issues, and environmental concerns.

♦ Students acquire information from a variety of sources written in the target language about a topic being studied in other school subjects.

♦ Students combine information from other school subjects with information available in the foreign language in order to complete activities in the foreign language.

♦ Students use a variety of sources intended for same-age speakers of the target language to prepare reports on topics of personal interest, or those with which they have limited previous experience, and compare these to information obtained on the same topics written in English.

Given the dearth of eight- to twelve-year foreign language programs currently available, it is unlikely that most learners will reach this stage with any degree of control by the time they reach grade 12. While the framers of the National Standards provide a framework that encompasses K–12 in an attempt to reinforce the importance of foreign language study at an early age, such a learning environment is, for the most part, still a desired development for the future. In the meantime, it is perhaps equally important to view the Standards as progress that continues through college, with Stage 4 of our model (and grade 12 of the sample progress indicators) being more likely when students pursue foreign language study at the college level. For this reason, our article deals less specifically with Stage 4, which would require elaboration of many complex issues not within the parameters of this discussion.

IMPLICATIONS OF THE DEVELOPMENTAL MODEL

To reiterate the key issue, the goal of foreign language courses is to teach/learn the foreign language. If the goal were content only, it could be argued that content would simply be provided to students in their native language or at least in the language of the culture in which they reside. In other words, the status quo could be maintained, in which interdisciplinary content is only minimally present in the foreign language classroom and the dichotomy of "skills" and content remains firmly entrenched in the curriculum. If, on the other hand, we wish to integrate skills and content successfully, it is important to recognize the following principle: For learning to occur, there must be familiarity with *either* the language needed to deal with the content *or* the content itself. If this principle is valid, it leads us to a reconsideration or expansion of the "input hypothesis" formulated by Krashen (1985).

> "For learning to occur, there must be familiarity with *either* the language needed to deal with the content *or* the content itself."

According to Krashen, "We progress along the natural order . . . by understanding input that contains structures at our next 'stage'— structures that are a bit beyond our current level of competence. (We move from i, our current level, to $i + 1$ [1985].)" Krashen's hypothesis focuses on progress in language proficiency without specifically addressing content. Since interdisciplinary content is becoming a major factor in language learning, we propose the following formulaic representation of language/content input that modifies and expands on Krashen's hypothesis:

Learner	Input	Description
c, l	c, l	content and language are at the same level as current level of learner; desirable for reinforcement and review
c, l	c, l + 1	content is familiar, language is raised by 1; desirable for learning to occur
c, l	c + 1, l	content is raised by 1, language is at current level of learner; learning is likely to occur in a systematic fashion
c, l	c + 1, l + 1	both content and language are one step beyond the current level of the learner; creates a "double bind" and comprehensibility is more difficult to achieve, i.e., learning may be inhibited
c, l	c + 2, 3, etc. l + 2, 3, etc.	both content and language input are so far above the current level of the learner that learning is unlikely to occur

c = content   l = linguistic proficiency

This type of hypothesized formula inevitably raises many issues and questions (as continues to be the case with Krashen's hypotheses). The most obvious ones concern the "level of the learner" and the "level of the input." How do we know exactly what the content and language level of the learner is? How do we know if a text is $c + 1$ or $l + 1$? Without reliable and accurate assessments of either students or text, our answer to these questions is necessarily limited to what we, the teachers, know about our students. As long as we are in a lockstep curricular system with 10 to 35 students per class and grades as measures of achievement (i.e., considerable student variability), the curriculum (goals, materials, performance) and experience are the general indicators of both student level and appropriate text levels. It remains true that, for example, a $c + 1$ text for one student may be a $c + 2$ text for another. To some extent, the variables can be reduced or at least somewhat neutralized through the pedagogical apparatus (advance organizers, drawings, photos, vocabulary glosses, etc.) and tasks (language and content activities) that accompany a text and thus make it comprehensible.

An analysis of the stages in the developmental model for content-oriented instruction reveals that the c and l formula can be superimposed so that meaningful learning will occur. At all stages, depending on the language and the topic, either the language or the content may alternatively be raised a level.

At Stage 1, in every instance, either the language or the content is familiar to the learner. In a math problem, for example, the mathematical concepts are familiar while the language is one step beyond the learner's current level ($c, l + 1$). The language of a simple poem or song may be at the learner's current level while the cultural content is likely to be unfamiliar and has to be made comprehensible ($l, c + 1$).

At Stage 2, the content of a biology lesson or a short novel is familiar and at the level of the learner; the language to express the content, however, is a step beyond the learner and must be made comprehensible ($c, l + 1$). This is the formula that predominates at this stage, although it can, of course, alternate with other combinations.

At Stage 3, the language is often at the level of the student, while the content may be unfamiliar ($l, c + 1$). For example, while learners may have the language required to talk about geography at this stage, the geography of a region of a target culture and its effects on the target population is likely to be less familiar. This is the formula that predominates at this stage, although it can, of course, alternate with other combinations.

At Stage 4, increasingly, learners are familiar with the language needed (particularly in terms of structures and functions), while the content is often unfamiliar ($l, c + 1$). At this stage, it becomes even more difficult to categorize either the current level of the learner or the level of the text. The learner's language competency and comprehension strategies are now such that they enable him or her to work with a text even if unfamiliar vocabulary and/or structures are embedded in it.

IMPLEMENTATION

If the hypotheses presented above are valid, the question arises: How can they be "translated" into classroom activities? The second part of this article will suggest some types of content materials (with possible sources) as well as some ways of working with them at the various stages identified in the developmental model above. Although the examples are in French, these suggestions apply equally as well to other languages.

□ STAGE 1: PREPARING FOR CONTENT CONNECTIONS

On the academic content side of the model, a good starting point is math. When beginning level students are learning numbers, they are frequently asked to do simple arithmetic operations: addition, subtraction, multiplication, division. Once they have a minimal comfort level with producing numbers, it is possible to spiral the task upward by including some simple math word problems (of the sort students begin to do in third or fourth grade) that combine the recycling of numbers with reading comprehension. For example:

Au cours d'éducation physique, les élèves font trois fois le tour de la cour qui a la forme d'un rectangle de 80 m sur 40 m. Quelle longueur ont-ils parcourue? Combien de tours doivent-ils faire pour parcourir au minimum 1 km?

During the physical education course, the students run three times around the courtyard, which is in the form of a rectangle measuring 80 m. by 40 m. How far have they run? How many times do they have to run around the courtyard to go at least 1 km?

With the help of the illustrations and, in some cases, a few vocabulary glosses, students can work individually or in pairs to solve the problem. The example above is taken from a math textbook from France used in 6^e (roughly the equivalent of seventh grade in the United States).

On the cultural content side of the Stage 1 model, an excellent source for materials at the beginning level is magazines written for students just learning the language. The content of these magazines reflects that of most beginning textbooks and adds topics of high interest to young people. In addition to short individual articles, the magazines frequently offer *dossiers* organized around a topic. For example, the following articles are excerpted from an issue dealing with music, television, and movies. The first article ranks the popularity of different types of music among French teenagers; the second provides statistics and reasons why teenagers like to go to the movies. In the third article, sixteen-year-old Sandrine talks about her preferences in music.

Vive le rock!

Le genre préféré des jeunes est la musique rock. Pour l'ensemble des Français, c'est la chanson française. Le jazz est en progression mais il est le genre le moins apprécié. Une surprise pour certains, peut-être: la musique classique est écoutée par huit jeunes sur dix! La musique rap, le reggae et la "World Music", appelée aussi la sono mondiale, sont très populaires.

Quel genre de film?

La moitié des Français ne vont jamais au cinéma! Mais soixante-quinze pour cent des 15–25 ans vont au cinéma au moins une fois par mois. Plus de quatre-vingt-deux pour cent y vont pour se divertir. Trente-huit pour cent y vont aussi pour rêver, un tiers pour apprendre quelque chose et vingt-trois pour cent pour découvrir une autre mode de vie.

Sandrine, seize ans

"Mon passe-temps préféré, c'est la musique. J'écoute très souvent de la musique, à la radio, sur mon walkman et je regarde les émissions musicales télévisées comme "Le Top", sur *Canal Plus*, ou "Boulevard des Clips", sur la M6.

J'aime un peu tous les genres de musique, sauf le rap. Le rap, c'est toujours la même chose! Toutes les chansons se ressemblent. Elles ont toutes le même air. Ma musique préférée, c'est la musique pop. Mes chanteurs préférés? J'aime bien le chanteur canadien Roch Voisine et le chanteur français Julien Clerc. Pour les chanteuses, j'aime Patricia Kaas et Liane Foly. Elles sont françaises toutes les deux. Parmi les chanteurs étrangers, j'aime beaucoup Prince, Phil Collins, Michael Jackson et Lenny Kravitz. Comme groupes, j'aime U2, 2 Unlimited et Take That..."

(*Bonjour*, no. 3, févr. 1994, pp. 4, 7, 10)

A *dossier* such as this one lends itself to a small group activity in which students, divided into teams, compete to see who can discover the most information from the article (with bonus points being awarded to any team that is the only one to come up with a particular piece of information).

Literary texts can also be used, even at the beginning level, provided they deal with familiar topics in simple language. Almost all French textbooks include poems by Jacques Prévert for this reason. For example, the poem on the next page:

Pour toi mon amour

Je suis allé au marché aux oiseaux
    Et j'ai acheté des oiseaux
    Pour toi
    mon amour
Je suis allé au marché aux fleurs
    Et j'ai acheté des fleurs
    Pour toi
    mon amour
Je suis allé au marché à la ferraille
    Et j'ai acheté des chaînes
    De lourdes chaînes
    Pour toi
    mon amour
Et puis je suis allé au marché aux esclaves
    Et je t'ai cherchée
    Mais je ne t'ai pas trouvée
    mon amour.

Jacques Prévert, *Paroles* (© 1949 Editions Gallimard)

When given a bit of help (four or five vocabulary glosses and, if the *passé composé* has not as yet been taught, a short explanation about the past tense), students are very capable of reading the text and then discussing it as a poem (i.e., in terms of not only meaning but also rhythm and repetition of sounds).

It is important to stress that at this stage content is dealt with *receptively*. Students should be allowed to use English for it is only then that they can fully profit from the fact that their receptive skills considerably outdistance their productive skills. Making use of their familiarity with the subject matter as well as their knowledge of standard reading strategies (recognizing cognates, guessing from context, linking words of the same family), they are able to begin to work with academic and cultural content in their first year of language study.

☐ STAGE 2: DEVELOPING THE CONTENT ORIENTATION (FAMILIAR MATERIAL)

Whereas at Stage 1 the student's relationship to content is primarily receptive (i.e., recognizing and understanding), Stage 2 introduces a productive element into this relationship. Students are now expected not only to understand the content but also to talk about it in the target language. Consequently, it is very important to work with content that is familiar. On the academic side, a fertile area is science, which tends to be fairly concrete. A good source once again is school textbooks and also books on science written for young people. These both have the advantage of dealing with material that American students also learn in late elementary or early middle school; moreover, the presentations of topics include many illustrations and photos, and the explanations contain numerous cognates.

Traditionally, beginning learners of a language are taught the parts of the body fairly early on. This vocabulary can be recycled and expanded at the next level as part of a short unit on human biology. For example, students can be given material dealing with breathing rates (at rest and when involved with various activities), with the composition of the air at different moments in the breathing process, and with the structure and function of the lungs. (See Figs. 2 and 3—these pages come from a textbook used in France in the equivalent of fifth and sixth grades.) With the help of activity masters, taken from the workbooks that accompany most textbooks or devised by the teacher, students can then check their reading comprehension and perform simple hands-on activities and experiments using the material of the lesson (see Fig. 4). Since the scientific information is for the most part familiar to the students, they can concentrate primarily on understanding it and then talking about it in the target language.

Figure 2. (L'air qui sort est différent de l'air qui entre.)

Figure 3. (À quoi sert l'oxygène?)

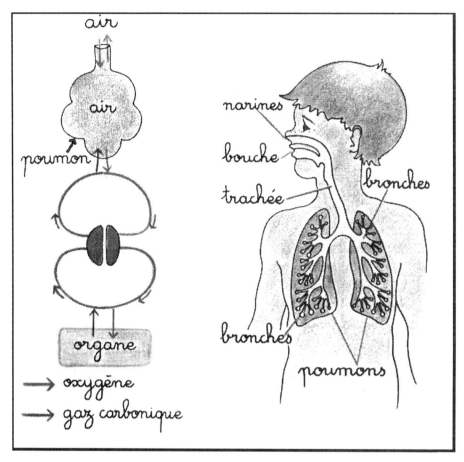

The above mini-unit on breathing can become part of a larger activity involving similar materials on circulation, digestion, and movement. The teacher can divide the class into four groups, each one assigned to become "experts" on the material of *one* of the mini-units. After each group has worked through its materials, the teacher can then reorganize the class into groups of four, one from each mini-unit. Each member of the new group has the responsibility of "teaching" the other three about his or her specialty. Alternatively, with the aid of posters created by the students and/or models borrowed from the biology teacher, each of the original groups can organize a display to help the others learn about their topic (in much the same fashion as a "poster session" at a professional conference). In either case, the final step could be a test on the content material from all four topics. Students would thus be using language to communicate information in a meaningful way.

Figure 4. Activity Master 1–12 (Des expériences)

I.   Ferme ta bouche et pince-toi le nez. Combien de temps peux-tu rester sans respirer?

   Demande à quelques camarades de classe de faire la même chose. Qui peut rester le plus longtemps sans respirer?

Nom	Secondes sans respirer
_____	_____
_____	_____
_____	_____
_____	_____
_____	_____
_____	_____

II.   Compte tes mouvements respiratoires pendant une minute...
   1. assis(e) sur une chaise
   2. après avoir marché pendant une minute
   3. après avoir couru pendant une minute
   4. étendu(e) sur le plancher

Maintenant compte les mouvements respiratoires de quelques camarades de classe.

Nom	Assis(e)	Après avoir marché	Après avoir couru	Étendu(e)
_____	_____	_____	_____	_____
_____	_____	_____	_____	_____
_____	_____	_____	_____	_____
_____	_____	_____	_____	_____
_____	_____	_____	_____	_____

III.   La capacité respiratoire est variable selon les personnes et elle triple entre 6 ans et 18 ans. Avec un mètre de couturière *(tape measure)* ou une ficelle *(string)*, mesure le périmètre de la cage thoracique d'un camarade (si tu es garçon) ou d'une camarade (si tu es fille). Ton (Ta) camarade fera de même pour toi.

While biology lends itself very nicely to content-oriented language instruction, other possibilities do exist. Areas in which to search for materials include: slightly more complicated math problems, such as volume and mass; social studies topics, such as world population and hunger; subjects from geography, such as the contrast between rural and urban living. The latter two subject areas (social studies and geography) also have the advantage of perhaps providing some new material (from the perspective of the target culture) while also reviewing familiar concepts.

Certainly, the productive ability of students at this level is still quite limited. Most of the talking and writing about the topics will initially take place at the word or phrase level—labeling diagrams, filling in missing information, answering questions with short phrases. A basic objective of these content units should be to lead students progressively to the point where they can use simple sentences to describe and explain the content material.

On the other side of the Stage 2 diagram, it is not as obvious how to find culturally authentic readings on topics familiar to students. In particular, most literary texts (with the exception of some fairy tales) represent a major jump both in language level and in content unfamiliarity. One solution involves using texts written in the target language *for* and *about* young people. While not all topics written for this age group will be of interest to American middle and high school students, it is possible to find some that will work. The following example comes from a series of books written for young readers in France (eight years and older). This particular story features a young girl who is wild about soccer. However, when her family moves to a new town, the girls at her school don't play soccer and the boys won't accept her. In the passage cited here she talks about the house in which she and her family lived previously. She says that in her former school there was no soccer goal cage, but she didn't care because she lived in a house with a garden, where she and her brothers could play. At first they used to use an abandoned washing machine as the goal; but it was too difficult to score because the opening was so small. Then they used a new rowboat that her grandparents stored at the house. The only trick was to get the boat back into the garage very quickly when her grandparents visited.

> Dans mon ancienne école, il n'y avait pas de but de football.
> Mais je m'en fichais pas mal parce qu'à Flagny, là où on habitait avant, notre maison, c'était une maison. Avec un grand jardin autour. Et dans le jardin, avec Seb—mon frère Sébastien qui joue en minimes—et mon autre frère Bertrand—Beb, qui joue en cadet—-, on ne s'était pas gênés pour en construire un, de but.
> Au début, on avait pris la vieille machine à laver que les voisins avaient abandonnée sur le trottoir. C'était trop dur pour marquer [un but]. Le tambour faisait à peine quarante centimètres d'ouverture. On a beau être entraînés, faut pas rêver. Ensuite, on s'est servi de la barque de

Papy. La toute neuve. Celle qu'il nous avait confiée parce qu'il n'a pas de garage chez lui. Le seul problème, c'est quand Papy et Mamy venaient: là, il y avait intérêt à rentrer le bateau en vitesse. Heureusement, ils ne viennent pas souvent. Et ils préviennent toujours avant.

(Fanny Joly and Christophe Besse, *Fous de foot* [Casterman], pp. 8–10)

On the one hand, clearly the language is difficult in spots. On the other hand, it's "real" French—as spoken idiomatically by young people. Moreover, American students can identify with the topic—the trials and tribulations of someone wanting to be on an athletic team. And, perhaps most importantly, unlike much of what students are asked to read, the story is genuinely humorous.

Obviously, the instructor will need to provide help, both in the form of vocabulary glosses and of multiple pre-reading and reading tasks. In terms of what to do before reading, advance organizers of the following type often prove useful: "You're going to read about playing soccer where Sonia used to live. Look for examples of her and her brothers' ingenuity."

After students have read the text, the teacher can provide basic comprehension exercises as well as more interpretive questions. (See Fig. 5.) At this transitional stage from receptive to productive work with content, it is essential to distinguish among different types of activities. The teacher should have students talk and write in the target language about the basic story line: who? what? where? when? why? At the same time, since these stories lend themselves to basic literary analysis (plot, narrative point of view, themes) and also raise issues that relate to the students' lives, the teacher should feel free to allow the use of English in certain limited situations.

Figure 5.

Où? Indique si les activités suivantes sont associées à **l'ancienne maison, au nouvel appartement** ou à **tous les deux.**

1. Sonia y jouait au football avec ses frères.
2. Ils y jouaient dans le jardin.
3. Ils y jouaient à l'intérieur.
4. On y a cassé quelques fenêtres.
5. On y utilisait une machine à laver comme but.
6. On y utilisait un bateau comme but.
7. Ils y voyaient leurs grands-parents.

Qu'est-ce qu'on peut en déduire? *(What can you deduce from the following passages?)*

1. «Le seul problème, c'est quand Papy et Mamy venaient: là, il y avait intérêt à rentrer le bateau en vitesse. Heureusement, ils ne viennent pas souvent. Et ils préviennent toujours avant.»
    a. The children didn't like their grandparents.
    b. The grandparents didn't like to visit the children.
    c. The grandparents didn't want the children to go too fast in the boat.
    d. The children didn't always tell their grandparents everything.

□ STAGE 3: DEVELOPING THE CONTENT ORIENTATION (LESS FAMILIAR MATERIAL)

On the academic content side of the model, materials for this stage can be found by looking for topics that are not stressed in American textbooks—for example, history of the target country—or for subjects not usually a major part of the high school curriculum—for example, art history. A relatively easy unit to develop would involve the study of a major artistic movement, such as impressionism. With the help of slides from the art teacher or from the teacher's own collection as well as of the readily available texts written to explain the movement to the general public, the teacher can help students explore the history of the movement as well as some of the artistic and/or technical aspects of that style. In the case of impressionism, students could learn in class about the *Salon des Refusés* and the origin of the term "impressionism"; they could be introduced to some of the main characteristics of impressionist painting (the choice of modern topics, the brush stroke, the use of light); and they could see one or two paintings of each of the most important impressionist painters. The teacher could then have them (working in small groups) do research (using classroom, library, and Internet resources) on an individual painter or theme; they could visit (in person or via the computer) a museum with a collection of works by the impressionists; or they could explore the connections between impressionism and a composer such as Debussy.

On the cultural side of the Stage 3 model, rich subject areas for content include the geography, history, politics, and popular culture of the target country and, in many cases, of other regions where the target language is spoken. Traditionally, student access to this content is often "filtered" through the numerous cultural notes in textbooks and through the anecdotal experiences related in class by the teacher. At this stage, it is possible to put students more directly into contact with the information by using sources designed for (young) people within the culture itself—for example, web sites in the target country or newspapers and magazines published in the target language for young people of that country or region. La francophonie (French-speaking areas of the world) offers a good illustration of such a cultural content unit. The teacher might begin to help students define francophonie by having them read not only official definitions of the term but also interviews with Francophone young people from different countries or regions talking about how they conceive of francophonie. After reviewing the general geography of the Francophone world, the teacher could give students an historical time line that would provide a context for discussions of colonialism and of independence. The in-class segment of the unit could end with the study of one Francophone country. This segment could then serve as a model for group projects as teams of students choose different Francophone countries on which to do research, again using classroom, library, and Internet resources.

At Stage 3, the productive aspects of working with content become even more important. Since students are working with less familiar material, they have the possibility of learning and of communicating more information to their fellow students. In addition, they are now capable of doing research on their own. However, to facilitate working with this more advanced level of content, it is important for students to begin speaking and writing in paragraphs. Students can then create more sophisticated presentations of their topics than those suggested at Stage 2. For example, both academic and cultural content topics lend themselves to more extensive poster sessions: i.e., the posters themselves can contain not only visual aides but also written material in the form of paragraphs, and group members can make short oral presentations of their projects as classmates tour the exhibits getting answers to questions (both their own as well as those provided by the teacher). Again, the unit can end with a content-based test on all of the material studied.

☐ STAGE 4: EXPANDING THE CONTENT ORIENTATION (UNFAMILIAR MATERIAL)

At first glance, Stage 4 would appear simpler to deal with. Although relatively few language students are asked to work with high-level unfamiliar academic content (the major exception being some experiments with foreign languages across the curriculum), most advanced students do come into contact with unfamiliar cultural content, primarily in the form of literature. Traditionally, fourth- and fifth-year high school courses (particularly those in the Advanced Placement Program), as well as post-intermediate college courses, work extensively with "content"—i.e., in particular, literature written in the target language. However, how successful is this traditional form of content-based instruction? Are students (other than the most gifted academically) able to work successfully with literary and cultural texts of increasing sophistication and difficulty? Do schools and colleges offer articulated programs that enable all students to move successfully from course to course and from level to level? One possible answer to these questions (a negative one) is suggested by the graph on the next page that represents a hypothesized representation of the relationship between (a) the way in which most language programs are organized, (b) the expectations that most teachers have, and (c) the real proficiency levels of most students.

The graph reflects the following hypotheses:

1. High school and college language/literature courses are organized in ways that create *sudden jumps* in difficulty level. These jumps are found both in content (the materials students are asked to work with) and in language (including the tasks students are asked to perform). Moreover, these jumps are sometimes greater than $c + 1$ or $l + 1$ and/or they involve both $c + 1$ and $l + 1$ simultaneously. Such an organization reflects the idea that there are distinct and identifiable levels of language learning: i.e., intermediate is different from beginning, etc.

2. Expectation levels of teachers do *not* correspond to the realities of student proficiency. Teachers, unaware of the jump in difficulty, expect steady, uninterrupted progress from one level to another or, if aware of the jump, expect that students somehow can "automatically" make the adjustment (in the same way the teacher may adjust teaching methods in moving from one level to another).

3. As a result of numbers 1 and 2, students, when learning a language, are confronted at regular intervals with major gaps between, on the one hand, their current level of linguistic proficiency and content knowledge and, on the other hand, the high expectations and increased difficulty level of the work they're asked to do. The result is often, at the beginning of each new level, both frustration and a form of "linguistic breakdown" (i.e., the deterioration of already existing skills and content knowledge).

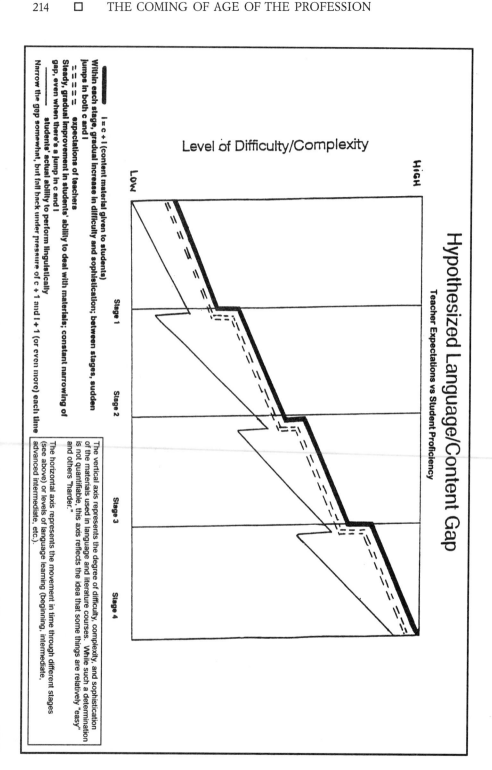

Hypothesized Language/Content Gap

Teacher Expectations vs Student Proficiency

Level of Difficulty/Complexity

l = c + l (content material given to students)

Within each stage, gradual increase in difficulty and sophistication; between stages, sudden jumps in both c and l

= = = = =   expectations of teachers

Steady, gradual improvement in students' ability to deal with materials; constant narrowing of gap, even when there's a jump in c and l

students' actual ability to perform linguistically

Narrow the gap somewhat, but fall back under pressure of c + l and l + l (or even more) each time

The vertical axis represents the degree of difficulty, complexity, and sophistication of the materials used in language and literature courses. While such a determination is not quantifiable, this axis reflects the idea that some things are relatively "easy" and others "harder."

The horizontal axis represents the movement in time through different stages (see above) or levels of language learning (beginning, intermediate, advanced intermediate, etc.).

If these hypotheses are valid, they hold several important implications for teachers. In particular, they offer two *explanations* and a *suggestion*.

1. These hypotheses provide a possible explanation for the complaint frequently heard at *every* level of language teaching (be it high school teachers talking about the middle school program, third-year teachers griping about students completing the second year, college teachers complaining about students from high school, or literature professors criticizing what has gone on in language classes): "The students coming in aren't prepared!" The above hypotheses suggest that these complaints are *not* valid; that students *are* "prepared," in the sense that most of them have progressed through their current stage; that what they are not prepared for is the jump in content and language expectations from one level to the next.

2. These hypotheses also provide a possible explanation for the dramatic drop in enrollment so often experienced from one level to another. The frustration occasioned by the jump in language expectations and content—particularly from first to second year, from beginning to intermediate, from language to literature courses—may well be a major factor in students choosing not to continue their language studies.

3. These hypotheses then suggest that a fundamental challenge for language teachers is to make our *expectations* (sometimes called "high standards") correspond to the linguistic and cultural possibilities of our student—i.e., to find ways to work at $c + 1$ or $l + 1$ (not the two together) in a more continuous progression. Doing this involves rethinking programs and then providing students with the support (information, vocabulary, preparatory activities, specific tasks) that help bridge the gap represented by the $+ 1$.

In conclusion, simply to introduce content into language programs will not automatically lead to the desired outcomes of the National Standards. Content can be used to help teachers reevaluate their programs in order to create a smoother, less frustrating jump from course to course and level to level. To the extent that this is done as set forth in Stages 1 through 3, students will be able to deal better with the unfamiliar content (both academic and cultural) of Stage 4. We believe that the model proposed here will help teachers and students connect language learning to the content of other disciplines and thus render language learning even more meaningful.

REFERENCES

American Council on the Teaching of Foreign Languages (1996). *Standards for Foreign Language Learning: Preparing for the 21st Century*. Yonkers, NY: ACTFL.

Biologie/Cahier d'activités CM2 (1992). Collection Tavernier. Paris: Bordas.

Bragger, J. D., and D. B. Rice (forthcoming). *Branchés... et au courant!* Boston: Heinle & Heinle Publishers.

Brinton, D. M., M. A. Snow, and M. B. Wesche. (1989). *Content-Based Second Language Instruction*. Boston: Heinle & Heinle Publishers.

Corrieu, L. et al. (1990). *Math 6ᵉ*. Paris: Delagrave.

"Guadeloupe, Martinique: Deux Françaises aux Antilles" (1994). *Clés de l'actualité*. Toulouse: Milan Presse.

Joly, F., and C. Besse. (1995). *Fous de foot*. Paris: Casterman.

L'Impressionnisme (1993). Collection Passion des Arts. Paris: Gallimard.

Krashen, S. D. (1985). *The Input Hypothesis: Issues and Implications*. London and NY: Longman.

Lafayette, R. C. (Ed.) (1996). *National Standards: A Catalyst for Reform*. Lincolnwood, IL: National Textbook Company.

Le Corps humain (1991). Collection Du Tac au tac. Paris: Larousse.

Met, M. (1991). "Learning Language through Content: Learning Content through Language." *Foreign Language Annals* 24 No. 4, 281–295.

Prévert, J. (1949). *Paroles*. Paris: Editions Gallimard.

Sciences et Technologie CM (1986). Collection Tavernier. Paris: Bordas.

_____ (1995). Nouvelle Collection Tavernier. Paris: Bordas.

"Vive le rock!," "Quel genre de film?," "Sandrine, seize ans" (1994). *Bonjour*, no. 3.

Widdowson, H. G. (1978). *Teaching Language as Communication*. Oxford: Oxford University Press.

SELECTED BIBLIOGRAPHY

Cantoni-Harvey, G. (1987). *Content-Area Language Instruction*. Reading, MA: Addison-Wesley.

Chamot, A. U., and M. O'Malley. (1994). *The CALLA Handbook: Implementing the Cognitive Academic Language Learning Approach*. Reading, MA: Addison-Wesley.

Crandall, J. (Ed.) (1987). *ESL Through Content-area Instruction: Mathematics, Science, Social Studies*. Englewood Cliff, NJ: Prentice Hall Regents.

Giauque, G. (1987). "Teaching for Content in a Skills Course: Greek Mythology in French." *Foreign Language Annals* 20:6, 565-569.

Iancu, M. (1993). "Adapting the Adjunct Model: A Case Study." *TESOL Journal* 2:4, 20–24.

Kang, H.-W. (1994). "Helping Second Language Readers Learn from Content Area Text through Collaboration and Support." *Journal of Reading* 37:8, 646–651.

Kasper, L. F. (1994). "Improved Reading Performance for ESL Students through Academic Course Pairing." *Journal of Reading* 37:5, 376–383

Leaver, B. L., and S. B. Stryker. (1989). "Content-Based Instruction for Foreign Language Classrooms." *Foreign Language Annals* 22:3, 269–275.

Moeller, A. J. (1994). "Content-Based Foreign Language Instruction in the Middle School: An Experiential Learning Approach." *Foreign Language Annals* 27:4, 535–544.

Mohan, B. A. (1979). "Relating Language Teaching and Content Teaching." *TESOL Quarterly* 13:2, 171–182.

Rosser, C. (1995). "Anne Frank: A Content-Based Research Class." *TESOL Journal* 4:4, 4–6.

Shih, M. (1986). "Content-Based Approaches to Teaching Academic Writing." *TESOL Quarterly* 20:4, 617–648.

Snow, M. A., and D. M. Brinton. (1988). "Content-Based Language Instruction: Investigating the Effectiveness of the Adjunct Model." *TESOL Quarterly* 22:4, 553–574.

Snow, M. A., M. Met, and F. Genesee. (1989). "A Conceptual Framework for the Integration of Language and Content in Second/Foreign Language Instruction." *TESOL Quarterly* 23:2, 201–217.

Creating Interactive Hypertext in German

Michael Geisler and Linnéa McArt, *Middlebury College*

Michael Geisler has been chair of the German Department at Middlebury College since 1992. His teaching and research interests include German language at all levels, German Studies, mass media, and studies in humanities and technology. He has published a book on literary journalism in Germany and a number of articles on topics relating to all of the areas mentioned above. Recent work includes an article on the depiction of Germans on U.S. television and a survey of German media theory. He is currently coediting a special issue of New German Critique *on contemporary German media and working on an interactive CD-ROM on the problem of German identity. His favorite authors, in the context of this article, are Walter Benjamin, Claire Kramsch, Roger Schank, and Benedict Anderson.*

======= ||| =======

Linnéa McArt is a recent graduate of Middlebury College, where she majored in Russian and Eastern European Studies while completing a minor in German. She also spent a year studying at the State University of Kazan, Russia; she plans to pursue a career in the social sciences.

NB. The following is a fairly conversational account of an experimental "collaborative learning" project I taught at Middlebury College during the spring of 1994. Since my professional background is in German media and cultural studies rather than in applied linguistics or the technology of language acquisition I have decided, in presenting the material below, to stick to a more reportage-like, narrative account, rather than writing a scholarly article in a discipline with which I have only a superficial acquaintance so far. However, over the course of various Mellon Workshops at Middlebury College, this project has been received with so much interest by colleagues from other institutions that I thought it worthwhile to report on the project (and its progress since then) in writing. In keeping with the original design of the course, I have asked Linnéa McArt, the only participant in the original seminar who is still at Middlebury College, to write up a separate report from her perspective.

Michael Geisler

In the spring of 1994 I taught a senior seminar at Middlebury entitled "Creating Interactive Hypertext in German." Nine students enrolled, one dropped the course early on (when he saw what was going to hit him!). Twelve weeks and countless sleepless nights later we presented our collaborative effort to an audience of colleagues and administrators: an interactive program of linguistic, literary, as well as social and cultural annotations to accompany Heinrich Böll's novel *Die verlorene Ehre der Katharina Blum* (*The Lost Honor of Katharina Blum*).[1] Going into this project, neither I nor most of the students taking the course had any significant experience with CAI (Computer Assisted Instruction) other than basic word processing skills.

WHY DID I PUT MYSELF (AND THE STUDENTS) THROUGH THIS?

On my part, the answer has to do with my dissatisfaction with existing "interactive" programs dating back to an experience I had as a young assistant professor at M.I.T. when I attended an early demonstration on CAI. After a generous amount of enthusiastic technobabble, the person demonstrating this breakthrough in modern language pedagogy revealed a program that enabled the student to play "Hangman." Since then, I have too often found that interactive technology, when applied to the classroom, put the cart before the horse, i.e., it satisfied needs that nobody had felt before. Filling in blanks on grammar exercises or building vocabulary lists are all things that can be done equally well on paper or in lab manuals—the computer may render these activities glitzier (and that is a point to be made in favor of such programs), but it does not really contribute anything new.

NEW TECHNOLOGIES

> "... *random access* ... (T)he possibility of putting in the student's hands an interface that enables him or her to create his or her **own individual encounter with a text,** with the program still supplying large amounts of information."

It was not until the advent of user-friendly Hypercard applications that the computer presented teachers with a real advance in technology. The difference between these and earlier programs is the potential for *random access*, i.e., the possibility of putting in the student's hands an interface that enables him or her to create his or her own individual encounter with a text, with the program still supplying large amounts of information. To put it in the most radical terms possible: new technologies are only as good as the medium-specific uses they allow us to make of them. The medium-specific use of the computer lies in its ability to provide significant amounts of information in nonsequential form. In other words the computer approximates parallel processing, whereas the print medium is based on a sequential, hierarchical epistemology.[2] In practical terms this means that an interactive computer program permits the user to maneuver through a text by following the map charted by his or her innate curiosity (unless pedagogical concerns suggest certain parameters). Some students may be more interested in literary intertext (themes, motifs, allusions to other works, etc.), some may be more fascinated by the social, cultural, or historic subtext of the work. All, presumably, would profit from a glossary.

> ". . . (**New technologies**) are only as good as the medium-specific uses they allow us to make of them. The medium-specific use of the computer lies in its ability **to provide significant amounts of information in nonsequential form**. . . "

Guided Reading, an interactive hypercard-based program developed by David Herren at Middlebury College is a user-friendly template both for instructors of language (or literature/culture) interested in creating their own annotated version of existing authentic texts and for their students who later work with these materials. Despite my inexperience in dealing with advanced computer applications and Hypercard, I could instantly see the possibilities this template opened for me. Precisely because of its gradual learning curve this program made it possible not just for me to quickly create my own hypertext version of a German text, but I could actually expect my students to learn the basic steps necessary for mastering the "instructor mode" of this program fast enough to make it conceivable to *collaborate* with them on this project over the limited time period of one twelve-week semester, i.e. to teach a class that would focus on the cooperative production of a common project.

PROJECT-ORIENTED LEARNING

I have always been convinced that "collaborative learning," or, as I like to call it with a slightly different inflection, "project-oriented learning,"[3] is the most exciting and the most challenging enterprise on which we can embark with our students. How much enthusiasm can we reasonably expect our students to muster for papers that they and we both know will be read once or twice by student and instructor and which then disappear in some desk drawer where they gather dust until we finally gather up enough courage to simply throw them out?

By contrast, the products of project-oriented classes, while by no means professional or ready to print, are usually sufficiently interesting to be presented and/or used by a group of people, whether it be through a theatrical performance (in the case of drama workshops), in-house presentations (skits, video documentaries etc.), or lower-level language classes, as was the case with our project on *Die verlorene Ehre der Katharina Blum*.

While it is true that one of the motivations in setting up this experimental seminar was the fact that no complete annotated edition of this quintessential German novel of the '70s exists in print, and that I thought that a group of students might be in the best position to provide future classes with some help in this area, it is nevertheless very important to understand that I embarked on this venture from the vantage point of "project-oriented (or collaborative) learning." Strictly speaking, the project had come to its completion as soon as a viable interactive text had been created by the eight participants in the senior seminar. Demonstrating the project to others and actually using it in the classroom was only a potential, secondary goal.

Students were divided into three different focus groups. Group One concentrated on the social/political intertext of Böll's novel, i.e., terrorism in Germany, the Baader-Meinhof Group, and the controversial practices of the BILD-Zeitung (the German equivalent of a cross between the *National Inquirer* and a Hearst paper, i.e., both hyper-sensationalist *and* on the extreme right politically). Group Two focused on the literary and intertextual resonances of the novel—Böll's *vita*, major related works, recurring themes and tropes, and stylistic questions. Group Three worked on a large number of what we referred to as "smaller cultural issues" necessary to understanding the novel, e.g., apartment living and social vs. private space in Germany, the German educational system, etc. In other words, Group One provided the macro background and Group Three the micro background in terms of cultural semiotics. As it turned out, Group Three was by far the most creative, exhaustive one: there are very few cultural signifiers on the level of the "micro" context that are not addressed in some way in the annotations.

GLOSSES AND CULTURAL ANNOTATIONS

All of us together, including myself, worked on the linguistic annotations (i.e., the glossary). This was rather an exhaustive process of first excerpting the entire vocabulary with the help of the Guided Reading program, then determining which vocabulary items *not* to gloss (because we assumed a second-year level basic familiarity with German), and finally deciding *how* to list forms such as separable verbs, plural forms, declined cases, etc. However, that was one of the most interesting, truly collaborative aspects of teaching this seminar, with students voicing their own creative ideas, quite a few of which were accepted over David's and my original suggestions because the students were better able to see the problem from an end-user perspective. There were also some pedagogical problems relating to the template itself: e.g., how to establish different *types* of links (glosses and cultural annotations) for the same word (answer: double-click vs. drag). Similarly, David Herren and I engaged in a running discussion on how to flag cultural annotations for students. Ironically, David, the "Techie" (with a strong background in Spanish language and literature), insisted that we not mark up the text in any way not intended by the author, while I, as the person coming from the discipline, felt an overriding practical concern: since, despite tremendous efforts by the students, the number of words sensitized for cultural annotations would be relatively small compared to the overall text of the novel (as opposed to the fairly comprehensive glossary), I wanted to avoid unneccessary frustration that might set in if students were to repeatedly click "blindly" on words for an annotation only to find that none existed. Ultimately, I prevailed in that argument even in the face of David's urgent protestations regarding the sanctity of the literary text: We bolded the sensitized words.

LITERARY THEORY

The course itself focused on a tripartite approach:

1. a very close rereading of the novel by the participants;

2. a survey of various literary theories brought to bear on the novel;[4]

3. the actual creation of the interactive program.

The three student groups then went off to do research on their own, and for the last half of the class I met several times a week with the individual groups rather than with the class as a whole. Students would write up their materials (including some scanned-in images) and deposit them on an electronic server where I went over each document, marked problematic passages in bold, or corrected problems that I felt they could not handle in italics. The bolded passages had to be corrected and redeposited by the students, so that each document was written and rewritten about two to four different times. Students also used the server to exchange documents with each other. (Warning: Like most technology-oriented courses, this is a challenging and interesting but very preparation-intensive type of endeavor!)

For me as the instructor, the most gratifying aspects of the course were the lengths to which some (obviously not all) students went to ferret out information for their respective areas. One woman even e-mailed her father in Germany to get a recipe for an Alsatian paté that was mentioned somewhere in the novel. (She got it!) However, I think students were skeptical about the actual usefulness of the project until they saw it coming together. At that point they got very excited and began to develop a sense of ownership. By the time we demonstrated the program to the Middlebury faculty and administration they were quite proud of what they had accomplished.

I am happy to report that we have since "road tested" the program in last year's German 202 class and that it passed with flying colors. With one exception, all the students in that class mentioned in their evaluations that the program had been extremely useful to them, with several of the respondents stressing the fact that they could not have gotten through the novel without it. The one dissenting voice also stated that he or she had never used the program. We are currently planning to use it again in the spring of 1997. What is more, at a recent curricular retreat, the German Department decided that we would use this model as a template for our capstone seminar, working with our seniors to create another annotated, interactive version of an important German text each year. If all goes well, in ten or twenty years we will have a small "Middlebury" library of student-annotated, authentic German texts to be used by future students in their class preparation. We are also looking into the possibility of making this part of a portfolio for each participant.

=========== ||| ===========

For myself, teaching this course was also a good way of overcoming my own subliminal technophobia. Guided Reading is so easy to learn that the instructor may focus on the logistics and methodologies of the *project* rather than on the pitfalls of the template he or she is using. For me, it was an incentive to try something more ambitious. Thanks to generous financial support from the Mellon Foundation, I am now working with my colleague Robert Smitheram on a new, somewhat more complex endeavor: an interactive CD-ROM on Germany's search for identity. The major difference between this project and the *Katharina Blum* program is that instead of working with a given text and just adding the annotation to it we are creating a complex Web-like *texture* of materials drawn from different discourses. The new template being created for this purpose will be entirely learner-centered. It will enable students to navigate the historical, ideological, and cultural discourses informing Germany's tortuous search for both a "usable past" and a present identity completely at their own pace, level of complexity, and personal interest, jumping from one link to a related issue in a different "subplot" of the German national narrative very much as they might on the World Wide Web. The idea is, as with Guided Reading, to create a template that can be used by different instructors working with different cultural or linguistic materials, but for similar methodological purposes. However, for those interested in providing annotations to existing texts Guided Reading would still be the most appropriate program.

The obvious limitations of this model lie in the fact that we cannot distribute our product, much as we would like to. Since the *Katharina Blum* project has been showcased at a number of consecutive Mellon Workshops here at Middlebury College, both David and I have received a number of inquiries asking us to share this program with colleagues at other institutions. Each time, we had to regretfully decline such requests, not because we would not have been happy to share it (even though it must always be kept in mind that the original focus of the seminar was the *process* rather then the *product*) but because of copyright restrictions. Since the project necessarily involved scanning the entire text of the novel so as to provide a platform for the annotations, I had to make a decision early on whether I would want to request copyright permission from the publisher for multiple usage of the program or go with the provisions of the fair-use act which would limit utilization of the scanned material to classroom and demonstration purposes.[5] Since I was working with non-professionals, and thus could not expect a marketable product, I decided to stick with the more restricted usage (a decision I have since come to regret). However, it is only the product that cannot be shared, whereas the Guided Reading template may be made available to others under certain conditions, so that the *process* may easily be duplicated at any institution with a strong undergraduate program in German.

I would like to conclude by listing the names of the students who collaborated on this project, for in the final analysis it is *their* project rather than mine. In alphabetical order, they are: Robert Curr ('95), Theodore Dolan ('94), George Elsener ('94), Susanne Horn ('96), Derek Lounsbury ('94), Linnéa McArt ('97), Robert Merrill ('94), and Stephen Pettibone ('95).

═══════ ||| ═══════

Linnéa McArt, *Russian Major/German Minor, Middlebury '97*

To preface what I have written, I should note that when I took the Creating Interactive Text course, my knowledge of the German language was on a third/fourth-year level, although I myself was a first-year student. For this reason I am the only student from our class who has had the chance to observe the success of our program. I consider the program to have been a success based on the results that are to this day achieved in classes in which it is used, as well as on the personal benefit I received in helping to create it.

I enrolled in the course, "Creating Interactive Text in German," with the expectation that it would provide me with not only a solid fourth-year level exposure to German literature but also introduce me to interactive computing technology. The novel idea of creating something new based on our regular discussions in class appealed to me. Instead of losing our in-class generated ideas to sheets of notebook paper, forever to be forgotten once the semester ended, our ideas would resurface over and over again in second-year classes, providing an insight into the reading that would serve as an informative "shooting-off point." My previous exposure to computer projects was very limited, therefore the idea of increasing my computer awareness, with my graduation day already in the back of my mind, appealed to me. The concept of being a proactive part of the creative process was a refreshing break from the routine first-year level courses I had taken.

Our class was divided into small groups of three students in order to thoroughly process as much information as we could within the short time-period of one academic semester. Each group was assigned a set of topics related to *Die Verlorene Ehre der Katharina Blum*, which they were to research, present to the class, and finally add to the computer program. My group was assigned the historical background to the novel; the Baader-Meinhof Group, terrorism, the *Bild* newspaper, the movement of Baader-Meinhof sympathizers and any relevant maps or historical pictures and films we might deem important in understanding the plot. Although the group initially consisted of three students, I eventually had to finish the project on my own, since one of my partners dropped the course and the other had to leave in order to attend to personal matters. He did however continue to contribute while absent from the college. This obviously generated some extra work and some logistical problems, but the bulk of the assignment was still successfully completed.

I was able to find some information about the Baader-Meinhof Group in our college library, but I also wrote to the *Bild-Zeitung* newspaper in Germany and attempted to use Library of Congress microfilm to locate articles and press clips. The information from *Bild-Zeitung* was eventually received, but only after the course had been completed. The limiting semester time-block interfered with the quality of the program in this case but only because the information was sent for too late. Had we realized that the information would be valuable to the course earlier in the semester, the problem could have been avoided.

We decided that it would be interesting to know the personality traits and histories of the individuals involved with the Baader-Meinhof Group rather than just the activities of the group as a whole. This proved to be not only interesting but pertinent to understanding the novel better. We also realized that we would have to write the backgrounds or provide a vocabulary list in simplified German, so that the second-year reader would understand it.

Vocabulary lists, in general, were a tedious but necessary task in developing the program. We were each given a list of words, a word-by-word list taken directly from the text, from which we were to isolate words that might challenge the second-year reader and define them. The definitions were to be written in English in order to avoid any further confusion. Verbs were put into their principle tense and all parts of them were given separately. For example, *versteht sich*, as it stands in the text really comes from the German verb *sich verstehen*. We had to determine how we would list this verb and other examples accordingly. It was also necessary to explain all of the hyphenations in the text, used frequently in the German language. Building the vocabulary lists became a true exercise in German grammar!

Along with the book-specific topics, we were given literary topics to be discussed in class. I made an oral presentation to the class about rhetoric and inter-textuality. Others tackled topics such as psychoanalysis, historicism, deconstructivism, and Socialist and Marxist analyses. These all applied directly to the course and proved very valuable to our understanding of the book, although they were not used in the eventual computer program.

Another valuable aid in understanding and getting a better feel for the text was watching a film that was based on Heinrich Böll's book. With the help of our computer assistant, David Herren, we were able to edit segments of the film into the hypertext program. The animated segments proved to be eye-catching and of high interest to students using the program.

I was surprised by the relative manageability of scanning the text and working through the hypertext program within the one-semester time frame. I did not expect that the program would reach such an advanced level so quickly. With help from our computer assistant and the continued interest of our professor, Michael Geisler, the program was completed to the extent that it could be used by students in other classes. As with every text, I am sure, a lifetime could have been devoted to explaining the historical and cultural background to the book, but within just one semester we were able to adequately cover the essentials. We provided users with enough encyclopedic and lexical information to understand the text.

In reading the book originally, we were to pick out sections, phrases, or words in the text that an uninformed second-year level student might have difficulty understanding without the assistance of reference material or research. This made reading the book especially challenging because we had to think like teachers rather than students. Even the concepts that we already understood became a challenge, since we had to convey our understanding to a specific audience. This process of absolute understanding rather than mere comprehension caused our appreciation of the text to extend far deeper than it would have in an average literary course.

The primary benefit I received from the course was a complete comprehensive knowledge of one book and its contextual, historical, and cultural background. The added benefits included exposure to computer programming through hypertext and the chance to think like a teacher instead of a student for a whole semester. I carry both of these side-benefits with me now as I embark on my career search.

It has been especially interesting to have had the chance to observe the effects of the program our class created. It has contributed to the strength of not only our German Department but to the college as a whole. Professor Geisler has been called upon to demonstrate the program for various groups at the college, including faculty interested in creating such programs of their own with their classes. Some of my classmates have had the opportunity to use the program and benefited directly from something that I helped create! It is definitely an exciting program, due to its continuing contribution to the college. It is nice to have helped create something tangible rather than just a notebook to be thrown away at the end of the semester. For this reason I highly recommend that all educational facilitators try such a project!

NOTES

1.   Heinrich Böll. *Die verlorene Ehre der Katharina Blum*. Cologne: Kiepenheuer & Witsch, 1974.

2.   Strictly speaking, that's a sleight of hand, of course. It is ironical that media theorists are picking up on the different epistemological implications of the two media at the very moment when scientists working in the field of Artificial Intelligence are searching for ways to get around the computer's own sequential limitations by experimenting with neural networks. However, for humans, the computer's speed creates at least virtual simultaneity, if not the real thing. The cinematic effect may be a useful metaphor here: just as persistence of vision renders the fact that we are only dealing with a large number of still pictures gliding by at the rate of 32 frames per second a purely academic concern, so the

far higher speed of the computer's integrated circuits create not just the illusion, but, from an anthropomorphic point of view, the practical reality of simultaneous processing.

For an interesting theoretical discussion of this problem, see Norbert Bolz *Am Ende der Gutenberg-Galaxis* (Munich: Fink, 1993), or his far more accessible (if slightly patronizing) *Das kontrollierte Chaos* (Düsseldorf: Econ, 1994). Unfortunately, neither book has been translated into English so far.

3. There is a slight semantic difference between the two in that I like to emphasize the creation of a tangible project as a partial goal of such a course.

4. This was meant as the "capstone" part of the seminar, but it flopped because the students, as I found out only after I had started into the course, had never been exposed to literary theory before and had a very hard time with this. Most of the students taking the course were seniors who had started at Middlebury before I had taken over as chairman of the department. I had not been at Middlebury long enough to realize that theory was very much underrepresented in the Middlebury curriculum. This has changed since then.

5. The legal advice I got was that I could scan in *one* copy of the text to be used at one work station or server for the purposes of classroom-related work only, provided that I also owned a hard copy of the text and each student was required to purchase one as well. Students were explicitly warned that copying the scanned text might constitute a copyright violation.

REFERENCES

Bolz, Norbert. *Am Ende der Gutenberg-Galaxis*. Munich: Fink, 1993.

_____. *Das kontrollierte Chaos*. Düsseldorf: Econ, 1994.

Böll, Heinrich. *Die verlorene Ehre der Katharina Blum*. Cologne: Kiepenheuer & Witsch, 1974.

APPENDIX

To give the reader an idea of what the program looks like, we have included a few sample pages as they would look when students are working with the program. Please keep in mind that all texts, except for the selections from the novel of course, are entirely student-generated with minimal editorial or stylistic interference from the instructor!

 File   Edit   Font   Style   Student   12:45 PM ② ◆

K. Blum 2.3

Pre-Reading

Rote-Armee-Fraktion (Die Baader-Meinhof Gruppe)

Den Hintergrund für Bölls Erzählung Die Verlorene Ehre der Katharina Blum bildet eine Welle von terroristischen Anschlägen (*attacks*), die damals die Bürger der Bundesrepublik Deutschland in Angst versetzten und auf die die Polizei mit sehr harten Maßnahmen (*measures*) reagierte. Hinter den meisten dieser Anschläge stand eine kleine Gruppe von linksradikalen Terroristen, die nach ihren bekanntesten Mitgliedern die "Baader-Meinhof-Gruppe" genannt wurde. Die Angst vor den Anschlägen selbst war damals in Deutschland genauso groß wie die Angst, zu den "Sympathisanten" (*sympathizers, supporters*) der Gruppe gezählt zu werden.

Wie kam es zur Bildung der Baader-Meinhof-Gruppe? Die deutsche Regierung behauptete, daß Amerika Deutschland nach dem zweiten Weltkrieg geholfen hätte und daß die Deutschen deswegen Amerika im Vietnam-Krieg unterstützen sollten. Das wollten die Studenten aber nicht. Es gab eine ganze Bewegung von Studenten in Amerika (*the lost generation, hippies*), die als Vorbild für deutsche Studenten galt. Im Mittelpunkt der Ablehnung stand die bedrohliche Möglichkeit der atomaren Selbstzerstörung, die anti-kommunistische Hexenjagd der McCarthy Ära, die Konsumideologie, Profitgier und Eigennutz (Aust 37). Als

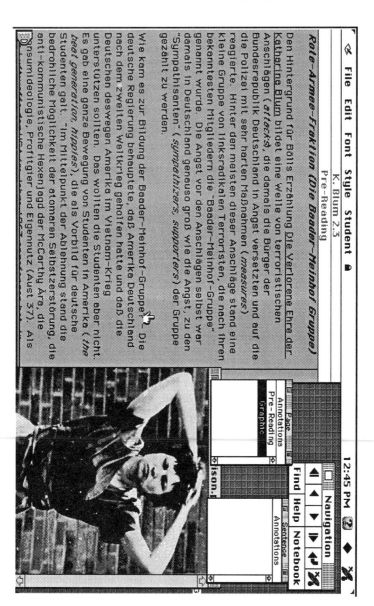

Page   Sentence
Annotations   Annotations
Pre-Reading
Graphic

Navigation   ◀ ▲ ▼ ▶

Find   Help   Notebook

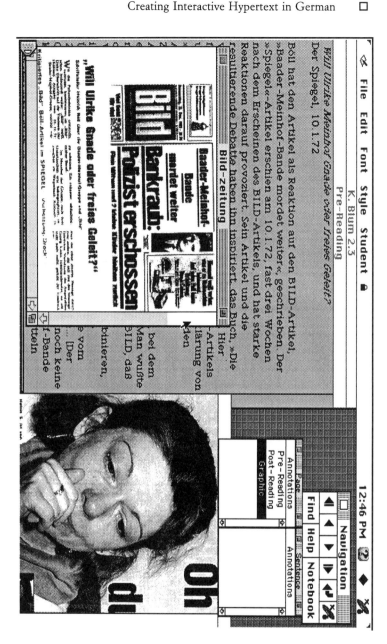

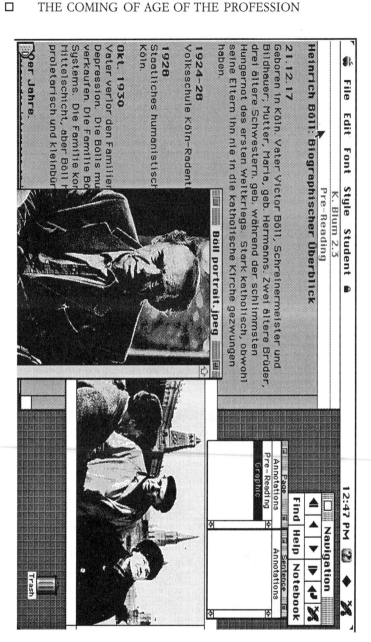

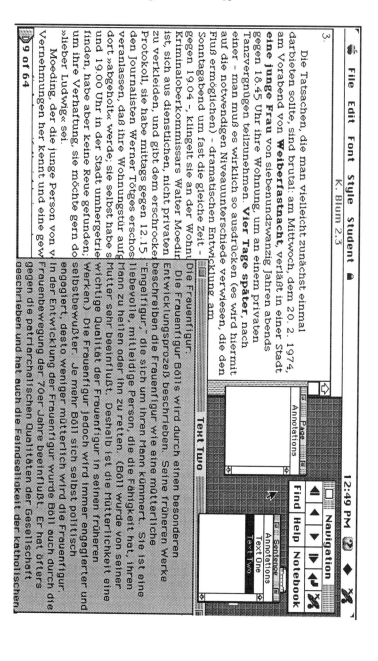

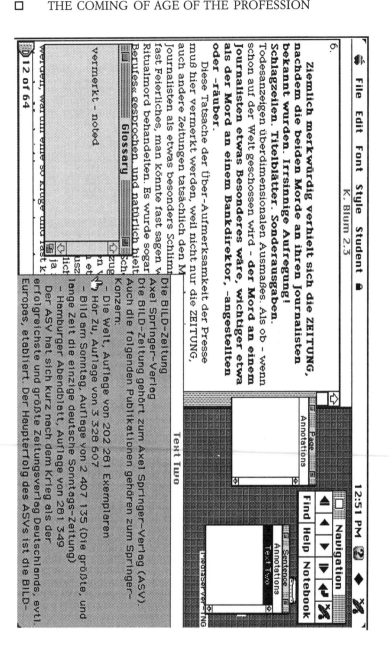

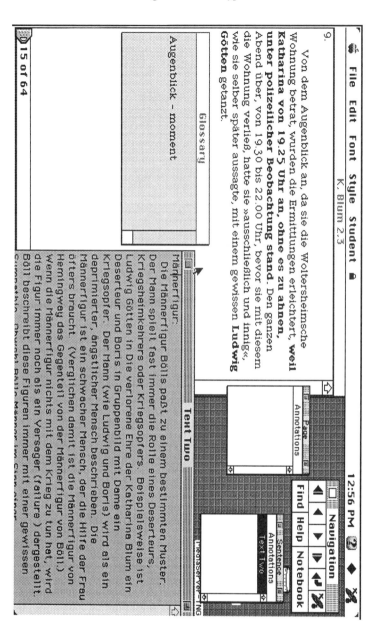

Thinking Workshops: Developing New Skills for a Changing World

Frederick Toner, *Ohio University*

Frederick Toner is coordinator of first-year French at Ohio University. Among his responsibilities are training and supervising the graduate student teaching associates. He teaches courses on foreign language methodology, as well as on French language, culture, and literature. He is the coauthor, with Katherine Kulick, of the intermediate French composition text Notez bien! Les contextes de l'écriture. *Research interests include developing critical thinking skills in a foreign language, developing writing proficiency, the interrelationship of the arts, and French for special purposes. Counted among Toner's favorite authors are Jeannette Bragger, Claire Kramsch, Robert Lafayette, Donald Rice, and . . . Stendhal.*

INTRODUCTION

The importance of critical thinking skills for effective teaching and learning is commonly accepted and well documented. This is generally true across the curriculum and is certainly the case in foreign language education. The "ACTFL Provisional Program Guidelines for Foreign Language Teacher Education" call for teachers to choose courses that emphasize the development of critical thinking skills (p. 73) and the "Professional Standards for Teachers of Foreign Languages" prepared by the AATF and AATG stress the urgency of developing such skills (p. 2):

> The United States is embarked on concerted efforts to prepare students for productive and rewarding lives in the global community of the 21st century. In order to function in that enlarged and ever-changing environment, students need to be able to reason and think critically and creatively.

The question is not should we be teaching and developing critical thinking, but rather the question is "how?" It is rare that foreign language teachers have any formal training in teaching critical thinking. In otherwise excellent books on teaching foreign languages, such as those by Shrum and Glisan or Omaggio Hadley, critical thinking is mentioned only tangentially and does not merit a listing in the index. Very few models

237

exist which systematically incorporate the teaching of critical thinking skills into the foreign language curriculum and fewer still offer any statistical proof of their efficacy. Some interesting models do exist, however, outside of our discipline, some of them a result of intense public and private pressure.

The demands of a new work environment have intensified the call for effective ways to develop critical thinking skills. The effort by many American and European companies to become ever more competitive by downsizing and reorganizing the workforce has created enormous social pressures. Workers who had been secure in their positions now find themselves looking for employment. The positions that are open often require the worker to attend to a wide range of responsibilities, make decisions, and activate higher order thinking skills. Workers who have "fossilized" in traditional jobs are rarely qualified for the demands of the new work environment. To complicate matters, potential employers periodically voice the opinion that recent graduates just entering the workforce are ill-prepared and are without the basic skills needed to do the job well. The need for qualified workers and the general disappointment expressed concerning the educational system have led various sectors of society to propose models designed to retrain the workforce and to develop critical thinkers.

> "Given **the intimate link between language and thinking,** any program which can improve thinking skills holds promise to improve language skills as well."

One such program in France, *les Ateliers de Raisonnement Logique*[1] (ARL), has inspired a great deal of interest. This article will investigate in some detail what we may learn from the ARL and how the ARL may be adapted to the foreign language classroom. The model of the ARL is of interest to language teachers for several reasons. Given the intimate link between language and thinking, any program which can improve thinking skills holds promise to improve language skills as well. As Chaffee explains, ". . . the process of using language generates ideas, and the language we (or others) use shapes and influences our thinking. In short, the development and use of our thinking abilities is closely tied to the development and use of our language abilities—and vice versa" (p. 294). Moreover, the situation of a worker being trained for a new job is somewhat analogous to that of a student studying a foreign language. In the new work environment and in the foreign language classroom, the learners find themselves operating at a much lower level of effectiveness than in any other area of their lives. Workers and students lack the basic skills to function well, they lack the vocabulary or terminology needed to express themselves in the new domain, and as a result they find their thinking short-circuited. In both cases the learner must acquire new skills and also transfer already-developed skills to a new content area.

THE MODEL: ATELIERS DE RAISONNEMENT LOGIQUE

Encouraged by powers in the business world, leaders in adult education, and members of the French government, Pierre Higelé and his colleagues in Nancy developed "tools of cognitive remediation," which are called into play and developed in a workshop setting (*atelier*). The ARL were first introduced in 1982 to retrain steel and iron workers in eastern France who had lost their jobs. Having met with some success with adult learners, the methods were adapted to a school setting six years later, primarily in the middle school grades, for students who were experiencing difficulties in their regular classes. The ARL are designed to make the students more aware of how they think and to help them to learn how to learn (Giry, 59). The focus of each lesson, in which students are called upon to understand, to solve, and to explain the solution of a written problem, is the *process* of problem solving, not the result. For each problem, the *formateur*—a kind of "enabler" or "facilitator"—leads the students in a three-tiered process which obviously draws its inspiration from computer science: Input, Processing (*traitement des données*), and Output. Each phase of the workshop will be discussed below.

APPLICATIONS OF THE ARL TO THE FOREIGN LANGUAGE CLASSROOM

There are several obstacles that would make implementation of the unmodified model into the foreign language classroom difficult. These obstacles have to do primarily with the availability of resources. Few school districts have the luxury of offering classes to five or a maximum of six students, as is the case in the model. Assuming funding and space could be secured, finding time for the workshops in an already crowded curriculum poses another problem. In addition to these obstacles, there is the matter of teaching materials. The ARL offer a wealth of generic materials for both students and teacher, but these materials are not readily available outside of France. The lessons of the ARL are carefully sequenced, using Piaget's Theory of Cognitive Development and its four basic stages[2] as a guide to the order and the focus of the exercises. In the absence of these materials, teachers would have to create their own problem situations without the benefit of extensive training in the field.

It is the method and the procedures suggested by the authors of the ARL, however, that are of most interest to language educators. These procedures can be adapted to function in other formats, and it is quite possible to implement a version of the ARL into the existing structure of the foreign language classroom without great difficulty. While some of the intimacy of the workshop format would necessarily be lost, the basic tenets of the ARL would hold true in sessions involving the whole class, just as they do in the original setting. Introducing the modified ARL would no doubt require planning and thought on the part of the teacher, but the "thinking workshops" should not further burden the curriculum. As already mentioned, thinking and language are intricately connected and improvement in thinking should lead to improved communication skills. Reading, writing, speaking, and listening are all part of the process of problem solving as outlined in the ARL.

As for the teaching materials, the exercises used in the ARL model are short and could be fashioned by the teacher with a minimum of effort. Furthermore, the materials could be designed to incorporate vocabulary and structures currently being studied in the classroom as well as to recycle previously learned material. If the teacher-created problems reflect the interests and concerns of the students, an argument could be made that these materials could be more effective for language production than the more generic materials produced by the authors of the ARL. Although it would be comforting to know that specialists in the field of cognitive development had designed the sequencing of the targeted skills, as is the case in the ARL, there are a number of researchers (Sadler; Marzano) who espouse a holistic rather than a sequential or hierarchical approach to cognitive training. The exact ordering of the exercises would then be of less importance, since "skills or processes interact in such a highly complex way as to be indefinable in a linear fashion" (Marzano, 7). In any case, the motivational and practical value of using problems that relate to student interests and to the target culture may outweigh the importance of precise sequencing.

Regular and sustained practice is essential to developing thinking skills. Therefore, it is suggested that the workshop sessions be scheduled at regular intervals, at least once or twice per week. The tripartite form of the ARL model offers some flexibility, since it is possible to interrupt the process and to partition the work on a given problem over two or three class periods. The teacher could thus decide to dedicate ten minutes a day over three days to problem solving, for instance, rather than spending one entire class period.

> "Regular and sustained practice is **essential** to developing thinking skills."

The students should be aware that the focus of the workshop is thinking. Although they will still be practicing the four skills, ideally in culturally authentic contexts, the focus has shifted and students should be able to sense the difference. The workshop sessions should stand apart from "normal" classroom routine and offer the students a change of pace. Critical thinking is an essential tool for the students' future success and is thus serious business, but teachers should also convey the fact that problem solving can be fun and useful. By emphasizing the fact that students will be practicing thinking, the teacher is able to link the language classroom to the work students are doing in other disciplines and reinforce the utility of the language. Selecting a title for the sessions that contains a descriptive term such as "thinking," "reasoning," or "problem solving," will remind the students of the focus. The positive attitude and the cheerful inquisitiveness of the teacher in the workshops will do much to foster the same dispositions in the students.[3]

CREATING TEACHING MATERIALS

The problem situation should reflect the linguistic level of the students and should elicit discussion that can be accomplished using known structures. The problem-solving workshops are easiest to implement at the intermediate or advanced level where the students' proficiency in the language enables the teacher to focus attention more easily on the thinking process. However, the workshop format can also be effective in lower-level classes if there is proper planning. At all levels, teachers will want to recycle previously learned material and link it to new vocabulary and structures. The problem situation is a good way to introduce new vocabulary, since meaning is often clear from the context. In all cases, care should be taken to think through what skills and strategies are necessary to solve the problem before presenting it to the students. This preparation will help the teacher to focus the students' attention on the process of problem solving and will facilitate the generalizing or formalizing of the strategy in the output phase.

The following three sample problem situations were written for students at the novice-mid or novice-high level on the ACTFL scale of speaking proficiency. The first is designed to use food vocabulary and practice the skill of ordering and comparing. The second reviews professions and adjectives describing character traits and practices combining. The third deals with modes of transportation and requires the skill of classifying.

(A) You want to sample a number of French cheeses and one of your friends suggests that you taste the mildest first and the strongest last. This advice meets with the approval of others at the table who offer the following opinions:

♦ Cantal is milder than Saint-Nectaire.

♦ Saint-Nectaire is stronger than Brie.

♦ Brie is milder than Cantal.

♦ Cantal is milder than Roquefort.

♦ Roquefort is stronger than Saint-Nectaire.

In what order will you taste the cheeses?

(B) You are helping a friend decide where people should sit at a dinner party. There are six guests and your friend would like to alternate men and women. Friends have given you the following descriptions of the people invited:

♦ Juan is a bank inspector. He is very organized and rather quiet. He doesn't like to talk about himself. He is very involved in politics.

♦ Pablo is a soccer coach. He is athletic and loves to talk about sports. He is a voracious reader but doesn't much like films.

♦ Carlos is a dentist. He is very knowledgeable about famous actors and actresses but has no interest in politics.

♦ María is a journalist. She is inquisitive and not at all shy. She isn't interested in sports but loves the theater and the movies.

♦ Teresa is a doctor. She is kind and a good listener. She doesn't like to be around smokers. She exercises daily at a fitness center.

♦ Isabel is a lawyer. She is relaxed and confident and is a trusted advisor of the mayor.

(a) How many combinations are possible? (b) How will you pair the dinner guests?

(C) It is 10:25 A.M. and you have an appointment with the hairstylist at 10:40. You have 45 Marks and you need 40 Marks for the stylist. It takes a half hour to walk to the stylist's. On the bus, which leaves in 5 minutes, it takes 20 minutes and costs 2 Marks. A taxi would take 10 minutes and cost 15 or 16 Marks. On the subway, it costs 2 Marks and it takes 15 minutes.

(a) How many options do you have for going to the stylist? (b) What are your options for returning from the stylist?

SAMPLE ACTIVITIES FOR THE THREE PHASES

☐ INPUT

In the input phase, the teacher makes sure that the problem will be at an appropriate level. Before distributing the problem, the teacher facilitates the task by highlighting vocabulary and structures necessary for comprehension. Traditional pre-reading activities such as brainstorming are useful in linking the problem situation and the language which expresses it to the students' experiences. Brainstorming can also provide good practice in categorizing and classifying if students are asked to regroup or reorganize the results of their brainstorming. For instance, if students are asked to brainstorm modes of public transportation, they could be asked to regroup their answers by speed, cost, comfort, etc. These are good organizational skills that will be useful in the processing phase of the workshop.

The teacher may also present exercises which combine vocabulary-building with logical thinking as a way both to prepare the comprehension of the problem and to practice problem-solving skills. Students can be asked to select the item that does not "fit" in a list of words and to explain why. For instance, as a review of food vocabulary and in preparation for problem situation (A), we could group "cheese, butter, cream, yogurt" (three are solids, one a liquid) or "brie, camembert, cheese, Pont-L'Évêque." ("Cheese" is the category, the others are examples of the category.) Another possibility is to ask students to find the logical link or the common element in a group of words. For situation (B), students could find the category for the following items, "banker, lawyer, doctor, coach" (all are professions) or "shy, talkative, inquisitive, patient" (all are personality traits).[4]

Questions specific to the context can tie the problem situation to the students' experiences and smooth the way to comprehension. By high-lighting the fact that the vocabulary can be useful in talking about what is important to the students, the teacher can also build motivation for learning. The same purpose is served by proposing a "Find someone who . . ." activity, where students interview their classmates to find someone who "eats a lot of dairy products," "would like to be a lawyer," or "takes the bus more than twice a week." The students could also be asked to invent questions on a topic and interview their partners, or to take a poll and report their results.

Personal questions can also be used to "warm up" the thinking apparatus and to practice formulating problem-solving strategies. If the problem situation concerns buying food for a party or traveling in the summer, for instance, you might ask: "How do you decide what to serve at a party? What criteria are important?" "How do you decide where to go on your summer vacation? What factors do you consider?" These cognitive "warm-ups" will be most successful in lower-level courses if students are asked to supply basic ideas and the teacher supplies the language that ties the ideas together. It is often useful to use a general heading written on the board under which there are spaces for suggestions (Criteria: personal taste, budget, healthfulness, availability; Factors: cost, interests, distance, time). The teacher then models the structures that permit a more complete rendering of the thought. ("John decides what to buy by considering how much things cost. If it is too expensive, he doesn't buy it.") Teacher modeling will be particularly important for structures that will enable the students to express their reasoning, such as those expressing cause and effect, ("if . . . then," "since," "therefore," "due to," etc.).

> ". . . (I)t is important **to create or strengthen the link** between the object or the action and the target language designation (**the sound and the symbol**)."

For all students, but especially for those at the novice level, it is important to create or strengthen the link between the object or the action and the target language designation (the sound and the symbol). TPR activities are an effective way to introduce new vocabulary without recourse to the native language. The students' ability to think in the language is thus enhanced, since the process is directly from the target language to the object or action and is not slowed by the "middleman" of the native language. Students can come to a clear understanding of key concepts in a relatively short period of time, and they generally enjoy the change in class routine.

Visuals of key vocabulary are also of benefit, since the representation of the idea can be linked directly to the target language. Exercises in visualizing or imaging can reinforce the association while personalizing it. For instance, if the vocabulary item is "car," the teacher can help students understand by a simple drawing on the blackboard. Once the concept is clear, the teacher can ask students to close their eyes and to create in their minds the clearest image possible of the car he or she will describe to them. Students are allowed to ask questions to clarify the image in their minds. The teacher may want to bring to class pictures of the car he or she describes and others that are similar. He or she would then ask students to select the car described and to explain how they knew. This kind of "TPR of the mind" improves concentration and helps to make the leap from the idea to the representation of the idea.

Alternatively, or as a follow-up activity, the teacher can ask students to close their eyes and to imagine their own idea of a car in as much detail as possible. Leading questions ("What color is it?" "Is it a two-door or a four-door?" "Is it a convertible?" "Does it have leather seats?" "Is it powerful?" "Is it economical?") will help the students solidify the image while reviewing and expanding the vocabulary of the lesson. To further reinforce the association of idea and word, the teacher can ask the students to imagine the word "car" written somewhere on their image, or the teacher can ask the student to imagine writing the word, one letter at a time, on the vehicle. After a few seconds, students open their eyes and work in pairs, one student drawing while the other describes.

> "By using **visuals** from the **target culture**, the teacher can help students learn **that language exists in a cultural context**."

Visuals such as slides, photos, or videos are also an excellent way to introduce students to the target culture while forging the link between idea and language. The term "cheese" would certainly not elicit the same image to a French teenager raised on Camembert and to an American whose only exposure to cheese was in individually wrapped slices. By using visuals from the target culture, the teacher can help students learn that language exists in a cultural context. Advertisements in target language newspapers or magazines often offer attractive visuals that are culturally significant and that can be exploited in the classroom. These images can be used in exercises to improve memory and to reinforce links between thinking and communicating ideas. For example, the teacher can select an appropriate visual and ask the students to study it carefully for five seconds, noting every detail. Students are then asked to close their eyes and to reproduce the image in their mind as exactly as possible. After a few seconds, the students are asked to draw the image they remember or to describe it to their partner. Subsequently, the students study the original visual another three seconds and add to their description.

> "... (P)recise language can improve memory and clarify concepts."

After this initial stage, there is a collective reconstruction of the image. The teacher draws attention to details the students may have missed and models the vocabulary and structures needed to describe them and then asks students to complete their drawings or descriptions. Students ordinarily find that their ability to reproduce an image is greatly enhanced by the teacher's intervention. In this kind of an exercise students learn an important lesson: Precise language can improve memory and clarify concepts.

Once properly prepared, the students read the problem. The teacher or a student may read the text through aloud, after which the teacher asks a number of questions to check general comprehension. One or more of the following questions might prove useful for this purpose: "What is the subject of the passage?" "What do we know?" "Do you notice any words that are related (that can be grouped in categories)?" "Where does the action take place?" "What are we supposed to do?" "What is the question?" "What do we need to know in order to solve the problem?" When students demonstrate a general understanding of the situation and of what is expected, they are given the time to think about the problem and process the information.

☐ PROCESSING

In the processing phase, the students work alone to find a solution to the problem. The teacher reminds the students that the interest of the exercise is the process rather than the answer. When first instituting the workshop, the teacher may wish to select a problem similar to the one chosen for the students and model the problem-solving process and the resultant visual representation (output phase) before asking students to work alone. By thinking aloud with the students, the teacher can make the point that the thinking process is recursive, that the effective problem solver stops to question his or her progress and may change strategies based on periodic evaluations. This kind of thinking aloud also enables the teacher to model language and structures that are useful for clarifying thought. The disadvantage of teacher modeling is that the students may be unwilling or unable to depart from the model and activate a different strategy. The class also becomes teacher centered rather than student centered and the students necessarily play a less active role. In subsequent sessions, students should be encouraged to work alone only consulting the *formateur* as necessary.

The role of the students in the processing phase is to write out the steps in the process that lead to the answer and to find a visual representation of the solution.[5] The teacher's role is to circulate through the classroom, observe the students' progress, and ask questions that will help the students find a solution or that will force the students to think about their reasoning. The teacher may also help students find the words to communicate their thinking as the need arises. In a larger class, a similar function can be performed by preplanned leading questions which are written out and included with the problem situation. The leading questions can help students get to the heart of the question, such as by asking the student to identify what information is essential to the solution. For instance, in sample problem (B) the student could be asked which of the following facts is not essential to solving the problem: (1) There are three men; (2) Teresa is a doctor; (3) Your friend wants to alternate men and women. Leading questions can also help the students verify the probability of their answers by helping them to approximate or by guiding them to make logical guesses. In sample problem (A), students could be asked to identify which of the following statements is clearly not possible and to explain why: (1) Brie is the strongest cheese; (2) Saint-Nectaire is the strongest cheese; (3) Pont-L'Évêque is the strongest cheese. (None of the three is possible because each is paired with a cheese that is stronger in the problem.) To help students represent their solution visually, leading questions can help students recycle other symbols that they have used in other contexts. Thus, in problem (A) a possible question would be, "Do you know a symbol that means 'greater than' or 'less than'?"

▢ OUTPUT

In the original workshop (ARL) setting, all participants are asked to put their visual representations on the board and each student is expected to explain his or her problem-solving strategy. This may be impractical in a whole-class setting. Instead, the teacher may wish to have students explain their procedure to a partner before asking four or five students to place their work on the board. This kind of "rehearsal" can be useful in that students often feel more at ease before a peer than before the whole class and thus are more willing to speak. The pair activity gives the students a chance to see if their explanations can be understood and, if not, to revise them. In addition, the students see clearly and quickly if they really do have the linguistic tools to express their thinking and to answer any questions their partner might ask.[6]

The students chosen to write on the board will each in turn explain how they solved the problem and then the teacher will open the floor for comments and discussion. The teacher helps the students to see any mistakes as a natural part of the process and as opportunities to learn, thus freeing the students from the anxiety of making a wrong answer. All students are encouraged to take an active part in the discussion and will be in a better position to do so after the pair activity. Naturally, the more different answers or representations presented, the more the students will be motivated to reexamine each step in the process. It is rare that all students in a particular class would design the same graphic representation, even if all the students came to the same answer. By circulating during the processing phase, the teacher will be able to select a variety of representations. The teacher should first direct the students' attention to the efficacy and clarity of the various models presented, but all aspects of the presentations should be examined, including the use of codes and symbols. If the students are slow to comment, the teacher can ask them more precise questions such as, "What are the advantages (positive aspects) of this presentation?" or "Which solution requires the fewest steps?" The questions the teacher asks will of course depend on the representations the students propose.

Following are two sample representations for problem situation (C) given above and repeated here for convenience:

(C) It is 10:25 A.M. and you have an appointment with the hairstylist at 10:40. You have 45 Marks and you need 40 Marks for the stylist. It takes a half hour to walk to the stylist's. On the bus, which leaves in 5 minutes, it takes 20 minutes and costs 2 Marks. A taxi would take 10 minutes and cost 15 or 16 Marks. On the subway, it costs 2 Marks and it takes 15 minutes.

(a) *How many options do you have for going to the stylist?*

(b) *What are your options for returning from the stylist?*

Student "X" chose the following representation:

Time available = 15 min (10:40–10:25 = 15 min)
Money available = 5 Marks (45M–40M = 5M)

WALK: time = 30 min.; money = 0 **BUS:** time = 20 + 5 = 25 min.; money = 2 M
TAXI: time = 10 min.; money = 16 Marks **SUBWAY:** time = 15 min.; money = 2 M

To Go:				To Return:			
	T	M			T	M	
w	0	x		w	x	x	←
b	0	x		b	x	x	←
t	x	0		t	x	0	
s	x	x	←	s	x	x	←

Student "Z" chose the following representation:

Time ≤ 15 mn	Cost ≤ 5 Marks } TO: subway = 1 option
subway taxi	subway bus walk
Time ≤ ∞	**Cost ≤ 3 Marks (5-2 = 3)}** FROM: w, b, s = 3 options
w, b, s, t	s, b, w

Both students arrived at the same answer and followed a logical strategy to find the solution. The representations make it fairly clear that both students have understood the problem, however the visual representations are very different. Discussion would focus on the strategy employed and the clarity of the representation. At first glance, the representation of student "X" seems clearer than that of the other student. Student "X" has included more information and the thinking process is easier to follow. The representation of student "Z" uses a rather sophisticated system of codes that requires some interpretation, but the thinking process is quite clear once the code is broken. Student "Z" has also found a very concise way to represent a great deal of information, and this point should come up in the discussion. At the end of the discussion the teacher may decide to offer a third alternative, such as the one below:

	Too slow	Too expensive	OK
To the stylist	walk, bus	taxi	subway
From the stylist	none	taxi	walk, bus, subway

The teacher might then ask students to decide which representation they prefer and explain why. In the ensuing discussion, the teacher should lead the students to generalize or formalize the strategies by identifying what the three models have in common.

The teacher's role in this phase is to serve as a model by asking questions that students need to ask of themselves when evaluating their own problem solving. The teacher also models an attitude of intellectual curiosity, a willingness to listen to various points of view, and attention to details. The teacher encourages and applauds careful planning and cautions against proceeding by trial and error or jumping to conclusions. The output phase also allows the teacher to model culturally appropriate ways to disagree with a speaker and to question thinking without attacking the thinker.

The final step in the workshop is to ask students to imagine instances in their personal life, in the work they are doing for other classes, or in situations in the target culture where they might use the problem-solving strategy that they have just formalized. This is an important exercise, for having the knowledge necessary to solve a problem in one situation does not insure being able to access the knowledge and apply it to a different situation. The teacher may wish to have students write out an analogous problem as homework, write out the solution, and include a visual representation of the process. This would furnish students with excellent thinking and writing practice and would ensure the teacher of having a good supply of problem situations for future classes. The best examples of problem situations could be revised and included in a bound volume with credit given to the authors. Publishing the students' work for the class or for other language classes would effectively instill a sense of pride in their linguistic ability and in their thinking and would serve as a motivational tool.

CONCLUSION

Much research has yet to be done in how thinking skills develop and how they can be fostered. How can we best enable students to transfer cognitive strategies from one content area to another? Do thinking skills build hierarchically one upon the other? How can we objectively measure progress in thinking skills and in the dispositions that appear to support them? As foreign language teachers, we are confronted with unanswered questions about how thinking skills transfer from the native language to the target language and back again. How can we best forge links between thought and the target language? Even with such seemingly basic questions unanswered, it is clear that something must be done and action must be taken. Highly developed thinking skills are a key to individual and corporate success in our ever more technologically sophisticated and information-rich world. Teaching thinking skills should be a common goal across the curriculum and should be fertile ground for interdisciplinary programs. Language teachers, as much or more than teachers in any other discipline, should be in a position to spearhead this effort in view of the obvious connection between good thinking and clear communication. How do we proceed?

The model of the ARL is somewhat limited in that it deals primarily with problem solving and not specifically with other forms of thinking such as decision making. It does, however, offer a structure and procedures to teachers wishing to strengthen the problem-solving skills of their students. The workshop model has a proven track record, having enjoyed some success in France, even when dealing with "difficult cases," and the method it propounds seems consonant with a large body of writings on thinking skill and strategy development and foreign language pedagogy. The role of the teacher in the ARL setting—the teacher as facilitator or coach—also provides an interesting model with implications for language teaching. On a practical note, the implementation of exercises such as those developed for the ARL would be relatively simple and could fit into existing course structures. Establishing such a program could be done reasonably quickly, while posing few risks and promising a number of benefits.

One of the most interesting aspects of the workshop model is the opportunity it offers to view language and language production in a new light. The information processing structure encourages teacher and student alike to investigate the mental operations that facilitate the acquisition of knowledge, rather than just focusing on the knowledge itself. Supplying language to describe thinking can make us more aware of what we do when we think and of the thinking strategies that are likely to be effective in various situations. As Tishman, Perkins, and Jay (1995, 12) point out, "the language of thinking helps students organize and communicate their own thinking more precisely and intelligently." There is good reason to believe that the skills we develop in the thinking workshops would transcend the foreign language classroom. By developing the metacognitive capabilities of our students, we can empower them to become independent learners who can plan a strategy, carry it out successfully, and evaluate the results. Instituting a thinking workshop in the foreign language classroom may be a step toward developing competent and productive workers who also have productive lives.

NOTES

1. For more information, see Gérard Teschner (1993) and Marcel Giry (1994).

2. Piaget maintains that the stages of cognitive development appear in a particular sequential order because of the basic principle of equilibration: the individual, by means of a particular cognitive stage, is partially adapted to his or her surrounding world, and this adaptation represents a particular degree of equilibrium between the organism and the environment. The four basic stages are: (1) the sensorimotor stage; (2) the preconcrete operational or intuitive stage; (3) the concrete operational stage; and (4) the formal operational stage. Due to the age of the learners in the ARL, the lessons concern primarily the last two of Piaget's developmental stages.

3. As French and Rhoder report, "fostering a positive attitude and strong motivation to higher level thinking is an important part of the teaching of thinking" (p. 34).

4. For a discussion of the importance of "superordination" and several activities to develop superordination, see "Adapting a Cognitive Apprenticeship Method to Foreign Language Classrooms" by Hosenfeld, Cavour, and Bonk, *FLA* 29.4: 588–96.

5. See Jones, Palincsar, Ogle, and Carr, Prawat, and Halpern who promote graphic organizers as a way of understanding information. Prawat maintains that "Concrete representations can crystallize or give form to concepts and procedures" (p. 8). As Halpern says, "The representation of a problem is often a good index of how well it is understood" (p. 167).

6. A key element in the workshops is the role of student interaction. This kind of social interaction is vital to language acquisition and growth according to theorists such as Long and Vygotsky. See also the interesting article by Williams, Lively, and Harper ("Higher Order Thinking Skills: Tools for Bridging the Gap," *FLA* 27.3 [1994]: 405–413) for a convincing discussion of the pivotal role of conversation in the development of higher order thinking skills.

REFERENCES

"ACTFL Provisional Program Guidelines for Foreign Language Teacher Education." *Foreign Language Annals* 21 (1988): 71–82.

Chaffee, John. *Thinking Critically.* 3rd ed. Boston: Houghton Mifflin Company, 1991.

French, J. N., and C. Rhoder. *Teaching Thinking Skills: Theory and Practice.* New York: Garland Publishing, Inc., 1992.

Giry, Marcel. *Apprendre à raisonner, apprendre à penser.* Paris: Hachette Education, 1994.

Halpern, Diane. F. *Thought and Knowledge: An Introduction to Critical Thinking.* Hillsdale, NJ: Lawrence Erlbaum Associates, Publishers, 1989.

Higelé, Pierre, G. Hommage, and E. Perry. *Ateliers de raisonnement logique, Exercices progressifs pour l'apprentissage des opérations intellectuelles.* Livret du formateur. Paris: Ministère de l'éducation nationale, 1989.

Hosenfeld, Carol, Isabel Cavour, and David Bonk. "Adapting a Cognitive Apprenticeship Method to Foreign Language Classrooms." *Foreign Language Annals* 29.4 (1996): 588–96.

Jones, B. F., A. S. Palincsar, D. S. Ogle, and E. G. Carr, eds. *Strategic Teaching and Learning: Cognitive Instruction in the Content Areas.* Alexandria, VA: Association for Supervision and Curriculum Development in Cooperation with the North Central Regional Educational Laboratory, 1987.

Long, M. H. "Input, Interaction, and Second Language Acquisition." *Native Language and Foreign Language Acquisition.* Ed. H. Winitz. *Annals of the New York Academy of Sciences* No. 379. New York: Academy of Sciences. (1981): 259–278.

Marzano, R. J. *The Theoretical Framework for an Instructional Model of Higher Order Thinking Skills.* Denver: Mid-Continent Regional Educational Lab, Inc. ED 248 045. (1984).

Omaggio Hadley, Alice C. *Teaching Language in Context: Proficiency-oriented Instruction.* Boston: Heinle & Heinle Publishers, 1993.

Prawat, R. S. "Promoting Access to Knowledge, Strategy, and Disposition in Students: A Research Synthesis." *Review of Educational Research* 59 (1989): 1–41.

"Professional Standards for Teachers of Foreign Languages." AATF and AATG. Draft 6/95. 27 pages.

Sadler, W. A., Jr. "Holistic Thinking Skills Instruction: An Interdisciplinary Approach to Improving Intellectual Performance." *Thinking Skills Instruction: Concepts and Techniques.* Eds. M. Heiman and J. Slomianko. Washington, D.C.: National Education Association. (1987): 183–188.

Shrum, J. L., and E. W. Glisan. *Teacher's Handbook: Contextualized Language Instruction*. Boston: Heinle & Heinle Publishers, 1994.

Sternberg, R. J. "Criteria for Intellectual Skills Training." *Educational Researcher* 12 (1983): 6–12, 26.

Teschner, Gérard. *Les Ateliers de raisonnement logique: Pratique et évaluation*. Paris: Retz, 1993.

Tishman, S., D. N. Perkins, and E. Jay. *The Thinking Classroom: Learning and Teaching in a Culture of Thinking*. Boston: Allyn and Bacon, 1995.

Vygotsky, L. S. *Mind in Society: The Development of Higher Psychological Processes*. Cambridge, MA: Harvard University Press, 1978.

Williams, Mary, Madeleine Lively, and Jane Harper. "Higher Order Thinking Skills: Tools for Bridging the Gap." *Foreign Language Annals* 27.3 (1994): 405–26.

APPLICATION OF IDEAS ON ACTIVITIES

1. Williams/Harper/Lively suggest that theme-based activities may be made relevant and engaging to the students in a number of ways, including:

   ◆ Making the topic engaging,

   ◆ Allowing for personalization,

   ◆ Engaging critical thinking,

   ◆ Establishing a summative goal,

   ◆ Using grids and forms,

   ◆ Emphasizing teamwork,

   ◆ Using the directions to stimulate ideas.

   Of course, several of these can be applied to a single activity simultaneously.

   Develop one or more activities on a theme to include in a syllabus for a course that you plan to teach during the next semester or quarter, employing at least four of the techniques listed above.

   (1) Select a theme that will require students to work with ideas, and to examine their knowledge and their world view.

   (2) Determine an angle from which you think that students will be affectively or intellectually engaged in the theme.

   (3) Develop a means for allowing students to consider their own experiences.

   (4) Select fairly concrete concepts with which students are familiar so that you can still engage them in analysis, synthesis, and/or evaluation.

   (5) Specify the summative goal of the activity, being sure that students must engage in meaningful communication of information and the use of that information in order to meet the goal.

   (6) Design a grid/form/chart to serve as a graphic organizer for the instructions to students.

   (7) Write carefully detailed directions, including examples of some of the expressions that students may need during the activity.

2. Bragger and Rice emphasize the importance of theme-based language instruction, using authentic target-language materials in a meaningful, contextualized form, supplemented to make them comprehensible, with primary focus on acquiring information and primary evaluation of the development of target language skills.

In what ways do your current language instructional practices fit this definition/description? Give consideration to at least the following criteria:

(1) Use of authentic materials

(2) Meaningful use of the materials in context

(3) Types of supplementation to make the materials comprehensible for students

(4) Focus on acquiring and/or using information from the materials

(5) Evaluation of language skill development (using the same or similar materials)

What changes could you make in your instructional practices that would bring your teaching/learning interactions with students closer to this model?

3. Bragger and Rice state that, "for learning to occur, there must be familiarity with *either* the language needed to deal with the content *or* the content itself."

Keeping this principle in mind, do the preparation for developing a theme-based unit of instruction for one of your classes.

(1) Consider the grade level, ages, interests, cultural/educational/ family backgrounds of your students.

(2) Make a list of topics or themes with which your students are familiar and around which you could possibly develop appropriate lessons.

(3) For each theme, make a list of authentic materials available for your use (e.g., magazines, brochures, schedules, announcements, newspapers, recordings, video clips)

(4) For each theme, make a list of possible sources of authentic materials (e.g., colleagues, library, mail-order catalogues, local college/university, travel agency/cultural attaché office, museums, professional collaborative, Internet)

(5) Explore these sources, collecting authentic materials on your possible topics.

(6) Based on the availability of authentic materials, decide on the best topic for development.

(7) Examine the materials on this topic, looking for examples of authentic language use that appear to be at your students' next stage, a bit beyond their current level of competence, but within their experience in terms of content. File these materials together for possible use.

4. Do the preliminary preparation for developing an annotated interactive version of a text in the language that you teach. (Review Geisler's report of his experience with students of German.)

(1) Select a text (keeping in mind the ages, grade level, maturity, life experiences, and interests of your students as well as their level of language proficiency). Indicate for which level of proficiency and general age group you will prepare the text.

(2) Determine the categories of documentation that you will provide for students (e.g., vocabulary for target-language definitions, vocabulary for translation, vocabulary for photo/graphic examples, grammar explanations, geographical information, historical reference, social/political intertext, literary references, other cultural issues).

(3) Using a variety of colored highlighters, mark on a copy of the text the words to be treated in each of your categories (in a separate color for each category).

(4) For at least five examples in each of your categories, write or describe the documentation that you would provide when a student "clicks" on a word.

(5) Select at least three pictures or maps or video clips or other graphics that you would include in your documentation.

(6) List at least three audio segments that you would include in your documentation.

5. Based on the French workshops, les Ateliers de Raisonnement Logique (ARL), Toner recommends a system for teaching higher order thinking skills in the foreign language classroom. He describes three phases of the teaching/learning activities: input, processing, and output.

Using this model, design an instructional activity which incorporates concepts, ideas, texts, or other materials from a culture where the language that you teach is spoken.

(1) Decide at which proficiency level and approximate age and maturity level you will construct the activity.

(2) Select a topic with which you can recycle previously learned material, and link it to new vocabulary and structures.

(3) Write a scenario that will require students to focus on problem solving. Use the examples in Toner's article to suggest ideas to you.

(4) Create two or more input activities to review and introduce needed vocabulary and structures. Select or design visuals for at least one of these activities. (You may want to review Ballman's descriptions of "setting the stage" and "providing input.")

(5) Do the processing phase of the activity yourself, writing out the steps in the process that lead to the answer and designing a visual representation of the solution. (You may want to articulate more than one process which you can anticipate that your students might use.)

(6) Do the output phase of the activity aloud to yourself, explaining your problem-solving strategy based on your visual representation of the solution. Notice any particular phrases that might be helpful to review with your students.

(7) Make a list of situations in the target culture where this problem-solving strategy would be useful.

(8) Try the activity on your colleagues.

6. In Terry Ballman's article in the Presentation section of this book, "From Teacher-Centered to Learner-Centered: Guidelines for Sequencing and Presenting the Elements of a Foreign Language Lesson," she identifies four segments of the instructional sequence: (1) *Setting the stage*, (2) *Providing input*, (3) *Guided participation*, and (4) *Extension*. The last two of these, as she notes, are "learner-centered."

Prepare at least one guided-participation paired activity on the same topic for which you prepared to set the stage and to provide input (in the Presentation section of this text).

(1) Review your objectives, key vocabulary, basic structural elements, visuals, and categories of contrasts/comparisons.

(2) Determine one or more kinds of information that your students would like to have from one another on the topic. (Identify a possible information gap.)

(3) Create an activity to motivate students to seek this information from a partner.

(4) Create a form (e.g., checklist, questionnaire, grid) to guide students through the process of eliciting and giving this information to each other.

(5) List possible phrases that can facilitate the information exchange, using targeted vocabulary and structures.

(6) Write a model of the anticipated dialogue between the partners.

(7) Try out the activity on your colleagues.

7. Now write an extension activity on the same topic that provides an opportunity for students to produce the targeted vocabulary and structures.

(1) Review the objectives, vocabulary, and structures.

(2) Write an activity that will require a pair of students to use the information that they acquired in the guided-practice activity above. The activity should require active listening, attending to meaning, negotiation, and design of a "product" agreed upon by both partners.

(3) Create any forms or materials needed to guide students through the process.

(4) Provide any authentic materials (or simulated authentic materials) needed by students for information.

(5) Test the activity on your colleagues.

8. Rewrite your guided-participation and extension activities to incorporate suggestions of your colleagues, more attention to higher order thinking skills, and/or greater emphasis on one or more of the "C's" of the National Standards.

9. Tschirner stresses that productive competence can only be developed by mapping a communicative intent to an expressive form. Thus, students must be allowed to express their own meanings in situations to which they relate.

Design an activity for Novice-high to Intermediate-mid students based on any one of the functions listed in activity 1 (Presentation Section, pp. 79–167) which will encourage students to express their own meanings. Take into consideration the ages, backgrounds, experiences, and interests of your students as well as such factors as current national and local political events, social events, sports events, entertainment, and advertising.

10. Tschirner emphasizes that the task of learners is to "map specific communicative intents to correctly phrased words, phrases, and sentences."

For the activity which you created in number 1 above, provide at least five preassembled phrases or clauses that students can use while expressing their own personal meanings.

11. Review and assess at least three multimedia foreign language programs. (Possible sources of foreign language software: your media

department at school, a local library, the language department and/or the instructional media center of an area college or university, publishers of foreign language materials. Samples of some of Heinle & Heinle's software are included on the CD-ROM accompanying this textbook.)

Evaluate each of these programs using the criteria identified by Cubillos, citing at least three examples for each criterion:

♦ Is it a rich source of input?

♦ Is it fully interactive?

♦ Does it support and encourage independent learning?

♦ Does it serve as a springboard for interactive and communicative activities?

♦ Does it facilitate the exploration of the target language culture?

♦ Does it maximize the use of resources?

♦ Does it enhance the role, rather than substitute for the foreign language teacher?

♦ Does it facilitate course administration?

12. Cubillos describes several "tendencies" toward effectiveness of technology for the teaching of foreign languages and gives examples of research studies in each of these categories.

Reread the section of his article on "What Does Technology Have to Offer?" For each of the following categories, explain at least one specific use that you would like to make of technology for this purpose (How do you see that technology can assist you as facilitator in the teaching/learning process?):

(1) To facilitate the acquisition of vocabulary

(2) To increase students' language awareness

(3) To support effectively input-rich activities

(4) To support and facilitate output activities

(5) To gain an insight into your students' second language acquisition processes

(6) To facilitate the exploration of the target language culture

(7) To enhance students' motivation

(8) To maximize the use of teaching resources

13. Aplevich and Willment express the concern common among instructors that students "will not be equipped to make the transition from a distance education course to the campus edition of the follow-up course." In order to alleviate this fear, distance education instructors must make certain that course goals, objectives, outcomes, tasks, activities, materials, and evaluations are equivalent to on-campus courses at the same level.

Plan a lesson to be delivered by distance education that would meet the same criteria that you have for a similar lesson in a traditional setting

(1) Choose a topic equivalent to two to four hours of class contact time to be taught by distance education. Assume on-line electronic capability.

(2) List prerequisites for the course in which this lesson will be included (e.g., Intermediate-high skills in listening and reading, Intermediate-mid-skills in speaking and writing).

(3) Note the demographics of the students to be served (e.g., age range, gender, level of education, prior language study, educational goals).

(4) Write two to four objectives for the lesson.

(5) Examine possible resources for students and for interaction with students (e.g., World Wide Web sites, e-mail, CD-ROM, video, audio, print, instructor notes, telephone numbers of businesses and agencies and individuals, telephone tutoring). Make a list of available resources.

(6) Design a cooperative learning task for a group of three or four students to accomplish that will allow them to show that they can meet the objectives.

(7) Write a series of incremental activities for input and guided interaction for students to acquire the skills needed to complete their task. Develop the activities to encourage student-student interaction as well as teacher-student interaction.

(8) Create the first encounter of the student with the program (e.g., first computer screen, title page of the study guide, first 30 seconds of a video).

(9) Determine how you would evaluate the student outcomes and assign grades.

(10) Create a brief assessment instrument for students to use in evaluating the lesson.

(11) List individuals (by name and/or position) with whom you would need to work in order to develop this lesson.

Part IV

Evaluation

Including articles by:

Jane Harper/Madeleine G. Lively/
Mary K. Williams
Robert M. Terry
JoAnn Hammadou

Testing the Way We Teach

Jane Harper, Madeleine G. Lively, Mary K. Williams,
Tarrant County Junior College, Fort Worth, Texas

INTRODUCTION

Over the last two decades, foreign language educators have developed a myriad of instructional techniques and activities to enhance the teaching/learning process in second language acquisition. These activities have been designed based on a number of underlying principles which have influenced the thinking of members of the profession during these twenty years. A partial list of some of the most significant of these would include communication as the primary goal (Canale, 1984; Hadley, 1993; Higgs and Clifford, 1982), Total Physical Response (TPR; Asher, 1982), the Natural Approach (Krashen and Terrell, 1983), comprehensible input (Krashen, 1981, 1982, 1985), input processing (VanPatten, 1993; Gass and Madden, 1985; Ballman, 1996), the use of authentic materials (Rogers and Medley, 1988), teaching toward proficiency (Higgs, 1984; Liskin-Gasparro, 1984 and 1987; Hadley, 1993), attention to higher order thinking skills (Met, 1991; Williams, Lively, Harper, 1994), task-based language teaching (TBLT; Breen, 1987; Candlin, 1987; Crookes, 1986; Long, 1985; Markee, 1997; Nunan, 1993; Prabhu, 1987), content-based instruction (Brinton, Snow and Wesche, 1989; Cantoni-Harvey, 1987; Curtain, 1986; Leaver and Stryker, 1989; Met, 1991; Mohan, 1986), attention to various learning styles of students (Claxton and Murrell, 1987; Horwitz, 1990; Oxford, 1990; Oxford and Crookall, 1989), cooperative learning (Johnson and Johnson, 1987; Johnson and Johnson, 1989; Johnson, Johnson, and Holubec, 1988), and the theory of constructivism (Gough, 1996; O'Neil, 1992).

At the heart of most language instruction is an emphasis on communication skills, both oral and written, in meaningful contexts in the classroom and/or other teaching/learning environments. Instructors of foreign/second languages have made great strides in the development and use of effective, engaging, thought-provoking, entertaining activities, frequently based on authentic materials from a target culture.

> "With the emphasis on communication comes the challenge of assessing students' ability to communicate." (Willis, 1996)

However, we too often have spent our energies on the activities/ materials development without a concomitant commitment to organize evaluation activities/materials that allow us to test the gains achieved by students in these instructional environments. Too frequently, content-based work emphasizing higher order thinking-skill development in communicative cooperative learning groups has been followed by an individually answered, fill-in-the-blanks test on discrete grammar points and a vocabulary quiz on the same words for everybody. Such testing gives a clear indication that the **real goals** of the instructor, in spite of published objectives and activity-rich class sessions, center on manipulation of language structure and memorization of vocabulary rather than the communication of ideas. In order for communication to be **valued** by students, the **evaluation** of communication must be central to the appraisal system. (Harper, Lively, Williams, 1992) "With the emphasis on communication comes the challenge of assessing students' ability to communicate." (Willis, 1996)

As Rebecca Valette points out in Omaggio-Hadley's *Teaching Language in Context*, ". . . the content of the tests and the method by which grades are assigned reflect more accurately than any lengthy statement of aims and purposes the real objectives of instruction." Thus, "our testing programs should, as far as possible, include measurements of all the skills that we wish students to acquire and should weight the measurements for grading purposes in relation to our instructional emphasis." (Harper, Lively, Williams, 1992)

> "We must not only test **what** we teach; we must also test **the way** we teach."

Moreover, students should not be expected to perform in a testing situation any tasks in any situation which they have not had opportunities to practice in the regular instructional setting. We must not only test **what** we teach; we must also test **the way** we teach. Evaluation strategies and materials should directly reflect instructional strategies and materials.

Therefore, for novice and intermediate learners, we recommend a variety of evaluation formats to achieve a balanced appraisal of structural and communication skills. "There's no one best assessment method. Whether to use multiple-choice tests, performances, projects, exhibitions, or portfolios depends on what's being assessed, for what purpose, and how results will be used." (Willis, 1996) The varying types of appraisals can be weighted to reflect a focus on listening and speaking skills, an emphasis consistent with the *ACTFL Proficiency Guidelines* (ACTFL 1986).

ACHIEVEMENT, PROCHIEVEMENT, AND PROFICIENCY TESTING

Achievement tests are used to measure how much learning has taken place in a prescribed content domain, generally based on explicitly stated objectives and goals of an instructional program. (Henning, 1987, 6) In foreign language education achievement tests are usually administered at set junctures in the course of study (e.g., after each chapter and/or unit and/or course), and the test items are taken from the content of the instruction.

Proficiency tests are global measures of ability in a language and are not developed and administered with reference to a particular course of instruction. (Henning, 1987, 6) Foreign language educators realize that the Oral Proficiency Interview is not generally applicable to classes of novice and intermediate speakers of a language, and that it is not a reasonable test for regular and frequent administration to large numbers of students at any level. (Gonzales Pino, 1988)

However, instructors who emphasize oral communication skill development in the classroom need to incorporate the speaking skill into their regular evaluation of student progress. Thus, these instructors tend to develop and implement some type of oral assessment, usually a blend of achievement and proficiency testing, often referred to as prochievement testing. A prochievement test incorporates specific lexical and structural items from the objectives of the teaching/learning syllabus so that students can demonstrate their control of those items and their achievement of those objectives. However, a prochievement test is also proficiency-oriented, permitting students to express their own meanings and to demonstrate their growing abilities to function effectively within a range of situations.

A sound and complete testing program probably will contain assessment samples of all three of these testing types: achievement, prochievement, and proficiency. The evaluation system that we recommend is composed of three major types of assessment, each different from the others in its balance of achievement, prochievement, and proficiency emphasis.

A Recommended Evaluation System

SOME TESTING FORMATS

> "It's hypocritical to teach in seven ways and assess in one." (Willis, 1994)

☐ COOPERATIVE ORAL TESTING

The cooperative oral test as a form of evaluation falls into the category of prochievement testing with tendencies toward proficiency testing. These guided-improvisation appraisal sessions measure a student's ability to deal with everyday social situations as well as with the linguistic content of the lesson, the current one under study plus opportunities for spiraling content and structures from previous lessons. In this role-play activity, students are encouraged to integrate their knowledge of culture (etiquette, body language) in order to avoid cross-cultural *faux pas*.

The cooperative oral tests are usually designed for two or three students. Although some may be adapted for larger groups, it often happens—as it does in normal speech in one's native language—that some individuals do not have adequate opportunity to speak when there are more than three participants.

Each test assignment provides explicit, carefully detailed objectives to guide students to successful performance of the activity. However, since this testing format is intended to promote synthesis and creative use of the language, students should be encouraged not to be confined by the assignments but rather to use them as a point of departure for expressing their own interests and ideas.

Some assignments include handouts for students to refer to during the activity (e.g., maps, charts, forms, telephone directories, pamphlets, schedules, classified sections of a newspaper, advertisements). Handouts may be the same for all participants or may be specified for Student A and Student B, in which case each should refer only to his or her own document. Occasionally an assignment may require the students to furnish their own materials, such as photographs of friends and family.

On the next page is a sample cooperative oral test assignment from a unit with objectives built around organizing leisure time activities, reading informational materials, and understanding conversations about leisure time activities, and talking about events in the past.

The cooperative oral test assignment should be given to the students in advance. If presented to students with the introduction to the entire unit of study, the activity allows students to see the purpose and intent of preparative paired work and cooperative learning activities as they are practiced throughout the classes leading up to the cooperative presentations. Thus, information about this assignment can help to focus student attention on vocabulary items and structural forms as they are presented, enhancing the possibility that students will select these elements as they subconsciously create their individual internal grammatical system. In other words, knowledge of the requirements of the cooperative oral test may help to produce some **cognitive Velcro** onto which students can stick lexical and grammatical forms. Furthermore, the more opportunity students have to prepare, the more effectively the task serves as the sort of organizing experience advocated by the National Council on Standards and Testing.

A Sample Cooperative Oral Test Assignment

Materials: Movie listings from theatres around Strasbourg (provided by the instructor). Each student will have a different set of listings.

Role-play the scenario in pairs, sitting back-to-back.

Scenario: Negotiate a decision to see a movie together. One of you should telephone the other to discuss specific plans.

(1) Dial the number and greet each other appropriately.

(2) Determine each other's preferences in genre and actors.

(3) Then, discuss the movies from your lists that you both might want to see.

(4) Verify your respective schedules and determine which of the movies you selected you are both free to see.

(5) Finally, set a time and place to meet.

In your discussion, you may want to say that you have already seen a film (see movie listings on the next page):

J'ai déjà vu ce film.   I've already seen that film.

Remember to use expressions like:

J'ai horreur de...   I have a horror of . . .
Il y a une séance à.../Il passe à... There is a feature at . . .
On se retrouve à...   Let's meet at . . .

At first glance, this form of testing may look daunting to schedule. However, if students have the assignment in advance, if they have a time limit (e.g., two to three minutes), and if they have practiced each step of the activity in class interactions, they come to this part of the evaluation well-prepared to show what they can accomplish. A group of two to four students can be heard in as little as five minutes, a class of 25 or 30 in an hour or so. In some academic settings, students may also enjoy the flexibility of doing their presentations during faculty office hours or, occasionally, recording them on videotape.

CHOIX DE FILMS

LES AFFRANCHIS de M. Scorsese avec R. de Niro, R. Liotta; J. Pesci. Un gamin élevé dans un quartier misérable rêve d'être un gangster. Il y réussit. Comédie dramatique — Club (16.10, 19.50) — 16 ans.

CHERIE, J'AI RETRECI LES GOSSES de J. Johnston avec R. Moranis. Un inventeur un peu fou réduit ses enfants et ceux du voisin à une taille microscopique. Comédie — Méliès (14.05, 16.05, 18.05, 20.05, 22.05)

GREMLINS 2 «La Nouvelle Génération» de J. Dante, de S. Spielberg avec Z. Galligan, P. Gates. Six ans après l'invasion à Kingston, les Gremlins contre-attaquent. Fantaisie — Méliès (13.50 uniq)

JEAN GALMOT, AVENTURIER de A. Malin avec C. Malavoy. Au début du siècle, un journaliste parisien devient un véritable héros en Guyane. Aventure — UGC (13.45, 16.30, 19.20, 22.10)

A LA POURSUITE D'OCTOBRE ROUGE avec S. Connery, A. Baldwin. Un as de la marine soviétique en route vers les EU à bord du sous-marin le plus sophistiqué du monde: transfuge ou agresseur? Suspense — Star (15.50, 22.10)

SPECTACLES

58 MINUTES POUR VIVRE de R. Harlin avec B. Willis. Un flic se bat avec des terroristes qui contrôlent un aéroport. Policier — Etoile ex-Omnia (13.45, 15.55, 20, 22.20)

MISS DAISY ET SON CHAUFFEUR de B. Beresford avec J. Tandy, M. Freeman. De 1948 à nos jours, l'amitié d'une vieille femme excentrique et son chauffeur noir. Comédie dramatique — Etoile ex-Omnia (13.45, 15.55, 18.05, 20.15, 22.30)

CYRANO DE BERGERAC de J.-P. Rappeneau avec G. Depardieu, A. Brochet. Par amour pour la précieuse Roxanne, Cyrano prête sa verve et son intelligence au beau Christian, aussi amoureux de Roxanne. Comédie dramatique — Club (14.05, 17, 19.40, 22.15)

JOURS DE TONNERRE de T. Scott avec T. Cruise, R. Duvall. Un pilote de courses rêve de participer aux plus grandes courses de stock-cars. Aventure — Espace-Vox (13.40, 15.50, 18, 20.10, 22.15, sam 0.25)

TOTAL RECALL de R. Verhoeven avec A. Schwarzenegger. Un homme part sur Mars à la recherche de son passé inconnu. Aventure — L'Etoile ex-Omnia (13.45, 16, 18.10, 20.05, 22.20, dim 10.15)

Film descriptions adapted from *Pariscope* N° 1171, 31 Oct. 1990.

The following grading form is offered to provide an efficient and straightforward means for evaluating performance of personalized speaking tasks, such as the *Causeries*. This form has several benefits:

First, the distribution of points demonstrates an emphasis on communication of ideas: Vocabulary (I) = 20%, Functions (II) = 20%, Appropriateness of responses (VI) = 8%, Creativity (VII) = 8%, Total for communicative ability = 56%.

Second, this form is flexible enough to accommodate a variety of tasks and levels. Note that the factors to be evaluated have generic labels (Vocabulary, Functions) so that they apply to almost any speaking situation. Also, the criteria for marking credit are expressed in general terms, allowing the instructor to determine what level of performance is satisfactory for a given class or student. (Of course, specific criteria for grading based on the unit objectives should have been established when the assignment was given.)

Finally, scales for marking points provide a clear, easy means for scoring. The point scale represents a range, allowing an individual instructor to distinguish between degrees of success in student language production. The criteria as stated also do not require perfection or mastery in each area, which are unreasonable expectations of novice and intermediate learners. Furthermore, instructors can use points written into the grading form to indicate expected performance and to recognize effort or risk that exceeds expectation by awarding bonus points.

This form has been well-accepted by both students and instructors using it for the first time. The comfort level of using the form to objectify what could be seen as a very subjective judgment of student performance appears to increase steadily with both groups with regular use.

Cooperative Oral Test GRADING FORM

I. Vocabulary within context

0	2	4	6	8	10

minimal   maximum

II. Functions/Use of language
(i.e., give basic information, enumerate/describe, ask basic questions, express likes/dislikes)

0	2	4	6	8	10

few   many

Continued on page 270

III. Accuracy in use of basic structures
(i.e., subject-verb/noun-adjective agreement, basic word order, negation)

0	2	4	6	8	10

very poor, interferes   few errors, does not interfere
with communication   with communication

IV. Fluency
(i.e., conversational pace of speech)

0	2	4	6

none   groping,   occasionally   confident
            slow   fluent

V. Pronunciation and intonation

0	2	4	6

no effort to   poor, greatly   occasionally   does not
to use French   interferes   interferes   interfere

VI. Reaction/Appropriateness of response

0	2	4

no reaction   sometimes   appropriate
                   appropriate

VII. Creativity/Recombination of learned material

0	2	4	MULTIPLY TOTAL POINTS BY 2

no attempt   some attempt   frequent attempts

Adapted from Bruschke Rating Scale in "Grading Classroom Oral Activities: Effects on Motivation and Proficiency" by Sidney L. Hahn, Tamara Stassen, and Claus Reschke in *Foreign Language Annals* 22, No. 3, 1989.

☐ THE ORAL QUIZ

An oral quiz can provide discrete-item testing in an oral format, providing a means to do achievement testing which leans toward personalization.

Achievement-oriented questions asked in an oral setting (one-on-one by the instructor or in a recorded format for administration in a laboratory setting) check listening comprehension, pronunciation, ease of speech, and control of vocabulary and structures.

Sets of sample questions on tape can allow listening comprehension practice on the topic of the unit, give an organization for study and review, provide a means of self-appraisal for students before testing, and enhance students' self-confidence in their ability to use the language. Examples of questions for the same unit as the guided improvisation above might include the following:

Quel est le dernier film que vous avez vu?	What is the last film that you have seen?
C'est un bon film?	Is it a good movie?
Qui a vu le film avec vous?	Who saw the movie with you?
À quel cinéma êtes-vous allé(e)?	To which movie theater did you go?
C'est un cinéma près d'ici ou en ville?	Is that a theater near here or in town?
Comment est-ce que vous êtes allé(e) au cinéma?	How did you get to the theater?
Qu'est-ce que vous avez fait ce week-end?	What did you do this weekend?

Although some testing objectives may require that students answer in complete sentences, to avoid fostering unnatural speech patterns, a better instruction might be simply not to give one-word responses. A grading system such as the following, which allows a student to earn 90% of the grade through accuracy with additional points being available only through personalized and creative responses, encourages students to express their own meaning and to take risks, pushing their own language development.

Name_____

GRADING FORM FOR ORAL QUIZZES

	Comprehension	Pronunciation	Grammar	Comments
1.	1	1 2	1 2 3	
2.	1	1 2	1 2 3	
3.	1	1 2	1 2 3	
.				
.				
.				
15.	1	1 2	1 2 3	

(From 1 to 10 additional points for personalized and creative responses.)
Comments:

☐ THE WRITTEN QUIZ

In a complete evaluation system, most instructors give a written quiz or chapter or unit quiz at regular junctures of a course. These tests are generally achievement tests with some opportunities for students to express their own meanings. They can include a variety of types of questions and activities to measure listening, reading, and writing skills, including the following:

- ◆ a range of listening-comprehension formats to check the diversity of goals, skills, and strategies needed for effective listening;

- ◆ multiple-choice questions and completions to check control of targeted structures and vocabulary as well as listening and reading;

- ◆ discrete-point grammar on morphology and syntax in contextualized reading and listening;

- ◆ open-ended responses that encourage creativity;

- ◆ realistic writing tasks based on chapter/unit topics;

- ◆ reading comprehension with functionally-oriented questions based on authentic materials.

In order to avoid testing memorization in the guise of comprehension (which is often the case when students have been exposed to the material before seeing it on the test), the reading selections on a test should be drawn directly from neither the textbook nor from the class exercises. Certainly care should be taken to assure that the reading selections are topically and structurally appropriate to the chapter and that the students have had ample practice in doing the same kind of activities that are asked of them on the test. However, they should be materials previously unseen by the students.

Testing materials should also be carefully selected to present linguistical and cultural authenticity. They need to be drawn from socially and geographically diverse sources, exposing students to the natural variation of an international language in its many everyday contexts, reflecting the classroom use of materials which meet the same criteria. Authentic reading tasks almost always draw on cultural information that encourages students to call upon global knowledge as well as reading strategies for comprehension. In order to assure that these extraliterate skills are used to enhance rather than to replace reading comprehension, it is essential that students be required to mark the segments of the reading that support their answers.

Writing activities on tests should be designed to simulate everyday, real-life tasks that anyone living or traveling in a francophone country or dealing with French-speaking travelers and business people might expect to do. Authentic materials (e.g., forms, brochures, postcards, schedules) can be used to provide a realistic frame for the activities. It is often possible to integrate the reading and writing sections of a test so that knowledge frames invoked and information given in the reading provide context and content for the function targeted in the writing. In all cases students should be given clear, point-by-point instructions for doing the required tasks.

GRADING

> "Whether we like it or not, a major question all students have is 'How will I be graded?'" (Bonwell, 1996)

One of the elementary principles of assessment is the prior knowledge of the criteria on which one is to be judged. Students should always know how they will be evaluated. Instructors need to make clear that they "use product criteria to assess the outcome of an assessment task [use], process criteria to assess elements such as effort and homework and class participation, and [use] progress criteria to assess how far students have come." (Willis, 1996) These criteria should be clearly explained and followed.

In general, when evaluating student work, following a few simple principles can enhance the students' willingness to pay attention to the instructor's comments and corrections:

♦ Respond to content, or at least respond to content first

♦ Focus on affirmative grading

♦ Value selective (personalized) learning

♦ Encourage risk-taking

♦ Carefully correlate objectives, instructions, and evaluation

A primary goal of testing (as well as of teaching) is to foster self-expression. Toward this end, we offer two recommendations:

1. In all instances, we advise instructors to think in terms of positive grading: Grant credit to students for demonstrating what they know rather than penalizing them for what they do not know. In the natural process of selective learning, students are more attentive to information that directly relates to their personal experiences. Therefore, we should expect each student to acquire a unique set of active vocabulary expressions on a topic.

2. Even though few bonus points may be explicitly written into a test, we encourage instructors to recognize and reward creative and personalized responses with bonus credit. Such responses entail a certain amount of risk-taking on the part of the students.

Students who are willing to take risks in their attempts to express their own meanings are among those who can ultimately become the best communicators in a language. It is more productive for us to reward their effort than to penalize errors that do not substantially impair communication. The sample grading forms offered for evaluating *Causeries* and oral quizzes have built-in mechanisms for awarding credit for personalized and creative responses. We suggest that similar measures be taken in the grading of written tests.

Testing is an extension of the learning process; it is another opportunity to present the topics, structures, and functions being studied in fresh contexts. The testing process provides students the exciting and cognitively challenging experience of dealing with familiar material in new situations and it is verification of their educational progress.

As you plan, develop, implement, and assess your own evaluation system and instruments, remember Rebecca Valette's statement that ". . . the content of the tests and the method by which grades are assigned reflect more accurately than any lengthy statement of aims and purposes the real objectives of instruction." Your students will rely on your evaluation system to inform their language study and practice and, ultimately, their language acquisition. Therefore, evaluate what you value and test the way you teach.

REFERENCES

ACTFL *Proficiency Guidelines*. Hastings-on-Hudson, NY: The American Council on the Teaching of Foreign Languages, 1986.

Asher, James J. *Learning Another Language Through Actions*. Los Gatos, CA: Sky Oaks Productions, 1982.

Ballman, Terry L. "Integrating Vocabulary, Grammar, and Culture: A Model Five-Day Communicative Lesson Plan." *Foreign Language Annals*, Vol. 29, No. 1, 1996, 37–44.

Bonwell, Chuck. "Building a Supportive Climate for Active Learning," *The National Teaching and Learning Forum*, Vol. 6, No. 1., 1996, 5–6.

Breen, M. P. "Learner Contributions to Task Design." In C. N. Candlin & D. F. Murphy (Eds.), *Language Learning Tasks, Lancaster Practical Papers in English Language Education*, 7. Hemel Hempstead, England: Prentice Hall International, 1987, 23–46.

Brinton, Donna M., Marguerite Ann Snow, and Marjorie Bingham Wesche. *Content-Based Second Language Instruction*. New York: Newbury House Publishers, 1989.

Canale, Michael. "Testing in a Communicative Approach," 79–89 in Gilbert A. Jarvis (Ed.), *The Challenge for Excellence in Foreign Language Education*. Middlebury, VT: Northeast Conference, 1984.

Candlin, C. N. "Towards Task-Based Language Learning." In C. N. Candlin & D. F. Murphy (Eds.), *Language Learning Tasks, Lancaster Practical Papers* 7 . Hemel Hempstead, England: Prentice Hall International, 1987, 5–22.

Cantoni-Harvey, G. *Content Area Language Instruction Approaches and Strategies.* Reading, MA: Addison Wesley Publishing Company, 1987.

Claxton, Charles S., and Patricia H. Murrell. *Learning Styles: Implications for Improving Educational Practices.* ASHE-ERIC Higher Education Reports, 1987.

Crookes, G. *Task Classification: A Cross-disciplinary Review.* (Tech. Rep. No. 4). Honolulu, HI: University of Hawaii, Manoa, Center for Second Language Classroom Research, Social Science Research Institute, 1986.

Curtain, Helena Anderson. "Integrating Language and Content Instruction." *ERIC/CLL News Bulletin* 9.2, 1986, 1, 8–9.

Gass, S., and C. Madden, (Eds.), *Input in Second Language Acquisition.* Rowley, MA: Newbury House, 377–393..

Gonzales Pino, Barbara. "Prochievement Testing of Speaking." *Foreign Language Annals*, 22, No. 5, 1989, 487–496.

Gough, Pauline B. "No More 'Pie in the Sky,'" *Phi Delta Kappan*, March 1996, 459.

Hadley, Alice Omaggio. *Teaching Language in Context.* 2nd ed. Boston: Heinle & Heinle, 1993.

Hahn, Sidney L., Tamara Stassen, and Claus Reschke. "Grading Classroom Oral Activities: Effects on Motivation and Proficiency." *Foreign Language Annals* 22, No. 3, 1989.

Harper, Jane, Madeleine Lively, and Mary Williams. *Testing Program, Allons-y!* Boston, MA: Heinle & Heinle Publishers, 1992.

Henning, Grant. *A Guide to Language Testing.* Newbury House Publishers, 1987.

Higgs, Theodore V., (Ed..), *Teaching for Proficiency, the Organizing Principle.* Lincolnwood, IL: National Textbook Company, 1984.

Higgs, Theodore V., and Ray Clifford. "The Push Toward Communication." In Theodore V. Higgs, (Ed.), *Curriculum, Competence, and the Foreign Language Teacher.* The ACTFL Foreign Language Education Series, 1982, 57–79.

Horwitz, Elaine K. "Attending to the Affective Domain in the Foreign Language Classroom." *Shifting the Instructional Focus to the Learner.* (Ed.), Sally S. Magnan. Middlebury, VT: Northeast Conference, 1990: 15–33.

Johnson, D. W., and S. Johnson. *Joining Together: Group Theory and Group Skills.* Englewood Cliffs, NJ: Prentice-Hall, 1987.

———, and R. Johnson. *Cooperation and Competition: Theory and Research.* Edina, MN: Interaction Book Company, 1989.

———, R. Johnson, and E. Holubec. *Cooperation in the Classroom.* Edina, MN: Interaction Book Company, 1988.

Krashen. Stephen D. *Second Language Acquisition and Second Language Learning.* Oxford, England: Pergamon, 1981.

———. *Principles and Practice in Second Language Acquisition.* Oxford, England: Pergamon, 1982.

———. *The Input Hypothesis: Issues and Implications.* New York: Longman, 1985.

———, and Tracy D. Terrell. *The Natural Approach.* Hayward, CA: The Alemany Press, 1983.

Leaver, Betty Lou, and Stephen B. Stryker. "Content-Based Instruction for Foreign Language Classrooms." *Foreign Language Annals*, 22, No. 3, 1989, 269–275.

Liskin-Gasparro, Judith E. *Testing and Teaching for Oral Proficiency.* Boston: Heinle & Heinle, 1987.

_____. "The ACTFL Proficiency Guidelines: Gateway to Testing and Curriculum." *Foreign Language Annals* 5, 1984, 475–489.

Long, M. H. "A Role for Instruction in Second Language Acquisition Theory." In S. Gass and C. Madden (Eds.), *Input in Second Language Acquisition*, 377–393. Rowley, MA: Newbury House, 1985.

Markee, Numa. "Second Language Acquisition Research: A Resource for Changing Teachers' Professional Cultures?" *The Modern Language Journal*, Vol. 81, No. 1, Spring 1997, 80–93.

Met, Myriam. "Learning Language through Content: Learning Content through Language." *Foreign Language Annals*, 24, No. 4, 1991, 281–295.

Mohan, Bernard. *Language and Content*. Reading MA: Addison Wesley Publishing Company, 1986.

Nunan, David. "Task-Based Syllabus Design: Selecting, Grading and Sequencing Tasks." In G. Crookes and S. M. Gass (Eds.) *Tasks in a Pedagogical Context: Integrating Theory and Practice*, 55–68. Clevedon, England: Multilingual Matters, 1993.

O'Neil, John. "Wanted: Deep Understanding," *Association of Supervision and Curriculum Development Update*, Vol. 34, No. 3, March 1992, 2.

Oxford, Rebecca L. "Language Learning Strategies and Beyond: A Look at the Strategies in the Context of Styles." *Shifting the Instructional Focus to the Learner*. (Ed.), Sally S. Magnan. Middlebury, VT: Northeast Conference, 1990: 35–55.

_____, and David Crookall. "Research on Language Learning Strategies: Methods, Findings, and Instructional Issues." *Modern Language Journal* 73, 1989, 404–419.

Prabhu, N. S. 1987. *Second Language Pedagogy*. Oxford: Oxford University Press.

Rogers, Carmen V., and Frank W. Medley, Jr. "Language With a Purpose: Using Authentic Materials in the Foreign Language Classroom," *Foreign Language Annals* 21, 1988: 467–88.

VanPatten, Bill. "Input Processing and Second Language Acquisition: A Role for Instruction." *Modern Language Journal* 77, 1993: 45–57.

Williams, Mary, Madeleine Lively, and Jane Harper. "Higher Order Thinking Skills: Tools for Bridging the Gap." *Foreign Language Annals* 27.3, 1994: 401–426.

Willis, Scott. "Foreign Languages: Learning to Communicate in the Real World." *Association of Supervision and Curriculum Development Curriculum Update*, Winter 1996, 7.

_____. "The Well-Rounded Classroom: Applying the Theory of Multiple Intelligences." *Association of Supervision and Curriculum Development Update*, Vol. 36, No. 8, October 1994, 3–8.

Authentic Tasks and Materials for Testing in the Foreign Language Classroom

Robert M. Terry, *University of Richmond*

Robert M. Terry received his Ph.D in Romance Languages from Duke University. He is Professor of French at the University of Richmond (VA). He was President of the American Council on the Teaching of Foreign Languages (ACTFL) in 1994. He has also served as Chair of the Board of Directors of the Southern Conference on Language Teaching (SCOLT). He was the editor of Dimension, *the annual publication of SCOLT, for seven years and has been a coeditor and associate editor of the ACTFL Foreign Language Education Series.*

INTRODUCTION

If, in today's communicatively focused classes, we are striving to enable our students to carry out realistic (if not authentic) tasks in their daily classroom activities, our testing should reflect that very same focus. After all, any material or technique that is effective for teaching a foreign language can also be used for testing. We are all aware that today's foreign language textbooks have gone far beyond those uniquely drab monochromatic books that contained gratuitous, space-filling black-and-white pictures of famous people and sites of the target culture. We now have at our access four-color textbooks and ancillary components that contain a wealth of authentic materials tightly integrated into the language program. Through the various elements included—model sentences, illustrations, readings, recordings (audio and video), exercises (textbook, workbook, computer-based)—we find the essence of language: representations of vocabulary elements and structures that reflect culture and civilization.

AUTHENTIC MATERIALS

Rogers and Medley (1988) state that:

> [. . .] students must [. . .] experience the language as it exists naturally, without the "pedagogical processing" so prevalent in most textbooks. If students are to use the second language communicatively in the real world tomorrow, then they must begin to encounter the language of

that world in the classroom today. They must see and hear the second language being used as the primary medium of communication among native speakers—as "language with a purpose." This can best be done through the use of authentic materials (p. 467).

However, we must first define just what is meant by *authentic materials*. Some argue that native speakers produce such materials for native speakers. Others claim that, on the contrary, it is the quality, appropriateness, and "naturalness" of the language, and not its source or purpose that make the materials authentic. Rogers and Medley (1988) hold that *authentic material* consists of "language samples, either oral or written, that reflect a naturalness of form and appropriateness of cultural and situational context that would be found in the language as used by native speakers" (p. 468). Authentic materials should be examples of authentic discourse. In fact, the first definition given above implies that authentic materials are authentic discourse. To resolve any problems of definition and distinction, Geddes and White (1978) separate *unmodified authentic discourse*, which refers to language that occurred originally as a real act of communication, from *simulated authentic discourse*, which is language produced for pedagogical purposes, but which exhibits features that have a high probability of occurrence in real communication (p. 137).

> "Just as we use authentic materials in our foreign language instruction, we must also use and insist on **authentic language** in **all** of our classroom activities, **including testing**."

COMMUNICATIVE COMPETENCE

Just as we use authentic materials in our foreign language instruction, we must also use and insist on authentic language in **all** of our classroom activities, including testing. Testing our students' knowledge of the foreign language is essentially testing their communicative competence: their implicit and explicit knowledge of the rules of the language and also the rules of language use (ACTFL 1989: G-1). Assessing a learner's communicative competence subsumes assessing many aspects of language (the functional trisection of grammar, content/context, and sociolinguistic appropriateness) and does not focus solely on grammatical accuracy. To be considered competent, a learner must be a fully active member in any communicative venture, be it productive or receptive—a reader or a writer, a speaker or a listener, an actor or a viewer.

In their listing of the four major components of communicative competence, Canale and Swain (1980) focus on the role of the language learner/user as a productive member of a communicative exchange. They talk about the following types of competence:

♦ *Grammatical competence.* To what degree has the language user mastered the linguistic code, which includes morphology, syntax, vocabulary, pronunciation, and spelling?

♦ *Sociolinguistic competence.* Is what is being said or written acceptable in the speech community in a given setting (ACTFL 1989: G-5), that is, can the language user vary his or her language according to the context, content, audience, and style called for by the situation?

♦ *Discourse competence.* Are the language user's ideas combined into a cohesive form and into coherent thought? We might also include *contextual appropriateness* in this category—Is the student "on task?" Is the sample of student performance, be it oral or written, relevant to the task that he or she was asked to carry out?

♦ *Strategic competence.* Can the language learner use verbal and nonverbal communication strategies to compensate for gaps in linguistic and lexical knowledge or in other cases of a breakdown in communication for whatever reason?

These same competences must be present in the receptive member of the communicative exchange—the reader or the listener—for if this person does not possess these same competences to relatively the same degree as the productive member (the speaker or the writer), then there will be a breakdown in communication. It is important to note here again that grammatical accuracy is not the only element that determines competence.

□ THE COMMUNICATION PROCESS

We can measure the effectiveness of the communicative effort by how much communication takes place between two (or more) language users— the *sender* and the *receiver*, the *speaker/writer* and the *listener/reader*. In order for communication to take place, there must be a significant overlap of both linguistic and extralinguistic elements and phenomena, ranging from the discrete elements that make up the code—be it written or spoken —to those elements we call *world experience* or *background knowledge.* In other words, the sender and receiver must have a significant amount of knowledge in common: language and experiences. Bertil Malmberg (1963, 26) illustrates this communication process (see Figure on the next page).

The problem, it would appear, would be to establish the needed degree of commonality—linguistic and experiential—between the sender and receiver. In our case, this is the role of the foreign language teacher: not only to teach the linguistic system of the language but also to help learners experience those extra-linguistic phenomena that make up one's background knowledge and increasing world experience. If we alter the shape and appearance of any text (and I am using the word "text" here meaning "any communicative output"—whether visual or auditory), we remove from it a significant portion of its context.

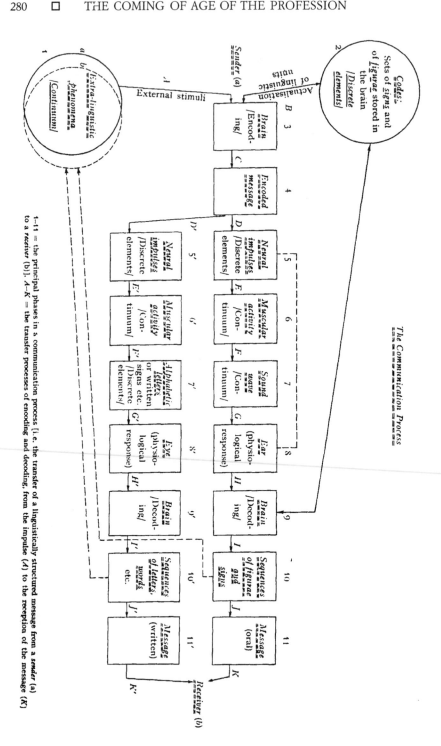

The Communication Process

1-11 = the principal phases in a communication process [i.e. the transfer of a linguistically structured message from a *sender* (a) to a *receiver* (b)]. *A–K* = the transfer processes of encoding and decoding, from the impulse (*A*) to the reception of the message (*K*)

For example, if we are teaching about housing in the target-language country, we must make the students aware that the concept identified as "house" in English is different from the concept *casa*, or *maison*, or *haus*, or ПОМ. Now, let us suppose that someone is moving to another country and needs to rent a house. This person consults the newspaper to find the classified ads. In most newspapers around the world, classified ads look very much the same. So we scan the newspaper to find these familiar pages. We then skim the pages to find a house—in the price range we want, containing the rooms we need, located appropriately, with or without certain features, and so on. We then begin putting circles around those ads that interest us, and we finally go back and concentrate on that group of circled ads for more detailed reading.

In classified ads for houses, I expect to find certain pieces of information and certain types of abbreviations. It is the format—the shape, the look—of what is in front of me that puts my mind "on the right track." If, however, a teacher were to take these same classified ads and retype them, they would no longer have that "telltale" format—that format that elicits certain expectations that I have as a reader. In short, the teacher would have removed the most revealing of all contexts—the *authentic* shape of the text.[1]

> "Whether the material is authentic and unmodified or whether it is simulated, the difficulty of the text is determined **only by the task(s)** that we ask the learner to carry out based on that material and *not* on the material itself."

AUTHENTIC MATERIALS AND REALISTIC TASKS

Authentic materials include print materials, videotapes, satellite broadcasts, audio recordings, films, most of which are now available to foreign language teachers and in their classrooms. These materials are logically unedited and not pedagogical in focus. They would, in fact, seem very unsuited for many academic uses, except perhaps for advanced-level students. After all, they were not prepared for use in the classroom, and native speakers of the language do not speak or write according to any given level of study. Access to authentic materials would appear even more problematic at certain levels of study, especially for FLES (Foreign Language in the Elementary School) students or lower-level language students.

On the contrary—whether the material is authentic and unmodified or whether it is simulated, the difficulty of the text is determined only by the task(s) that we ask the learner to carry out based on that material and *not* on the material itself.

In speaking of using authentic video materials, Pusack and Otto (1996, 36) state that:

> The drawbacks of using authentic materials must be recognized, especially in matching available footage to curricular sequences, but the advantages are manifold. They lie in the motivational effects, in the richness of the material (not least of all for the instructor who must experience the documents semester after semester), and in the head start that is gained by students who begin to confront difficult authentic material from the earliest days of language study. Without such early training, many students are ill-prepared to view authentic materials when they suddenly crop up in later semesters.

It is apparent that as teachers, we must often find authentic materials and create realistic tasks that are not only linguistically appropriate for various levels of language study but also for a variety of ages of learners. It is only reasonable to point out that what might be considered a realistic or authentic task for a college-age student might be totally inappropriate for a student of FLES, for a middle or high school student, or at times, for an adult learner. For example, it would be difficult to have a middle school student fill out a registration form for a hotel room in Paris, since students this age do not make such arrangements on their own! This student could, however, fill out a different kind of form that calls for the same type of information—a subscription or a membership form, for instance. Similarly, a rather dated college textbook directs students to introduce their Martian fiancé(e) to their parents. This is hardly a realistic task even for anyone who is old enough to have a fiancé(e)!

When we choose authentic materials, there should be a purpose—not simply to decorate the page or to fill (or kill) time but to introduce learners to a specific cultural concept, to illustrate something that has just been taught (or that is going to be taught), to serve as a stimulus for an activity or test item. Materials that we present to learners should be of potential interest to them or of possible need or relevance to them. Just as the hotel registration form is not generally relevant to a middle school student, so a reading on the latest Michael Jackson concert will be of very limited interest to an adult learner. At the outset of language study, it is more feasible to select materials that are of interest to the student and not those that are of interest to the instructor or ones that he or she *thinks* the students will (or even should) enjoy.

TESTING AND DIVERGENT ANSWERS

In principle, we expect students to produce essentially the same quality and quantity of language on tests that they would produce in real life in a communicative situation. Since each student is different, we would expect their abilities in the language and their performance to differ in both in-class performance and in testing. There are obviously times when evaluation that calls for convergent (uniform or consistent) answers and discrete-point (right or wrong) scoring is relevant, warranted, needed, and appropriate: on quizzes for evaluating the demonstrations of mastery of isolated, focused grammar points; or of a given lexicon; or for determining if an answer is basically right or wrong; or if a communicative effort succeeds or fails.

There are also times when we need to evaluate the learners' ability to communicate in the target language in a more unstructured situation, i.e., when the learner has to call on his or her entire linguistic arsenal, communication strategies, and general competencies. Such times replicate reality in which the train of thought in a conversation or text makes unexpected turns and stops, when we have to react to situations spontaneously . . . and appropriately, when we least expect it.

In all fairness to our students, and in order to get a true picture of their abilities, we should not ask them to carry out any task for which they have not practiced. Yet, as just mentioned, reality is not like a test for which one can prepare, cram, and study—*das Leben ist keine Probe* ["Life is not a rehearsal"]. In an academic environment (which as we all know rarely duplicates reality!), there are times when we need to "do things academic," such as give quizzes, tests, final examinations, interviews, . . . and grades. To prove that I can drive a car, I go to the Department of Motor Vehicles (DMV) and pass written, driving, and vision tests. To prove that I can fly an airplane, I must fly with an FAA (Federal Aviation Administration) examiner and provide documentation (and proof) of my skills and training. To prove that I can "perform acceptably" in another language, I similarly need to demonstrate my abilities . . . and successfully so. I can drive acceptably because I have practiced; I can pilot a plane because I also practiced (and practiced and practiced). I can use another language because I have practiced using it—I have done the same thing in training that I am going to be asked to do on a test or called on to do in real life. That is practice, and that is why we need to practice. I need to feel comfortably at ease as I prove my abilities, even when there will inevitably be unexpected elements thrown in front of me. We practice so that we can learn. We practice so that we can do something well. We are tested to find out just how well we have learned, how well we can do something.

Driving a car or flying a plane is essentially an either-or process. You either *pass* the test and receive a license or you do not. Learning another language is slightly different. I can use the language very well, rather well, well, rather poorly (but still be understood), poorly (the degree of comprehension is minimal), or not at all. I can be declared proficient to drive a car or fly a plane. The license attests to my abilities. A lack of proficiency will not take me over the mountain . . . but into it! In learning another language, however, I have many resources available to me to prove my proficiency. After all, being proficient in a language is *not* like being proficient in driving or flying! It is not a case of either-or; there is a continuum of abilities. I am not simply proficient in another language (contrary to the wording of many college/university requirements!), but I am proficient to do specific things at a given level and with a certain degree of acceptability. One only needs to read any descriptor in the ACTFL Proficiency Guidelines to realize this point. Can anyone imagine any DMV or the FAA examiner handing out a license to any candidate who performs the tasks he or she was asked to do and got only a "D-" on some of them?!

In both driving and flying, we are trained to expect the unexpected, to have sufficient knowledge to be able to get out of an unexpected situation with which we simply do not know how to cope. That is what the training in languages also does—we begin by working with materials that are "learned phrases," "learned utterances," "learned materials," "recombinations of learned elements in a limited number of content areas," to borrow phrases from the ACTFL Proficiency Guidelines (1986). My affective filter must be low enough so that I am willing to try to learn and not be threatened by the thought of failure or incomplete mastery.[2]

However, as my learning increases, I should be challenged to use that "learned" language in new ways—to use the models, phrases, structures, lexical items in *new, creative* ways, to *recombine* those items into something that is relevant and perhaps that I have not uttered before. Higgs and Clifford (1982: 74) contended that:

> . . . the premature immersion of a student into an unstructured or "free" conversational setting before certain fundamental linguistic structures are more or less in place is not done without cost. There appears to be a real danger of leading the students too rapidly into the "creative aspects of language use," in that if successful communication is encouraged and rewarded for its own sake, the effect seems to be one of rewarding at the same time the *incorrect* communication strategies seized upon in attempting to deal with the communication situations presented.

I am not convinced that this is the case. When students have a minimal amount of linguistic and lexical baggage, it is only logical to assume that they cannot produce language that is of the same level or quality as that in their native language, regardless of their age. Nonetheless, students can indeed be put into a situation in which they need to create language to convey a given message. *If* the instructor provides a clearly delimited situation with no extraneous interfering elements, students can rise to the occasion very well and be quite inventive *and* communicative, even though they are somewhat constrained by (1) their limited linguistic and lexical bases, and (2) the instructor's clear delimitation of the task at hand. This in no way means that the language produced by the student is of the highest quality, but it does mean that students can produce effective (although maybe not quite efficient) personalized communication with only a modicum of raw materials.

Again, it is only by practicing that language learners will develop and refine their linguistic abilities and, dare I say, their proficiency. The moment they begin writing their test or participating in an interview is

> "[. . .] Any material or technique that is effective for teaching a foreign language can also be used for **testing**."

assuredly not the time for them to realize that they have never been asked to carry out such a task before. As stated in the opening sentence, "Any material or technique that is effective for teaching a foreign language can also be used for testing." Students should have ample opportunities to practice tasks with teacher direction in the classroom. Then and only then is it reasonable to ask the students to carry out a similar task in an evaluation, be it a quiz, test, final examination, or oral interview. Note that I say a *similar* task, not an identical task. Memorization does not prove learning and communicative ability. However, practice is very justifiable since it helps provide that common experience and success that are key features of interactive communication.

Imagine that I am testing my students on the use of the subjunctive in Spanish or in French. Rather than have them fill in the blanks with the correct form of the subjunctive of the infinitives in parentheses (sound familiar?), I want to put them in a situational context in which the use of the subjunctive is logical and anticipated—sending regrets. "Imagine that you have been invited to a dinner party for Saturday evening, two weeks from now. Unfortunately, you have already made plans and will have to miss the dinner. The invitation indicates R.S.V.P. Send your regrets."

Students cannot be expected to know the social protocol of a formal R.S.V.P. unless they have seen examples of one. They can model their response on that of an appropriate sample. They need to make their sample look like the example. Such a sample does *not* come from Miss Manners' latest book, but from a book on Spanish or French etiquette (*savoir-faire*).

> ". . . (T)he writing of appropriate test items based on authentic materials call(s) for . . . a **reasonable, fair,** and **equitable** system of scoring or evaluating that performance."

Not only does the writing of appropriate test items based on authentic materials call for a new creative frame of mind and different expectations of performance, but also for a reasonable, fair, and equitable system of scoring or evaluating that performance. Many of these communicative test items will call for divergent answers that cannot or should not be scored using a discrete-point method. For example, one student might write:

Je regrette que je ne puisse pas venir à la fête à votre maison samedi prochain. Mes parents veulent que je les accompagne pour visiter des amis. Quel dommage que je n'assiste pas à la soirée. [I'm sorry that I can't come to the party at your

house next Saturday. My parents want me to go with them
to visit some friends. What a shame that I can't come to
the party.]

And another might respond:

*Je regrette de ne pas pouvoir venir au dîner chez vous d'ici
deux semaines. Il faut accompagner mes parents chez des
amis. Comme il est dommage de ne pas passer une soirée si
agréable parmi vous.* [I'm sorry that I can't come to dinner
at your place two weeks from now. I have to go with my
parents to some friends' place. What a shame it is, not to
spend such a pleasant evening with all of you.]

In the first sample, there are indeed subjunctive forms (although the
first of them is incorrect). In the second sample, there is not one instance
of the subjunctive, yet this student has carried out the task quite well and,
by avoiding the subjunctive, proves to me that he or she in fact knows it
well by using structures which have the potential to call for the
subjunctive but which, in this particular context, can be avoided.

Is the second student to be penalized because there are no
subjunctive forms? Is the first student to be rewarded because there are
subjunctive forms used, although one of them is incorrect? Just what
degree of penalty, if any, should be levied against either or both students?
And these are only two samples of student writing! What must we do
when we have about 25 more student papers to correct, all of which are
assuredly going to be different?

EVALUATION—THE COMMON YARDSTICK

Evaluation implies measuring against a standard, against a common
metric, for it is only by determining how far a student's performance is
from the median—that level of work that is considered "average"—that we
can determine a student's level of competence. For academic purposes in
which grades are necessary, this common yardstick cannot be based on a
minimal standard. A standard should not be unrealistic or unattainable,
nor should it be so low that all who are measured against it exceed it
unrealistically. The standard should represent the level of performance
expected of the majority of students in the class, that basic 66.67% of
students in the middle that make up the traditional "bell-shaped curve."

> "With the emphasis on **language-learning for** *all* in
> the newly adopted foreign language standards, we
> must in fact **pay attention to** and **learn to evaluate**
> the foreign language performance samples **of** *all*
> **learners at** *all* **levels of ability.**"

We must evaluate student performance against what we, in our expert judgment, consider to be "acceptable" according to the level of study, the psychological level of the students, and their age.

With the emphasis on language-learning for all in the newly adopted foreign language standards, we must in fact pay attention to and learn to evaluate the foreign language performance samples of **all** learners at **all** levels of ability. This includes the entire gamut of learners:

♦ the learner who is only minimally on task but who is willing to take the risk to be creative or who is at least adventuresome in his or her test-taking;

♦ the student who can reproduce verbatim vocabulary lists and model sentences, and who can manipulate previously learned materials but who cannot communicate creatively;

♦ the typical, average student who, by dint of memorization and the internalization of selected aspects of the language, succeeds in communicating and in sharing some personal information or thoughts.

Evaluation is going to have to take on a different form. As mentioned earlier, of course we will still administer discrete-point quizzes and test items. These types of items are strongly oriented toward achievement testing, in which the material tested is based on a given curriculum, a specific textbook (and ancillaries), and a planned course of study.

With the focus now on more communicative uses of language in relatively realistic situations and conditions calling for the use of naturalistic language, we are moving more toward proficiency-based testing which is independent of time, teacher, and textbook. However, instead of totally open-ended tasks that call for divergent answers—no more just right or wrong, but logical and appropriate and effectively communicative—we add in the basic curricular component and constraint of a finite corpus of material as determined by the textbook and ancillary materials. This is what I have referred to elsewhere as *hybrid testing* (Terry, 1986, 522–23; although the term *prochievement testing* is also applicable here):

> . . . hybrid tests retain certain features of achievement tests (a limited corpus and a focus on specific grammatical features) and incorporate proficiency-based tasks eliciting and encouraging performance using acquired knowledge. Hybrid tests combine specified features of the target language within naturalistic discourse. Such tests provide more specific feedback on recently learned material than is often possible on truly global proficiency tests.

> "Learners should . . . be given the opportunity **to demonstrate just what they have learned**."

We teachers know what we have tried to teach our students. Learners should then be given the opportunity to demonstrate just what they have learned. I actually prefer the term "internalized" to "learned," since the latter can be (and often is) a synonym of "memorized." Internalized language is what they feel comfortable using when called on to "perform" in the language. I can give them every opportunity to employ object pronouns, for example, in answering personal questions. I can either (1) *tell* them to answer my questions using the appropriate pronoun(s) for the underlined words or phrases, or I can (2) *tell* them to answer my questions using the appropriate pronoun(s) in their answers but not cue them to which words can be replaced, or I can simply (3) *ask* the question and tell them to answer it. Any of these three options is acceptable, provided the students have had practice in such activities before test time and depending on the level of language that is being studied and tested.

The more open-ended the test item, i.e., the less teacher direction that is given, the more flexible the grading must be. *If* students are given the option to use whichever language samples they feel most comfortable using, then we simply cannot penalize them for avoiding the very element we were trying to test. We all know from experience how creative students can be in answering a question correctly while completely skirting any new grammar points that might have been studied in the past few weeks.

TEST OR QUIZ? WHY?

It is at this point that we must clarify (or explain) what has just been said. The rigor that we apply in scoring a test is dependent on what we are testing. If we want to determine the degree of mastery of any given point of grammar or topical vocabulary list, then we can administer a quiz which is narrow in focus, tends to call for convergent answers and discrete-point scoring. By *mastery*, I simply mean the degree of accuracy which the learner demonstrates in using those specific elements.

If we examine many traditional tests, we find that we have nothing more than a series of small quizzes that are hooked together by sequential numbering into what we call a test. If, on the other hand, the primary focus of our foreign language instruction is to give our students a degree of facility in communicating in the target language (and by "communicating" I mean being an active participant in the communicative process as reader, writer, listener, or speaker), we must give them the opportunity to prove their skill and abilities in coping with situations that replicate what they might encounter in a real-life encounter with a text or user of the target language. As either a *sender* or a *receiver* of communication, have they been successful in demonstrating the four components of communicative competence—grammatical, sociolinguistic, discourse, and strategic competence?

The method of evaluation that we use will have to be determined by the purpose of the evaluation instrument—quiz, test, interview, final examination. If we want to find out basic right or wrong answers, we can use completely discrete-point scoring with fill-in-the-blanks, multiple-choice, or true-false types of items. If we want to find out how much of the course content has been mastered for assigning course grades and/or for continuation to the next level of study, we might use hybrid or prochievement tests, which can be a mixture of convergent and divergent answers, still tightly enough controlled by the teacher so that students do not have the opportunity to go far beyond their capabilities and knowledge, i.e., to find out how much of the course content they have mastered. Finally, if we want to determine the learners' linguistic and lexical prowess in demonstrating how much of the language they have at their control, we must give them the opportunity to do just that, without the constraints of predetermined responses that contain a very limited (and predictable) number of grammar points, structures, or vocabulary items.

CONCLUSION

Authentic materials are used in foreign language teaching to show students just how the language they are studying works, how it communicates, and how it reflects the culture(s) of those who use that language. With our training, we are not trying to develop that "near-native speaker" of the 1960s. We are developing competent users of the target language—those who can communicate effectively, whether they are readers or writers, listeners or speakers. The word *communication* should not be interpreted as being only productive in meaning because a fully engaged member of a communicative exchange both uses the language and lexicon appropriately *and* comprehends the message that is being sent.

We should expect our students to demonstrate grammatical accuracy, since poor grammar bears the stigma of being poorly educated. We should expect our students to demonstrate sociolinguistic appropriateness in the language they produce, since a linguistic, lexical, or social *faux pas* also carries a judgmental stigma. Finally, we should expect our students to demonstrate their functional ability in the language—they should certainly be on task. They should be able to use the language and the lexicon (and their resourcefulness) that are called for in any given context. They can demonstrate their complete communicative competence by carrying out tasks in a variety of class activities and evaluation instruments. Insofar as possible and feasible, they should be asked to use real language in realistic (if not real) situations using authentic materials. This is when language becomes real for our students.

NOTES

1. This is the principle of *schema theory* as discussed in Alice Omaggio-Hadley (1993). *Teaching Language in Context*, 2nd edition. Boston: Heinle & Heinle Publishers, 134–137.

2. According to Krashen (1982), ". . . a variety of affective variables relate to success in second language acquisition [. . .]. Most of those studied can be placed into one of these three categories:

   a. *Motivation*. Performers with high motivation generally do better in second language acquisition.

   b. *Self-confidence*. Performers with self-confidence and a good self-image tend to do better in second language acquisition.

   c. *Anxiety*. Low anxiety appears to be conducive to second language acquisition, whether measured as personal or classroom anxiety (p. 31).

REFERENCES

ACTFL. 1986. *ACTFL Proficiency Guidelines*. Yonkers, NY: The American Council on the Teaching of Foreign Languages.

Buck, Kathryn, ed. 1989. *The ACTFL Oral Proficiency Interview Tester Training Manual*. Yonkers, NY: The American Council on the Teaching of Foreign Languages.

Canale, Michael, and Merril Swain. 1980. "Theoretical Bases of Communicative Approaches to Second Language Teaching and Testing." *Applied Linguistics* 1: 1–47.

Geddes, Marion, and Ron White. 1978. "The Use of Semi-scripted Simulated Authentic Speech for Listening Comprehension." *Audiovisual Language Journal* 16, iii: 137–45.

Hadley, Alice Omaggio. 1993. *Teaching Language in Context*, 2nd edition. Boston: Heinle & Heinle Publishers.

Higgs, Theodore V., and Ray Clifford. 1982. "The Push Toward Communication." In Theodore V. Higgs, ed., *Curriculum, Competence, and the Foreign Language Teacher*. The ACTFL Foreign Language Education Series, 57–79.

Krashen, Stephen D. 1982. *Principles and Practice in Second Language Acquisition*. Oxford: Pergamon Press.

Malmberg, Bertil. 1963. *Structural Linguistics and Human Communication*. New York: Academic Press, Inc., Publishers.

Pusack, James P., and Sue K. Otto. 1996. "Taking Control of Multimedia." In Michael D. Bush, ed., *Technology-Enhanced Language Learning*. The ACTFL Foreign Language Education Series. Lincolnwood, IL: National Textbook Company, 1–46.

Rogers, Carmen V., and Frank W. Medley, Jr. 1988. "Language With a Purpose: Using Authentic Materials in the Foreign Language Classroom." *Foreign Language Annals* 21, v: 467–88.

Terry, Robert M. 1986. "Testing the Productive Skills: A Creative Focus for Hybrid Achievement Tests." *Foreign Language Annals* 19, vi: 521–28.

A Blueprint for Teacher Portfolios:
Concerns That Need to Be Addressed When Embarking on Teacher Assessment via Portfolios

JoAnn Hammadou, *Department of Modern and Classical Languages & Literature*

JoAnn Hammadou is Associate Professor of French at the University of Rhode Island, where she teaches Foreign Language Methodology, Advanced French Composition, Second Language Acquisition Theory and supervises preservice secondary foreign language teachers. She holds a Ph.D in Foreign Language Education from the Ohio State University, and her areas of active research include teacher assessment and second language reading comprehension. In addition to numerous conference papers, Dr. Hammadou has authored and coauthored numerous articles on foreign language pedagogy and authored a French composition text.

> "Teachers are being asked to prove that they have demonstrable competencies and can 'produce' competent students. As a result, foreign language teachers now must struggle with the task of **defining foreign language teacher competencies and the problem of providing evidence of these competencies.**"

FOCUS ON ASSESSMENT AND EVALUATION

Like it or not, educators currently find themselves in the center spotlight of public scrutiny. In the recent past, educators in general, and certainly foreign language educators in particular, have focused their attention on the role of methodology or the role of individual learners' differences in learning (Bernhardt and Hammadou; Moore). Currently, all eyes are on the teacher himself or herself as a key variable in the classroom, and foreign language teachers are no exception. In a recent Public Agenda poll, when asked "What is the most important thing public schools need in order to help students learn?" the most common answer, by a wide margin, was "good teachers" (Wise, 1). With this focus of attention have come calls from various directions for greater accountability from classroom teachers to legislators, parents, administrators, and students (see D'Costa and Loadman). Teachers are being asked to prove that they have demonstrable competencies and can "produce" competent students. As a result, foreign language teachers now must struggle with the task of defining foreign language teacher competencies and the problem of providing evidence of these competencies.

The era of teacher assessment is upon us. But teacher assessment, like student assessment, is a frustratingly complex task, not easily reduced to a single test or checklist. Indeed, there is a burgeoning interest in alternative forms of assessment as a result of the belief in the importance of teachers. Traditionally, assessment is the term used for the collection of information, and evaluation is the term used for the subjective judgments made about this information. When the only format of assessment of teaching is a score on the National Teacher Examination or a transcript of courses taken, the kinds and depth of evaluation that one can accomplish are limited. Dissatisfaction with these limitations is what currently is driving the search for alternative assessments.

This article contains a blueprint for educators interested in the use of portfolios in foreign language teacher assessment. The portfolio as both an instrument and a process of assessment requires that teachers consider a number of new criteria for what quality testing is and new procedures for initiating evaluation. It is a promising example of a movement toward direct rather than indirect measures of proficiencies. For foreign language educators, the move toward such direct measures may have a familiar echo from earlier, similar moves toward more direct measures of second language proficiencies spearheaded by ACTFL's Oral Proficiency Interview (Henning).

PROMOTING FAIRNESS

Most of the common current assessment formats are pencil-and-paper tests. They are the products of good faith efforts to minimize subjectivity in evaluation. The attempt to separate the concept of objective measurement from subjective evaluation has been an ongoing struggle and subject of much debate within the field of educational testing. Many educators disagree on both the feasibility and the advisability of this dichotomy. In fact, no measure (assessment) is completely objective; subjective judgment always plays some role in assessment—and educators will be on firmer ground when they strive to acknowledge when and where in any given assessment system this subjectivity is most at work. For many years in American education, objectivity has been equated with fairness. The elimination of subjectivity has been equated with justice, and subjectivity has come to mean bias or prejudice. However, despite good faith efforts to promote fairness through "objective" tests, paper-and-pencil tests do not remove subjectivity from assessment. Rather, they move the test developer's subjectivity "behind the scenes," where it is harder for others to see. In this traditional form of assessment, much of the subjectivity is in the selection of questions asked, the phrasing of the questions, and in the sampling of content done entirely by the test writer in a process invisible to the test taker. Much of the test's "objectivity" is based on keeping this very subjective process a secret from test takers. Perhaps other alternative assessment formats are not the antithesis of "objective" tests after all; instead they are assessments that have their subjective features elsewhere in the assessment process.

DEFINITIONS OF PORTFOLIO

One popular alternative assessment currently is the portfolio. Actually, in the singular, the term "portfolio" is misleading, because there are many assessment procedures that each carry the name of portfolio that are, in fact, very different one from the other. Portfolios, then, are a broad category of assessment that can be used to meet a variety of evaluation needs. Current interest in portfolios can be demonstrated by the number of recent articles listed by Educational Research Information Center (ERIC) on the topic. The search label of portfolio and assessment yielded 769 entries for 1992–1996, and portfolio and teacher education yielded 172 entries for the same period. Not all of these authors are talking about the same thing, but, clearly, the topic has generated considerable interest. The largest number of articles on the topic discuss elementary school children's writing portfolios, but discussions of teachers' professional portfolios are increasing.

> "In broad terms, it [**a portfolio**] consists of multiple pieces of evidence created over time to represent a broad set of proficiencies or understandings."

What is a portfolio and how can it be helpful to teachers? In broad terms, it consists of multiple pieces of evidence created over time to represent a broad set of proficiencies or understandings. Educational portfolios are often grouped into four different categories. There are **showcase**, or best-work portfolios, in which entries are usually selected by the creator of the portfolio (the portfolio developer), and self-evaluation takes priority over standardization of evaluation. In other words, the developer must decide which pieces of his or her work are the best, and justifying these choices is an important part of the portfolio. As a result, each developer's portfolio will be necessarily different. **Documentation** portfolios are similar to the compilation of materials that teachers have gathered in the past to show at parent conferences. They usually have more entries than a showcase portfolio and show some self-evaluation and some outside evaluation. Some entries are selected by the portfolio designer, others by the portfolio developer, with frequent sampling over time. This portfolio may resemble a scrapbook. **Evaluation** portfolios consist of specific tasks that all portfolio developers are required to complete. Efforts are made to standardize the tasks and the evaluations for all developers. All tasks and activities are selected by the portfolio designer, and the results are judged by outside evaluators to maintain consistency. An example would be Vermont's Literacy Assessment Project (Koretz) that is a statewide assessment of students' writing portfolios. The fourth category is the **process** portfolio that permits the greatest student freedom in entry selection, focuses on students' self-reflection on the learning process, and is usually not graded. For example, student portfolios that show outlines, rough drafts, rewrites, and peer reviews of a single writing assignment are process portfolios used during process writing instruction.

These four categories are rough attempts to classify portfolio types. Each type rarely exists in its pure form, but the categories do highlight different purposes and characteristics of the portfolio concept. Differences among the models are not trivial; they reflect different assessment methods, evaluation criteria, goals, and audiences. They have different strengths and weaknesses. And, all important, they fit differing contexts and are not interchangeable.

RATIONALE AND IMPETUS FOR TEACHER PORTFOLIOS

Foreign language teachers often find themselves in the solitary context of being the only teacher of a given language in a school. Those charged with teacher supervision and evaluation often do not understand the very medium of instruction in the language teacher's classroom. These teachers may be especially helped by training in self-evaluation, which can come from the practice of selecting pieces of evidence to include in a professional portfolio and from articulating one's decision making process.

Newer understandings of "fairness" in assessment and evaluation draw educators to think less in terms of cookie-cutter sameness for all and more in terms of diverse, individualistic solutions. Portfolio assessment may be the method to permit such individualized evaluations of a diverse teaching staff. The portfolio also is considered a useful vehicle for teachers to demonstrate what they know and what their strengths are. Rather than having supervisors document via an observation checklist what is missing from the annual lesson they happen to observe, portfolio assessment allows teachers to document their own teaching strengths. It can be a way for teachers to articulate what they know and highlight what they contribute to their school, rather than highlight what is absent from a given lesson. Many educational researchers are interested in "pedagogical content knowledge," the subject matter knowledge a teacher possesses and his or her understanding of how best to convey that knowledge to students, as the key component of good teaching (Hammadou; Shulman). In other words, in order to research the qualities of good teaching, it is necessary to look at subject-matter specific understandings and how they are conveyed to students. The individualized nature of portfolio assessment in which each individual teacher's portfolio is unique may be an especially promising procedure for gathering information about teachers' pedagogical content knowledge. The result may be to free supervisors from checklists that are uniform for all disciplines but therefore vague and to provide more helpful information to supervisors and researchers alike.

Portfolios are often grouped under "authentic" assessments, those assessments that are linked directly and obviously to the proficiencies they are trying to measure. Fill-in-the blanks tests are indirect measures of writing proficiency; letter writing is a direct "authentic" writing assessment. Similarly, portfolios of lesson plans, videotaped segments of actual teaching, and samples of student work can be more authentic measures of teachers' work than a score on the National Teachers Examination or a principal's checklist results. Portfolios may be more amenable to the context of schools than other traditional measures as well. Assessment via portfolios can include evidence of aspects of teaching that other assessments miss, such as collaboration with colleagues. Since collaboration with others is another useful teaching skill that needs to be practiced in order to be learned, portfolios can be used to encourage or to demonstrate collaboration when work is done by teams of colleagues, · for example. Finally, portfolios can be built over any time period desired. Building a portfolio over a year's time can eliminate the potentially distorted view that a single annual observation provides. They also can demonstrate a teacher's growth and professional development. Evidence can be made for improvement on almost any dimension desired. In this way, they can be helpful tools for the life-long learner.

If you are curious to know whether portfolio assessment could meet your assessment needs, what follows are the assessment decisions that must be made to select an appropriate assessment portfolio. The author approaches the process with a program to evaluate in-service teachers in mind. Only minor adjustments need to be made to consider the same procedures for pre-service foreign language teachers at any level, and just a little imagination is needed to consider the procedures for language learners.

KEY COMPONENTS OF THE ASSESSMENT PROCESS

□ MAIN PURPOSE OF THE PORTFOLIO

> "In principle, portfolio assessments are either **summative evaluation, formative evaluation, or a record of a process**."

First in the assessment process must come the decision of what type of evaluative information is desired out of the assessment. In principle, portfolio assessments are either summative evaluation, formative evaluation, or a record of a process.

Expected use of the portfolio

If its expected use is to make a summary statement of the teacher's skills, proficiencies, or knowledge, the portfolio is a **summative** evaluation. It may be an exit requirement of a course or a program of study or a prerequisite to final state certification or master teacher designation. It can be used to demonstrate competency to current or future employers.

If the portfolio is used to show strengths and weaknesses of teaching performance with an eye toward self-awareness of strengths and chances to work on weaknesses, the purpose of the portfolio is **formative**. As a result, the process of creating the portfolio is likely to be a different experience. Willingness to expose weaknesses will clearly be greater when the purpose is to find areas to improve than when the purpose is to make a summary statement of proficiency.

For example, one set of preservice foreign language teachers was given the task of providing evidence that they used a repertoire of different strategies to maximize the use of L2 (second language) and minimize the use of L1 (first language) in their teaching. Under the pressure of summative evaluation, one student teacher advised his peers: "Just don't show yourself teaching a grammar point." This advice was a logical response to the assignment: to display one's strengths to best advantage for a summative evaluation. With a purely formative evaluation, no such advantage would be gained from hiding one's weaknesses or avoiding challenging tasks. It is quite possible that the portfolio designer may wish to derive both types of evaluation from the same portfolio. However, some tensions seem inevitable if the designer tries to establish a balance between formative and summative evaluation with the same assessment instrument. In-service teachers may need to demonstrate ongoing growth in their teaching to maintain employment, or for promotion, or may wish to participate in formative evaluation as part of staff development.

Other portfolios are intended as records of the teaching/learning process, much as a diary can be a record of a process (a trip or growing up, for example). Internal reflection is sufficient and outside evaluation is not necessary. Some proponents of this purpose for portfolios advocate using them to make teaching a more social experience by sharing with others via the portfolio. Schram, Mills, and Leach purport that "talking about one's teaching becomes just as important as the actual doing of it" (p. 2). Others maintain that the portfolio record is personal and private and should be used for internal reflection on prior experiences leading to personal formative evaluation (see J. Thompson). Most portfolio users seem to attempt to achieve more than one purpose with a single portfolio. For example, the teacher education portfolios used at Wichita State University are intended to serve as "a tool for reflection, a mechanism to assist integrating theory and practice, a foundation for goal setting, and documentation of program goals" (Carroll, Potthoff, and Huber, 259).

Portion of time required

Formative evaluation tends to take longer and need more frequent evaluations and feedback to learners. Since the purpose of formative evaluation is to direct subsequent learning and teaching, it must occur early enough in the learning sequence to allow for change and further learning. Portfolio development that is to be part of formative evaluation will need numerous steps in the process. Summative evaluation can be done less often. Record portfolios can be maintained for any length of time along the continuum.

Kinds of conclusions drawn from the evaluation

Summative evaluations will typically lead to broad summary statements about teaching abilities. For example, the National Board for Professional Teaching Standards investigates many different features of teaching, but the final outcome is a simple pass/fail statement. Formative evaluation, on the other hand, has specific feedback to the learner as its hallmark. Ideally, the feedback is specific and early enough to allow the learner to respond and change. For example, preservice teachers could receive feedback on the amounts and kinds of L2 they use in the classroom, and objectives for improvements during subsequent lessons could be set.

Educators preparing to use portfolios for the first time need to be aware of the major rift that exists between supporters of portfolio-as-formative evaluation and those of portfolio-as-summative evaluation. Proponents of the former worry about an obsession with grades in education and wish to be freed of them to establish supportive learning environments. Proponents of the latter worry about eroding standards and wish to give students every opportunity to meet standards of excellence (Sommers, 153). Proponents of the portfolio-as-descriptive record appear to value highly either the metacognitive ability to understand one's own learning or the collaborative process of finding interesting teaching dilemmas to be investigated (Schram, Mills, and Leach; J. Thompson).

☐ STAKEHOLDERS AND DECISION-MAKING

Many different societal groups express an interest and concern in the process of educating children. The list goes well beyond just teachers to include administrators, parents, legislators, the media, and the general public. Any number of these stakeholders may be part of the decision-making process. Any combination of groups may act as the portfolio designers that guide, monitor, or assist the actual portfolio developers. However, who makes what decisions should be clearly spelled out.

Most portfolios contain some prescribed evidence required by the portfolio designer and some elected evidence decided by the portfolio developer. Barton and Collins report being more satisfied with prescribing form (e.g., a video of a science lab) rather than prescribing specific content (e.g., a lesson on photosynthesis; p. 204). This decision must be based on the portfolio's purpose: If the portfolio is to be used to grant state certification or as an exit requirement for a teacher education program, it seems reasonable for some aspects of the portfolio to be prescribed by the designers of the project; or if the portfolio is to be a private descriptive record, all aspects may be elected.

Collaboration on portfolio development can be seen as a necessary skill to foster, an appropriate option, or as cheating. The role of collaborating with others should be determined early in the portfolio process. If collaboration is a requirement, tensions and conflict may result among collaborators, especially when important job evaluations are at stake. If collaborators are also evaluators, conflicts of interest can arise. Collaboration typically occurs when portfolio developers either build evidence together as part of work or study teams or when they select pieces of evidence with input and advice from colleagues. Control over the kind and extent of collaboration that may occur will be less than in other traditional testing contexts.

☐ OWNERSHIP

One of the major benefits that portfolio proponents claim from portfolio use is that it can increase a sense of "ownership" of one's own evaluation. Since meaningful feedback on their teaching can be so hard to come by for many teachers, especially the lone teacher of a given foreign language, supported practice in self-evaluation may be very useful in the long run for novice teachers. In fact, "we must constantly remind ourselves that the ultimate purpose of evaluation is to enable students to evaluate themselves" (Costa, 36). Although it is frequently a goal of portfolio assessment projects, it is a difficult claim to prove.

Some of the confusion about portfolio ownership is in its definition. For some, ownership comes from taking responsibility for personal goal setting and the personalizing of learning. For others, it is the ability to defend choices or the ability to determine the quality of one's own work, even when the tasks are assigned by another.

In a survey of teacher education faculty who were using a program-wide portfolio assessment of preservice teachers, Carroll, Potthoff, and Huber found that faculty disagreed most often with the survey statement that the university's portfolio plan convinced most students that they were the owners of their portfolio (p. 257). Despite good intentions to the contrary, portfolio developers can still find that portfolios are evaluation done *to* them, not *by* them (p. 260). Schram, Mills, and Leach cite a novice teacher who states: "When I began my portfolio I felt an immediate sense of ownership and control . . . Several months into the internship, my definition of ownership reached a higher level" (p. 11). She abandoned the practice of writing explanations to the university faculty about why an event had been noteworthy and began to write why it was important to her. Participants' understanding of ownership can shift during the portfolio development process.

☐ USE OF THE FINAL PRODUCT

Once the all-important portfolio development process has come to an end, the resulting products are put to different uses. Some portfolios are used to showcase the portfolio designer in order to graduate or complete a program of study. Others are sent or given to prospective employers to market the designer in the job market. Others are used to evaluate the program itself—its successes or congruence with stated goals or needs to change. Some are used as records of growth and improvement—of individuals or of a program. Others are not allowed to "stand alone" but are used as props to assist portfolio designers to describe their learning process, often in rite-of-passage oral evaluations. Some portfolio proponents claim that explanatory captions written to accompany each piece of evidence are sufficient for a portfolio to be understood alone; others insist that a portfolio should always be narrated and presented by its creator.

□ BEST WORKS VS. SIGNS OF IMPROVEMENT

Will the portfolio be a sample of best works or evidence of "growth and progress?" Although this question is clearly redundant from the first problem of identifying the assessment's purpose, it is repeated separately here because it is a question often asked in discussions about portfolios. If teachers are asked to demonstrate improvement from a baseline sample or asked to explain what they learned from a less than stellar lesson, the portfolio can be used as evidence of growth or progress. If teachers are asked to highlight their most successful work in a given area and to defend those choices, the portfolio can be a showcase of best works. If the finished portfolio is meant to demonstrate growth or baseline samples "worst case" evidence will be needed.

□ INTENDED "AUDIENCE"

The portfolio may be presented to any number of different interested constituencies, or it may be a private matter for the portfolio developer alone. Different audiences will have differing influences on the portfolio development process and therefore must be considered carefully. A teacher's portfolio may be shared with peers, future teachers, prospective employers, administrators, the general public, parents, or students. The portfolio developer's expectations of what differing audiences may want to see will clearly affect the creation process. Some stakeholders' expectations may be better known ahead of time than others'. Traditionally marginalized groups to teacher evaluation, such as parents or students, may add a new agenda to the portfolio process if included substantially in it. But every group included in the process can be expected to influence or change it in some way.

The forum for participation also needs to be considered. Many portfolios are evaluated in settings similar to an oral exam or a hearing with a panel or team of evaluators to receive the presentation. Others are simply handed over as stand-alone documents. The receivers may or may not be collaborators in the development process, which can be expected to change their understandings of the process and the manner in which they evaluate it. The varying perspectives of each group will interact, sometimes in unexpected ways.

☐ DEFINING QUALITY

For most portfolio projects, evaluators will be called upon to gauge the performances of the portfolio developers. Prior to being able to do so, stakeholders must define the standards and expectations against which portfolios can be judged.

Success with questions of validity seems to be a common strength of portfolio projects. At least face validity (Is the connection obvious between the "test" and the knowledge it is supposed to measure?) is much easier to establish with portfolios than with most pencil-and-paper tests. Content validity (Is the "test" a fair sampling of the body of knowledge learned?) can be addressed in part with Haertel's "value-added principle" (Barton and Collins). The portfolio developer selects a document that provides the most compelling evidence for a given goal; then, he or she considers several more pieces of evidence to support the same goal. Once several new pieces are rejected for communicating nothing more of importance, the goal has been met (pp. 204–205). This presupposes, of course, that the goals and content standards are thought out carefully and are explicitly articulated throughout the assessment project. Content standards can be written by any and all stakeholders, including, of course, the portfolio developers themselves with no threat to the integrity of the assessment.

☐ JUDGING PORTFOLIOS

Evaluators of portfolios face the challenge of applying common standards to unique works. To apply content standards for portfolio evaluation, each portfolio segment may be given a score and all the segments' scores tallied, or all segments can be judged holistically, using the same scoring rubrics across all segments of the portfolio. For example, evidence of the teacher's planning skills, communication skills, and community involvement might be judged separately using separate scales, then summed. Or a general scale, such as 1–4 or 1–5, might be used to indicate different levels of competence, and clusters of characteristics might be used to describe each level of the scale, often based on exemplars from either inside or outside of the group being evaluated. In the Teacher Assessment Project (TAP) at Stanford University, trained examiners evaluated all pieces of evidence in teacher portfolios according to five criteria, such as "manages and monitors student learning" along a five-point scale from "unacceptable" to "superb." A descriptive paragraph describing the main features of a performance at that particular level was used to rate each portfolio. Based on experiences with TAP, Wolf warns that "without some kind of structure or guidelines, people tend to go to one extreme or the other—either they retreat to unsubstantiated global impressions based on first reactions or gut feelings, or they try to simplify the assessment task by looking for specific, objective criteria and become overly narrow in their evaluation" (p. 13).

One of the thorniest problems with portfolios is the reliability with which such rubrics are applied to products that, by their very nature, are supposed to be dissimilar in significant ways.[1] Portfolio evaluation needs to be consistent among judges and among the differing types of portfolio entries. Valencia and Calfee cite evidence from first language writing portfolios and the judging of skating and diving competitions to support the notion that reliable evaluation of differing and complex tasks is possible when the evaluators are knowledgeable and thoroughly trained (p. 338). Similar evidence of the possibilities exists in the high inter-rater reliability that has been possible for some time in evaluation of oral proficiency in foreign languages (I. Thompson). The level of consistency required for a given project and how that consistency will be confirmed is an important decision to be made in each assessment project.

The traditional, statistical procedures used to analyze testing's numerical results are difficult to apply fairly to portfolio evaluation. The more standardized the test, the higher and "better" the ratings of reliability and validity, but (sometimes forgotten) the lower the authenticity of the task. Paulson and Paulson express hope that the emerging science of Chaos Theory, the study of complex patterns in natural events, may eventually provide us with more accurate techniques of analyzing authentic assessment results. They report that chaos theory's use of the mathematics of nonlinearity is already finding some practical applications in medical treatment. Meanwhile, they urge all educators experimenting with portfolio assessment to experiment freely with methods of analysis as well.

The fact that portfolio evaluation scores may vary significantly from other test scores is not always viewed as a negative feature of portfolios. When Alabama courts threw out the state's traditional certification exam because of the disproportionate number of minority students doing poorly on it, Tuskegee University tried portfolio and performance assessments of their preservice teachers in its stead. They found no statistical relationship between portfolio score and GPA or between portfolio score and the performance measure. They determined that portfolios were measuring teaching skills and abilities that are relatively independent of those elicited by traditional tests as represented by GPA or by performance measures. They thereby concluded that "portfolio measures show good promise for diversifying assessment for teacher certification" (Nweke and Noland, 2).

CONCLUSION

Portfolios are versatile components of assessment that can take many forms. They are both an assessment process and a tool of subjective evaluation. Educators may select to use them for summative evaluations of teaching proficiencies or as formative evaluation of any dimension of teaching during ongoing professional development. They, like all assessments, require their users to identify clearly where subjective decisions are being made in order to protect teachers against bias and to promote fair evaluations.

The potential benefits of portfolio assessment for teachers include the opportunity to take greater charge of their own assessment. This is a long awaited opportunity to make staff development more relevant to individual teachers' needs and to make learning more learner-centered with the teacher as the life-long learner. When portfolio development is supported by knowledgeable, experienced educators, teachers will have the greatest opportunity to improve their skills of self-evaluation. Due to the isolated nature of much of teaching, this benefit may be most critical to sustained growth and satisfaction in a teaching career. Finally, practicing the skills and procedures of portfolio development on themselves may give teachers useful assessment skills that can, in turn, be taught to their own students for similar benefits.

Given the current enormous attention to teacher assessment in general and portfolios in particular, a real danger exists, however, that teachers will be pressured into using the new tool incorrectly. Stakeholders, whether they be administrators, parents, legislators, the media, the general public, or teachers themselves, who push for the quick fix of a hastily implemented new procedure will harm the educational process if care is not taken to do the job thoroughly and conscientiously. There are really no shortcuts to a valid and reliable evaluation of teaching. If what is really desired is to use evaluation to aid and improve schools, the commitment to do the job to the best of our abilities must be made. The educational landscape is strewn with the litter of many bandwagons that have come too hastily and been abandoned consequently.

A proponent of teacher portfolios, Mary Dietz, claims: "Creating a learning environment for *all* must begin with the staff ('you cannot give away what you do not have'). Our initial studies reveal that the portfolio process is indeed successful in helping school leadership become architects of learning environments for all and for staff development to be truly learner-centered" (pp. 42–43). If the teacher as learner is given the time, opportunity, and support to pursue her own goals and to develop self-evaluative skills, it stands to reason that he or she will be better prepared to help students learn similar skills and in a similar fashion. But, as Darling-Hammond reports: "These days the talk is tough: Standards must be higher and more exacting, outcomes must be measurable and comparable, accountability must be hard-edged and punitive, and sanctions must be applied almost everywhere—to students and teachers, especially . . ." (p. 5). Teachers should resist any assessment process or instrument that is devised to be part of that "hard-edged and punitive" evaluation. Instead, teachers have the more important, and much more difficult, task of searching for teaching assessments that will aid them evaluate their own levels of understandings and teaching proficiencies while helping them develop their individual talents *and* those of their students.

DECISION-MAKING PROCESS FOR PORTFOLIO ASSESSMENT:
Key Ingredients and Major Interactions

Program	Stakeholders	Procedures	Evaluation
1. What are the program's goal?	1. Who is affected by the portfolio? (teachers, students, colleagues, parents, legislators, general public)	1. What kinds of evidence will be used?	1. What criteria will be used to determine portfolio excellence?
2. What aspects of teaching do you wish to gather information about?	2. Which stakeholders determine the following:	2. What forms will the portfolios take? (handwritten, video, multimedia)	2. How will the validity of standards be confirmed?
3. What type of evaluative information is desired? (summative, formative, descriptive, combination)	• program tasks • Define goals	3. How much time is allotted to creating portfolios?	3. Will the portfolio be scored?

4. How much time, and how many resources do you wish to invest? (If time is limited, select a different assessment)	• Set standards
	  • Write scoring rubrics
	  • Select types of evidence
	  • Select individual pieces of evidence
		4. What feedback will developers receive?	• How will the criteria be scored? (holistically, by separate sections)
			  • How many different rating levels will the scoring use?

• Which instruments do you wish to use? (written test, observation checklist)	• Provide feedback to the developers	5. How will feedback be provided? (written critique, oral interview)	• What will be the procedures for scoring?
• If more time is available, a formative evaluation is an option	3. Which stakeholders will collaborate and which will evaluate?		4. How will the reliability of the evaluation be determined?
5. What kinds of conclusions can be drawn?	4. Who is the audience for the final project?		5. How satisfied are all stake-holders? (with outcomes, with procedures)
• summary statements of proficiency (from summative)			6. How will one know that program goals been met?
• detailed feedback (from formative)			

NOTES

1. In school portfolio projects, not many inter-rater reliability coefficient have been reported in the literature. Herman & Winters (1994) report finding 13 reliability data reports among 46 projects reviewed (p. 49). This author found none in ten teacher education portfolio conference reports reviewed for the year 1995. Those that have been reported have tended to be low. Herman & Winter's review of the 13 reports find inter-rater reliability ranging from .28 to .60 in one project to an average of .82 between pairs in another (p. 50). Nweke & Noland (1996) report disappointing low coefficients from .0 to a high of .38 between cooperating teachers and faculty raters and from .02 to .81 among teacher education faculty (p. 7). In contrast, the lowest published inter-rater reliability coefficients reported for the ACTFL's Oral Proficiency Interview (OPI) scores are .70 in English as a Second Language (I. Thomson). Also, the Advanced Placement Studio Art portfolio of the College Entrance Examination Board, one of the nation's oldest large-scale portfolio assessment programs, reports average between-reader reliability of .89 for overall portfolio scores and from .65 to .81 for portfolio subsections (Myford & Mislevy). Teacher education portfolio projects have not yet reported reliability data as consistent as the AP (Advanced Placement) Art or OPI.

REFERENCES

Barton, James, and Angelo Collins. "Portfolios in Teacher Education." *Journal of Teacher Education,* 44 (1993): 200–210.

Bernhardt, Elizabeth B., and JoAnn Hammadou. "A Decade of Research in Foreign Language Teacher Education." *Modern Language Journal,* 71 (1987): 289–298.

Carroll, Jeri A., Dennis Potthoff, and Tonya Huber. "Learning from Three Years of Portfolio Use in Teacher Education." *Journal of Teacher Education,* 47 (1996): 253–262.

Costa, Arthur L. "Re-assessing Assessment." *Educational Leadership* 46 (1989): 35–37.

Darling-Hammond, Linda. "The Right to Learn and the Advancement of Teaching: Research, Policy, and Practice for Democratic Education." *Educational Researcher* 25 (1996): 5–17.

D'Costa, Ayres G., and William Loadman, eds. *Assessing Tomorrow's Teachers. Theory into Practice.* Columbus, OH: The Ohio State University. (1993).

Dietz, Mary, E. "Using Portfolios as a Framework for Professional Development." *Journal of Staff Development* 16 (1995): 40–43.

Hammadou, JoAnn. "Beyond Language Proficiency: The Construct of Knowledge." In Ellen S. Silber, ed. *Critical Issues in Foreign Language Instruction.* New York: Garland. 1991. 251–274.

Henning, Grant. "The ACTFL Oral Proficiency Interview: Validity Evidence." *System* 20 (1992): 365–72.

Herman, Joan L., and Lynn Winters. "Portfolio Research: A Slim Collection." *Educational Leadership,* Oct.: 48–55.

Koretz, Daniel. "The Evolution of a Portfolio Program: The Impact and Quality of the Vermont program in its Second Year (1992–93)." ERIC ED 379 301. (1994).

Moore, Zena, ed. *Foreign Language Teacher Education: Multiple Perspectives.* Lanham, ML: University Press of America, 1996.

Myford, Carol M., and Robert J. Mislevy. "Monitoring and Improving a Portfolio Assessment System." ERIC Document Reproduction Service ED 388 725. (1995).

Nweke, Winifred, and Juanie Noland. "Diversity in Teacher Assessment: What's Working, What's Not?" ERIC ED 393 828. (1996).

Paulson, F. L., and Pearl R. Paulson. "How Do Portfolios Measure Up? A Cognitive Model for Assessing Portfolios." Paper presented at the Annual Meeting of the Northwest Evaluation Association, Union, WA. (ERIC Document Reproduction Service No. ED 324 329). (1990).

Schram, Tom, Donna Mills, and Wendy B. Leach. "Teacher and Intern Portfolios: Creating Norms of Inquiry and Support." Paper presented at the Annual Meeting of the American Educational Research Association, San Francisco. 1995.

Shulman, Lee. "Knowledge and Teaching: Foundations of the New Reform." *Harvard Educational Review* 57 (1987): 1–22.

Sommers, J. "Bringing Practice in Line with Theory." In Pat Belanoff and Marcia Dickson eds., *Portfolios: Process and Product.* Portsmouth, NY: Boynton/Cook, 1991. 153–164.

Thompson, Irene. "A Study of Interrater Reliability of the ACTFL Oral Proficiency Interview in Five European Languages: Data from ESL, French, German, Russian, and Spanish." *Foreign Language Annals* 28 (1995): 405–422.

Thompson, Joan. "Shaping an Emerging View of Teaching: Portfolio Development in the Teacher Education Program." Paper presented at the Annual Meeting of the American Educational Research Association, San Francisco. 1995.

Valencia, Sheila W., and Robert Calfee. "The Development and Use of Literacy Portfolios for Students, Classes, and Teachers." *Applied Measurement in Education* 4 (1991): 333–345.

Wise, Arthur E. "Shattering the Status Quo: The National Commission Report and Teacher Preparation." *NCATE Quality Teaching,* 6.1 (1996): 1. [Newsletter of the National Council for Accreditation of Teacher Education]

Wolf, Kenneth. "The Schoolteacher's Portfolio: Issues in Design, Implementation, and Evaluation." *Phi Delta Kappan*, (1991): 129–136.

APPLICATION OF IDEAS ON EVALUATION

1. Harper/Lively/Williams distinguish among achievement testing, pro-chievement testing, and proficiency testing. Give and explain at least one circumstance in which you would place primary evaluation emphasis on each of these types of assessment.

2. Based on your *real* goals of instruction, what percentage of your students' grades should be dependent on their performance in each of the following areas?

   ♦ listening comprehension

   ♦ speaking

   ♦ reading comprehension

   ♦ writing

   ♦ grammatical accuracy

   What percentage of your students' grades currently are achieved based on their performance in each of these areas?
   How could you modify your assessment system to reflect more nearly your instructional goals?

3. Develop a Causerie (*charla, chat*) based on a topic or unit of instruction that you will be teaching next semester (or quarter or month or week):

   (1) Study the objectives of the unit to identify those that are functionally driven. Select objectives that can be logically woven into a scenario.

   (2) Determine the overall goal of the scenario. (What should students accomplish in their interaction?)

   (3) List the steps of the performance expected of the students.

   (4) Note any targeted structures useful for the activity. Make a short list of reminders of phrases that students may want to use.

   (5) Select or create any needed supportive materials (e.g., maps, graphs, charts, schedules, ads, brochures).

4. Terry states that "any material or technique that is effective for teaching a foreign language can also be used for testing." He encourages the use of authentic materials and realistic tasks both in classroom activities and in evaluation situations.

Select an unmodified authentic text (print, video, audio, film, satellite broadcast, Internet). For two different levels of students (e.g., novice-mid learners in first semester and Intermediate-mid learners in fourth-semester classes at a specified educational level), write:

(1) one of more objectives for student interaction with the materials;

(2) at least one example of activities for input with students;

(3) at least one example of guided-practice or extension activities with students;

(4) at least one evaluation device to allow students to show their control of the task;

(5) a scoring system for determining grades on the evaluation instrûment.

5. Hammadou comments that different kinds of portfolios are appropriate for different purposes.

List possible items for a teaching portfolio that you might assemble in each of the following situations:

(1) To accompany your application for a teaching position in a new high school

(2) To document the effectiveness and problems of a new network-centered unit of instruction with your students

(3) To record your professional growth during a four-week program of language/culture immersion in another country

(4) To present to students' parents at a regularly-scheduled school open house to show your students' progress

6. Create a portfolio that you could use in one of the above situations. Prepare to present it to your colleagues.

7. With a group of your colleagues, develop a set of rubrics to be used in the evaluation of portfolios. Determine the criteria that you wish to measure, a rating scale for measuring each, descriptors or examples of each level on your rating scale, and any other elements that you wish to include. Then use your common instrument to evaluate one another's portfolios. Using the suggestions of your colleagues, create an improved version of your portfolio.

8. Develop an annotated interactive version of an authentic text in the language that you teach to include in your teaching portfolio:

(1) Use your preliminary preparation from the Activities Section as a basis for this project, if you wish.

(2) Complete your mark-up of the text with colored highlighters.

(3) Write or describe the documentation to be provided for each student "click."

(4) Use a variety of pictures and other graphics that you can scan into your program.

(5) Use at least two types of audio input (e.g., music, sound effects, reading of the text, conversation).

(6) Include one or more video clips that are appropriate and available.

(7) Copy your project onto a disk to be included in your portfolio.

(8) Design and print a title page to describe your project.

List of Abbreviations Used in this Book

AATF	American Association of teachers of French		ISDN	Digital telephone network services
AATG	American Association of Teachers of German		L1	First language
			L2	Second language
AATSP	American Association of Teachers of Spanish and Portuguese		LAN	Local Area Network
			Mgb	Megabyte
ACE	American Council on Education		MHz	Megahertz
			MLA	Modern Language Association
ACTFL	American Council on the Teaching of Foreign Languages		NLP	Natural Language Processing
ALM	Audio-Lingual Method		OPI	Oral Proficiency Interview
AP	Advanced Placement		RISC	Reduced Instruction Set Computer
ARL	*Les Ateliers de Raisonnement Logique*		SCOLT	Southern Conference on Language Teaching
CAI	Computer Assisted Instruction		SISC	Complex Instruction Set Computer
CALICO	Resource Guide for Computing and Language Learning		SLA	Second Language Acquisition
CD-ROM	Compact Disc Read-Only Memory		TA	Teaching Assistant
CPU	Central Processing Unit		TAP	Teacher Assessment Project
DMV	Department of Motor Vehicles		TBLT	Task-Based Language Teaching
DVD	Digital Versatile Disc		TCJC	Tarrant County Junior College
ERIC	Educational Research Information Center		TESOL	Teaching English as a Second Language
ESL	English as a Second Language		TL	Target Language
FAA	Federal Aviation Administration		TPR	Total Physical Response
FLES	Foreign Language in the Elementary School		UNC	University of Northern Colorado
FLI	Foreign Language Instruction		VR	Virtual Reality
GALT	Glossing Authentic Language Texts		WinCALIS	Computer Assisted Language Instruction for Windows
GPA	Grade Point Average		www	World Wide Web
G.T.A.	Graduate Teaching Assistant			

Credits